Conventional
Wisdom

Conventional Wisdom

The Alternate Article V Mechanism
for Proposing Amendments to
the U.S. Constitution

JOHN R. VILE

THE UNIVERSITY OF
GEORGIA PRESS
Athens

Paperback edition, 2020
© 2016 by the University of Georgia Press
Athens, Georgia 30602
www.ugapress.org
All rights reserved
Set in 10.75/13.25 Garamond Premier Pro by Kaelin Chappell Broaddus

Most University of Georgia Press titles are
available from popular e-book vendors.

Printed digitally

Library of Congress Cataloging-in-Publication Data

Names: Vile, John R. author.
Title: Conventional wisdom : the alternate Article V mechanism for
proposing amendments to the U.S. Constitution / John R. Vile.
Description: Athens : The University of Georgia Press, [2016] |
Includes bibliographical references and index.
Identifiers: LCCN 2015025660| ISBN 9780820349008
(hardcover : alk. paper) | ISBN 9780820348995 (ebook)
Subjects: LCSH: United States. Constitution. Article 5. |
Constitutional amendments—United States.
Classification: LCC KF4555 .V555 2016 | DDC 342.7303/2—dc23
LC record available at http://lccn.loc.gov/2015025660

ISBN 9780820357850 (paperback : alk. paper)

CONTENTS

PREFACE

Throughout my academic career, I have been fascinated by the process of formulating and amending constitutions. My earliest book, as well as one of my most recent, highlight proposed alternatives to the U.S. Constitution, many of whose authors call for convening an Article V convention.[1] Although I wrote the second largely to update the first, I realized about midway through writing it that I was dealing with an ever-proliferating number of proposals. Not surprisingly, even though they cover shorter time spans, the chapters detailing recent proposals are thus much longer than are those dealing with earlier periods.

Even after sending the latest of those books to the press, I have discovered an increasing number of works devoted to proposing constitutional amendments. Many of their authors have advocated adopting such amendments not through the mechanism of congressional proposal and state ratification but by calling for an Article V convention. Although this swelling tide of proposals is partly due to the rise of self-publishing, it may also express both rising discontent with American government and a greater willingness to consider changes to the current system. Solid treatments of the amending process and the history of constitutional amendments are available, and I will cite them in a subsequent chapter. By contrast, relatively few systematic works consider the Article V convention process. Aside from governmental reports and legislative handbooks, often written by advocates of one or another proposal, that tend to focus chiefly, if not exclusively, on the probable mechanics of such conventions, the two best contemporary scholarly studies of the convention are both more than twenty-five years old.[2] Moreover, although Thomas E. Brennan's recent book on the subject is a welcome addition to the literature,[3] it is far more concerned with outlining a possible agenda for such a convention than with addressing specific details about its operation.

Recent Developments

As this book will detail, even though the Constitution was created by delegates to a convention that met in Philadelphia in 1787, and despite the presence of numerous extralegal conventions in its history, the United States has never used the provisions of Article V of the U.S. Constitution to call a constitutional convention. However, there are other signs that interest in the subject appears to be increasing.

Although their proponents largely come from different sides of the political spectrum, both the Tea Party Movement, which was initially devoted to reducing governmental powers, particularly over taxation, and the Occupy Wall Street movement, which was largely directed toward protesting the inequality between those whose wealth is in the top 1 percent and the remaining 99 percent, have indicated substantial dissatisfaction with the current political system. Claiming to be seeking to restore prior constitutional understandings rather than to introduce new amendments, 116 delegates from forty-eight states heeded a call by Bob Schultz to meet in St. Charles, Illinois, September 11–22, 2009, in a Continental Congress that articulated considerable criticisms of existing policies.[4]

Largely inspired by a book by Professor Lawrence Lessig on the need for campaign finance reform,[5] Harvard University hosted the Conference on Constitutional Conventions (ConConCon) in September 2011, which drew individuals from both the right and left of the political spectrum who wanted to consider the convention option. A related movement is the Wolf PAC launched by Cenk Uygur for the purpose of calling an Article V convention to overturn the Supreme Court's decision lifting the lid on campaign contributions by corporations.[6] The previous year, Charles Kacprowicz, the founder of Citizens Initiatives, published a book on Article V conventions, which his organization has mailed to approximately fifteen thousand state legislators.[7] John J. Rodenkirch mailed copies of the first edition of his book favoring a Constitutional Balance Amendment to all state governors and copies of the second to all state attorneys general.[8] The *Boston University Law Review* hosted a symposium on dysfunctional government.[9] Francis Fukuyama says that America has so emphasized separation of powers as to become a "vetocracy,"[10] while a noted political scientist has authored a book titled *Constitutional Failure*,[11] *The New Yorker* featured an article called "Our Broken Constitution,"[12] and another political scientist has asked, "Is the American Constitution Obsolete?"[13]

In the meantime, Robert G. Natelson, a retired law professor whom this work will cite frequently, has written extensively on Article V conventions, including a handbook published by the American Legislative Exchange Council (ALEC), which has created the Jefferson Project as what has been described as a "new lobbying arm" for a convention,[14] that he has designed specifically for state legislators.[15] Colorado state senator Kevin Lundberg and New Mexico state representative Yvette Herrell are cochairs of the State Legislators' Article V Caucus, which "believes that an Article V convention is the most efficacious means of meeting our goals."[16] A group called Citizens for Self-Governance, which is led by Mark Meckler, cofounder of the Tea Party Patriots; Michael Farris, founder of the Home School Legal Defense Association; and Eric O'Keefe, a leader of the term limits movement, has published a similar handbook, which is now in its third edition and is most likely to appeal to political conservatives.[17] The Madison Coalition, affiliated with former Indiana representative David McIntosh, is attempting to restore "a balance of state and federal powers" by calling for a state law that would strictly limit the authority of delegates that states sent to a constitutional convention and for state constitutional amendments to prohibit states from considering any amendments that exceeded state calls.[18] I Am American .org, apparently organized by novelist Loren Enns, has created a website advocating an Article V convention.

States have once again begun petitioning in a serious way for an Article V convention to propose a balanced budget amendment, with a group called the Compact for America setting a target of July 4, 2015, for ratification of a proposal it hopes to facilitate through an interstate compact.[19] Radio commentator Mark R. Levin has gathered widespread attention for his latest book proposing a series of amendments,[20] which in turn has spawned numerous imitators. At least nine authors have published recent novels on the subject,[21] while two coauthors have linked what they perceive to be current crises in U.S. government to a worldwide movement to "reinvent the state."[22] Moreover, more than 100 lawmakers from more than thirty states have gathered, first at Mt. Vernon in 2013, and again in Indianapolis in 2014, to make plans for what Natelson has called "an Article V Convention for Proposing Amendments."[23]

Although there has been a lot of activity, this does not mean that states will soon succeed in calling an Article V convention. The constitutional bar requiring two-thirds of the states to issue such a call has historically proven to be quite high. Moreover, many current calls for conventions (and opposition to them) appear to be led by individuals who are considerably to the right or left of the American mainstream,[24] and some opponents are convinced that "the Convention of the States (cos) is an Article V Constitutional Convention (Con-Con) supported and funded by the elitists."[25] Furthermore, as this book demonstrates, on at least three occasions, states have come close to calling a convention but have ultimately fallen short of the necessary petitions from two-thirds or more of the states. Moreover, in addition to numerous scholars who oppose the idea that an Article V can be limited (and thus contributing to ever-present fears of a "runaway" body), there are some groups, most notably Phyllis Schlafly's Eagle Forum[26] and the ultraconservative John Birch Society, that remain adamantly opposed to calling a convention precisely because they fear that a new convention might in fact repeal existing constitutional protections.[27]

My Previous Work on the Amending Process

All of this is of great interest to me. I have written and edited a number of books dealing specifically with the Constitutional Convention of 1787 and its participants,[28] have published several books that focus specifically on the constitutional amending process,[29] have compiled lists and explanations of amendments and proposed amendments,[30] participated in a workshop in Greece dedicated to looking at constitutional change from a comparative perspective,[31] and regularly revise books that seek both to explain what the Constitution means and how it has been interpreted.[32]

When I attended graduate school at the University of Virginia, I concentrated on political theory, but when I took my first teaching job, I found that my chief teaching responsibilities focused on constitutional law. In part to buttress my knowledge of this subject, I attended a seminar sponsored by the National Endowment for the Humanities titled "America's Continuing Revolution: the Role of the Supreme Court," which was directed by Professor Alpheus Mason at Princeton University, where I proposed as my outside project to investigate the possibility of an Article V convention. At the time, I found the subject to be somewhat overwhelming, and I decided instead to focus on U.S. Supreme Court decisions relative to amending issues.[33]

In one of my early books on issues surrounding the constitutional amending process, I devoted a chapter to questions connected to the Article V convention mechanism.[34] It was, however, only after doing some research for testimony before the Joint Government Operations—Legislative Advisory Subcommittee of the Tennessee legislature in November 2013 that I realized that the issue might again be growing in importance. As I continued my scholarly research, I began to think that it was time to revisit it in greater detail. The result is a book that examines the subject from a perspective that I did not think other scholars have yet fully articulated.

Differentiating Circumstances

Although I seek in the early chapters of this book to provide historical context, I have come to believe that the primary difficulty in discussing Article V conventions is that individuals do not adequately differentiate among the occasions where they might be called and the tasks in which such a convention might engage. In my judgment, the arguments both for and against using an Article V convention are both too predictable (the term "knee jerk" comes to mind) and too generic. There are some tasks that seem far more appropriate for the process that Congress and the states have already successfully used to adopt twenty-seven amendments and that would accordingly require considerable justification for using an alternate mechanism. There are other jobs for which an Article V convention may be the only appropriate mechanism. Individuals who favor one or another constitutional change or set of changes should give serious consideration to whether the method of congressional proposal and state ratification is better or whether there is a reason specifically to go the convention route. To paraphrase a poem by Robert Frost, choosing one or the other path could make all the difference!

Moreover, although existing literature sometimes portrays an Article V convention as sovereign, the fact that three-fourths of the states would have to adopt its recommendations is a strong indication that it is not. Other writers urge Congress to ignore petitions that call for a limited Article V convention, an act that would likely enrage public opinion and further confirm existing beliefs that Congress is out of touch. Still others, in what I believe to be a perversion of the doctrine of original intent, adamantly assert that an Article V convention would have to follow the same scheme of representation as was used when states were equally represented in Congress, which last happened in 1788, and when senators were appointed by state legislatures, which went out in 1913!

My Stance on Amendments

I need to begin with a disclaimer. Although I am deeply interested in politics and have views on a number of proposed amendments, my chief interest in the amending process is academic. If I am able to contribute to my country as a scholar of the Constitution, I am most likely to do so not as a partisan favoring or disfavoring a particular amendment but on behalf of maintaining the validity of the process itself. If I may preemptively answer a variant of the question that congressional committees sometimes asked in the 1950s, I am not now, nor have I ever been, a proponent of a particular Article V convention, either to adopt a specific amendment or set of amendments or to rewrite the Constitution.

I hope that had I been alive in 1787 I would have supported the convention that proposed the current document, and I just as surely hope that I would have opposed the Confederate Constitution and the Rebellion that accompanied it had I been alive in 1861. Having written extensively about proposed amendments and proposed constitutions, I can think of changes in the Constitution that I believe are worthy of consideration, but I have no ax to grind, and I am not writing this book in hopes that it will aid or hinder a particular outcome other than the obvious one of hoping to perpetuate representative institutions that secure civil rights and liberties.

I think it is important that those of us who consider ourselves to be defenders of the U.S. Constitution recognize that Article V of the Constitution specifically created a mechanism whereby states can petition Congress to call a convention. I do not think it is any more appropriate to denigrate this mechanism in general than it would be to criticize the constitutional machinery for impeachments or for expelling members of Congress by a two-thirds vote, even though neither such mechanism is appropriate except in specific times and circumstances. The Article V convention is first and foremost a *constitutional* mechanism. It is not intended to be a blunderbuss but is designed to address situations that arise in particular times and circumstances, and those who criticize its use on all occasions do not, in my judgment, fully appreciate the mechanism or its larger part in the American constitutional system.

Despite the lack of experience with this mechanism, I have further come to believe that the historical evidence demonstrates that an Article V convention could, under proper circumstances, be a relatively safe and effective means of re-formulating fundamental law or bypassing institutional roadblocks. No method, especially one that is untried, can be completely failsafe, but irrational fears could stymie progress. Indeed, the Constitution formulated in 1787 was, in part, an act of faith in the possibility of progress. Moreover, I would rather seek to delineate how such a convention might effectively operate so that it is available for use if future occasions so demand than to hope that uncertainty will serve as an independent deterrent to ever using the mechanism.

Terminology

Throughout this book I will consistently refer to the topic at issue as an Article V convention. I do so as a fairly strict grammarian with consciousness that some individuals, including those under whom I have studied, oppose using a noun (in this case, Article V) as an adjective. In so doing, I hope to distinguish the mechanism that the Constitution outlines in Article V from the noble but extra-constitutional convention that drew up the current Constitution, the far more questionable convention that met in Montgomery, Alabama, in 1861 to unite rebelling states (most of whom refused to allow their own citizens to cast ballots) in opposition to the Union, or other irregular meetings without specific constitutional sanction. I further hope that the use of Article V will emphasize that, however exotic it may seem, an Article V convention is a *constitutional* process, which our forebears included for good reasons and that might, on certain occasions, prove helpful.

In the course of this book, I will introduce some additional terminology. I will, for example, distinguish between deliberative and nondeliberative conventions and between those that tackle single issues and those that seek to rewrite the entire document. I will present four models by which to understand how an Article V convention would be governed, and advocate what I call the federal, or mixed, model. Although some of my terminology is new, I believe the analysis is otherwise largely consistent with existing scholarship on the subject.

Organization of this Book

I have organized this book into a series of chapters that form a coherent whole, although most of the individual chapters should be able to stand on their own. The first chapter examines the origins of the convention mechanism and the dynamics that most contributed to the success of the Convention of 1787 with a view to the paradigmatic nature of this convention and to factors that might be relevant to future conventions. The second chapter discusses how amending and ratification mechanisms in Article V and Article VII of the Constitution, including convention options, emerged at the Constitutional Convention of 1787. It also analyzes the key arguments that Federalist proponents of the new document made on their behalf. I argue that many existing interpretations of Article V are incomplete because they do not also consider the arguments on behalf of Article VII. Chapter 3 proceeds by recounting the history of constitutional amendments in the United States, all of which have followed the method of congressional proposal and state ratification, which James Madison initiated in introducing the Bill of Rights in part to forestall extralegal conventions. This chapter will pay particular attention to the factors that appear to lead to the success or failure of individual amendments.

Chapter 4 devotes special attention to a number of extralegal conventions that were held in the nineteenth century and that may by false association have discouraged and raised fears about the use of their constitutional counterpart. Chapter 5 further focuses on the views of key scholars from throughout early U.S. history who have examined the constitutional amending process, and especially the issue of whether Article V conventions can be limited to a single topic or topics (though most did not give that specific question much attention). Chapter 6 continues this discussion by highlighting key arguments that scholars have advanced in the last several decades as to whether Article V conventions can be limited. I believe these arguments weigh on the side of those who believe that states can petition for, and Congress can call, a convention to address a single issue or issues without great fear, albeit not with absolute certainty, that it will attempt to rewrite the entire document unless that is what the states commission it to do. By the same token, I question the value of convening nondeliberative conventions on issues that can just as easily be addressed through congressional proposal and state ratification.

Chapter 7 examines the criteria for a successful convention and discusses four ideal types of how it would be governed. After considering what I describe as the sovereign-delegate convention model, the state-dominated convention model, the congressionally dominated convention model, and the mixed, or federal, convention model, I conclude that the latter is the best, in part because it is most consistent with the Framers' wishes and with the goal of facilitating constitutional changes when they are required. Such a model would recognize that the states are responsible for petitioning for a convention and that Congress is responsible for convening it, but that both entities should allow convention delegates to make key decisions on their own.

Chapter 8 focuses on how delegates to a convention would be selected and what kind of people they would likely be, as well as how they should be apportioned among the states. Contrary to a number of current convention advocates, I take the position that precedents prior to 1787 offer relatively little guidance, and that the norms both the U.S. Constitution of 1787 and subsequent amendments have established suggest that delegates to the convention should largely, if not wholly, be apportioned according to state populations.

Chapter 9 examines other organizational and logistical issues related to Article V conventions but concludes that most of these are fairly manageable. Chapter 10 further identifies four different kinds of constitutional conventions according to their deliberativeness and the scope of their objects and focuses on those occasions where Article V conventions are best used and those where it is not. It specifically identifies three occasions—when Congress as a whole is seriously malfunctioning, when rules effectively block all amendments, and when institutional interests block needed amendments—that especially call for using the Article V convention mechanism. This chapter further advocates the adoption of congressional legislation on the subject and outlines what I believe to be the most desirable provisions that should be included in proposed legislation on the subject.

Acknowledgments

As with all my books, I am indebted to my family, which has supported me; to the colleges and universities that have educated and employed me; to colleagues who have served as sounding boards; to scholars who have published their ideas;

and to my publishers. I appreciate Tennessee state representative Judd Matheny who whetted my appetite for this topic by inviting me to speak to the Joint Legislative Oversight Committee of the General Assembly of Tennessee about the topic of Article V conventions; Dr. Derek Frisby at MTSU for gathering information about the Confederate Constitution; Dr. Mark Byrnes at MTSU and Dr. Frank Guliuzza at Patrick Henry University for useful discussion on the subject; Toby Heytens and Larry Sabato at the University of Virginia for leads; David T. Young for providing a copy of his insightful undergraduate thesis at the University of Virginia on Article V conventions; Richard Albert at the Boston College Law School for sharing publications; Nick Dranias of the Goldwater Institute for sharing essays that he had written; Matthew Spalding at Hillsdale College for sharing information on the topic; Stephen M. Griffin at Tulane University and Peter J. Galie at Canisius College for helping me find sources; Dean Ken Paulson of MTSU who provided critical encouragement at an early stage of this manuscript; John Davenport at Fordham University for useful correspondence; Susan Lyons at MTSU for helping with ideas for the book title; staff members in the Honors College and fellow administrators at Middle Tennessee State University who continue to make my job a pleasant one, and especially to Drew Sieg and Susan Lyons who helped with formatting the document; Bobbie Patray of the Tennessee Eagle Forum who provided useful information explaining that group's opposition to an Article V convention; and Pam Middleton in the MTSU interlibrary loan office for finding relevant sources. I am especially grateful to Professor Brannon Denning of the Cumberland Law School at Samford University, who in addition to serving as coauthor on a number of previous articles volunteered to read the entire manuscript for me and offered some helpful comments.

I am also grateful to the University of Georgia Press for publishing this book and to the two anonymous reviewers who vetted the book before its acceptance and raised critical questions that spurred me to improve it. I am pleased to thank Patrick Allen, acquisitions editor; Sue Breckenridge, copyeditor; Kaelin Chappell Broaddus, cover designer; Michelle Moran, proofreader; and John Joerschke, project editor.

Conventional
Wisdom

CHAPTER 1

The Constitutional Convention of 1787 and Its Origins

One of the most fascinating and elusive provisions in the U.S. Constitution is the clause in Article V (the amending article) that provides that Congress "on the Application of the Legislatures of two thirds of the several states, shall call a Convention for proposing Amendments."[1] According to a group known as the Friends of the Article V Convention, one of a number of organizations currently advocating such a convention, as of April 19, 2014, forty-nine states had filed a total of 745 petitions for an Article V convention.[2] To date, no such Article V convention has been held, and there is general, albeit not universal,[3] agreement that Congress is not currently obligated to call one because the amendments that states have requested have varied widely, and two-thirds of the states have neither contemporaneously petitioned for a convention to revise the Constitution as a whole nor proposed a single amendment or set of amendments on the same subject.

As chapter 3 describes, states have come close to calling conventions to propose amendments: for direct election of senators (something Congress eventually decided to propose on its own); to modify U.S. Supreme Court decisions relative to legislative apportionment; and more recently, to adopt a balanced budget amendment. The mechanism has stirred considerable debate, most of it centered on two questions. The first is whether states can call, or whether Congress can enforce, provisions for a "limited" convention, or whether such a convention might become a "runaway" body. The second concerns the practical matters of how such a convention would be organized, how delegates would be selected and apportioned, who would finance it, how long it would meet, and similar housekeeping issues.

I will deal with both these questions in considerable detail. However, I believe that most of the current discussion of the convention mechanism is misdirected away from a more important question. That question centers on identifying the circumstances, if any, under which the convention mechanism can best be used to advance needed amendments versus those where the nation would do well to employ the more familiar process of congressional proposal and state ratification of amendments. The answers emerge from a closer examination of the origins of the current U.S. Constitution and of the amending process.

Origins of American Constitutionalism

One can trace American history through a trail of documents that articulated the structures and powers of governments and outlined individual rights and responsibilities.[4] Many colonists arrived in the New World under the authority of charters from British monarchs. Pilgrims in Massachusetts did not even debark from their ships without drawing up an agreement respecting self-government among themselves. In the controversies that arose between the thirteen colonies and Great Britain after the latter ended its policy of "salutary neglect" in the aftermath of the French and Indian War (1754–63), the colonists appealed to rights that had been articulated in the Magna Carta (1215) and other charters of English liberties.

When Americans declared their independence from Great Britain in 1776, they began phrasing complaints that they had previously couched in terms of their perceived rights as Englishmen in terms of human rights, or their rights as human beings. Their central quarrel was with a parliament that was seeking to tax them without allowing them to be directly represented in that body. The British thought that American representatives in Parliament were unnecessary since they believed that Parliament virtually represented all Englishmen. Although Americans could and did appeal to ancient documents like the Magna Carta, they were reacting to a body that claimed to exercise parliamentary sovereignty under an unwritten constitution consisting chiefly of established customs and usages. Largely because of their own experience with colonial charters, the colonists preferred what they believed would be the more secure foundation of written constitutions.[5]

Early State Constitutions

Indeed, although the Second Continental Congress had few written constitutional moorings until the belated state ratification of the Articles of Confederation in 1791, on May 10, 1776, this Congress authorized states to "adopt such Governments as shall, in the Opinion of the Representatives of the People, best conduce to the Happiness and Safety of their Constituents in particular and America in general."[6] This launched one of the most creative periods of constitution writing in U.S. history. Donald Lutz notes that states composed seventeen such constitutions between this call and the writing of the U.S. Constitution in 1787.[7]

At the time of American independence, it was common for state legislatures to draft, and sometimes even to adopt constitutions. The trend from 1776 through the early 1780s, however, was toward increasing differentiation between legislatures, which made the laws, and conventions, which proposed constitutions. In his classic work *The Revision and Amendment of State Constitutions* (1910), Walter F. Dodd observed that in the fertile constitution-writing period from 1776 to 1784, the states of South Carolina (1776), Virginia, and New Jersey had operated under the authority of "constitutions framed by purely legislative bodies, which had received no express authority from the people for this purpose," and with no submission to them.[8] Indeed, Thomas Jefferson had criticized his state's constitution for being the product of a legislative assembly rather than a separate convention convened for that purpose.[9] The states of New Hampshire (1776), Delaware, Georgia, New York, and Vermont had operated under a constitution framed by legislative bodies that the people had expressly delegated for this purpose but had no role in ratifying. The constitutions of Maryland, Pennsylvania, North Carolina, South Carolina (1778), and Massachusetts (1778) had been framed by legislatures designated for this purpose and (aside from Massachusetts, which formally did so) informally submitted to the people. Finally, only New Hampshire (1779–83) and Massachusetts (1779–80) had operated under constitutions formulated by a special convention "chosen for that purpose" and subsequently submitted to the people.[10]

Further State Constitutional Developments

This differentiation would continue throughout the nineteenth century. After the New York State Council of Revision recommended the convening of a convention to redraw the state constitution, Chancellor James Kent (1763–1847), one of the better-known judges of the nineteenth century,[11] wrote a decision joined by Chief Justice Ambrose Spencer and affirmed by Governor DeWitt Clinton (over the dissents of Justices Yates and Woodworth) in which they vetoed the proposal and demonstrated how thinking was progressing in this area. Acknowledging "that free governments are founded on the authority of the people, and that they have at all times an indefeasible right to alter and reform the same as to their wisdom shall seem meet,"[12] Kent argued that the state constitution should not be rewritten without the authorization of the people. He explained that it "may well be doubted whether it belongs to the ordinary Legislature, chosen only to make laws in pursuance of the provisions of the existing Constitution, to call a Convention, in the first instance, to revise, alter and perhaps remodel the whole fabric of the government, and before they have received a legitimate and full expression of the will of the people that such changes should be made." He thought the doubt was especially strong when it applied to a body like the Council of Revision, "which was instituted for the express purpose of guarding the Constitution against the passage of laws 'inconsistent with its spirit.'"[13] Kent cited a variety of precedents from other states that established that it was common practice to consult state voters before calling for wholesale constitutional reform.

On a related matter, Kent also ruled that it was improper for the people to be presented with a straight up-or-down vote on a new constitution (this argument was arguably weaker, in part because it conflicted with the federal precedent). Kent explained, "If the people are competent to pass upon the entire amendments, of which there can be no doubt, they are equally competent to adopt such of them as they approve and to reject such as they disapprove."[14]

The Development of the Convention Mechanism

Just as the term "congress" originally referred to a meeting, and not necessarily a legislative body, so too the term "convention" initially referred to a meeting (much as it continues to do today, as when referring to meetings, or conventions, of professional organizations),[15] usually of short duration,[16] which was often characterized as (to use a non-original pun) being somewhat unconventional, or irregular. Parliaments held in the 1650s under Oliver Cromwell (the self-proclaimed "Protector" under whom Charles I was beheaded) and that of 1689, which offered the throne to William and Mary after James II fled England, were thus called "convention parliaments" because they met in the absence of monarchical sanction.[17] Henry Baldwin, who served on the U.S. Supreme Court from 1830 to 1844, explained that "another striking feature of affinity in the great political institutions of both countries, is in the *convention* of the *estates* of the one, and the *states* of the other, as its organic power; they pass *ordinances* rather than *acts of parliament*."[18] He further expostulated:

> In England it is called a "*convention* parliament," because the two houses meet, as *representatives* of their *several estates*; each sitting and acting separately, as in their legislative capacity, but acting as a *constituent convention*. There can be no constitutional parliament without a king: the houses meet in convention, and declare the rights heir to the throne to be the king, as at the restoration, or, as at the revolution of 1688, when the houses as conventions, declared *the throne vacant*, by the king having abdicated the crown; *name the person to fill it*, and fix the *succession* in future; but in both cases acts of parliament were passed, when all the constituent parts were assembled, to confirm and validate the acts of the conventions.[19]

Historian J. Franklin Jameson further hypothesizes that modern usage may have come to America largely from Scotland, where a body known as the Convention of Estates acted as "a less formal parliament, not requiring the warrant or concurrence of the Crown."[20] Such conventions, which exercised both legislative and regime-forming powers, were often governed chiefly by the laws of necessity.

Robert G. Natelson, a retired law professor and the most prolific recent writer on constitutional conventions, has recently documented a dozen multicolony and multistate conventions, some of which were called congresses, that preceded the Annapolis Convention and the Constitutional Convention of 1787. They included the Albany Congress of 1754, the Stamp Act Congress of 1765, the Continental Congress of 1774, the Providence Convention of 1776–77, the York Town and Abortive Charles Price Conventions of 1777, the Springfield Convention of 1777, the New Haven Convention of 1778, the Hartford Convention of 1779, the Philadelphia Convention of 1780, the Boston Convention of 1780, the Hartford Convention of 1780, and the Providence Convention of 1781.[21]

Not everyone distinguished the earliest conventions from those that followed. In the nineteenth century, delegates to a number of state conventions asserted that, as representatives of the people, they were sovereign bodies. Members of a committee referring to the Illinois Convention of 1862 thus claimed:

> When the people, therefore, have elected delegates, ... and they have assembled and organized, then a peaceable revolution of the State government, so far as the same may be effected by amendments of the Constitution, has been entered upon, limited only by the Federal Constitution. All power incident to the great object of the Convention belongs to it. It is a virtual assemblage of the people of the State, sovereign within its boundaries, as to all matters connected with the happiness, prosperity, and freedom of the citizens, and supreme in the exercise of all power necessary to the establishment of a free constitutional government, except as restrained by the Constitution of the United States.[22]

Speaking to that same assembly, General James W. Singleton asserted, "That this Convention of the people is sovereign, possessed of sovereign power, is as true as any proposition can be. If the State is sovereign the Convention is sovereign. If this Convention here does not represent the power of the people, where can you find its representative? If sovereign power does not reside in this body, there is no such thing as sovereignty."[23]

Distinguishing Constitutional Conventions from Revolutionary Conventions

In one of the greatest legal commentaries of the nineteenth century,[24] Judge John J. Jameson (1824–90) authored a classic book largely to refute this thesis. With a penchant for classification that pervades his work, Jameson drew from his vast knowledge of previous conventions, most at the state level, to distinguish among four types of conventions. He identified the spontaneous convention simply as a voluntary meeting, like that which the First Amendment currently protects, that called for "agitation or conference in respect of their industrial, religious, political, or other social interests."[25] Jameson identified general assemblies, or legislative bodies, as a second type of convention, but his most important distinction was that between his third and fourth categories, which he identified as a revolutionary convention and a constitutional convention.

Jameson described the former conventions as "a part of the apparatus of revolution." As he described them, "They either supplant or supplement the existing governmental organization." According to him, they arise "from necessity" and "*are not subaltern or ancillary to any other institution whatever, but lords paramount of the entire political domain.*"[26] Under Jameson's description, the First and Second Continental Congresses were both revolutionary conventions, because they exercised legislative powers as they were attempting to create formal governmental frameworks. Moreover, the Second Continental Congress, like a number of revolutionary state legislatures, drew up a constitution, albeit one that it submitted to the states for approval.

Jameson took great pains to distinguish the revolutionary convention from the constitutional convention, like that authorized by Article V of the Constitution or by most state constitutions. He explained:

> It differs from the last preceding [the revolutionary convention], in being, as its name implies, *constitutional*; not simply as having for its object the framing or amending of Constitutions, but as being within, rather than without, the pale of the fundamental law; as ancillary and subservient and not hostile and paramount to it. This species of Convention sustains an official relation to the state, considered as a political organization. It is charged with a definite, and not a discretionary and indeterminate, function. It always acts under a commission, for a purpose ascertained and limited by law or by custom. Its principal feature, as contradistinguished from the Revolutionary Convention, is, that at every step and moment of its existence, it is subaltern,—it is evoked by the side and at the call of a government preexisting and intended to survive it, for the purpose of administering to its special needs. It never supplants the existing organization. It never governs.[27]

As a subsequent chapter will demonstrate, not all scholars have agreed with Jameson's conclusions, but most have recognized that the functions of legislating and constitution making are distinct.

The Development of Formal Amending Mechanisms

Likely drawing from Protestant respect for Holy Scriptures, former colonists expected written documents to provide greater security for liberties than unwritten customs and usages, but they also recognized that the people would need to change such documents both as the people discovered flaws and as circumstances altered. The idea of providing a formal amending mechanism was born in the New World with William Penn's *Frame of Government for Pennsylvania.* Observing that "I do not find a model in the world that time, place, and some singular emergencies have not necessarily altered,"[28] he permitted changes in most provisions of the document with "the Consent of the Governor his heirs or Assigns and six part of seven of the said freemen in Provincial Council and General Assembly."[29]

Revolutionary state legislative bodies drafted a number of constitutions, and not all included amending processes. However, by the time of the Constitutional Convention, nine states formally provided for amending the constitution—four through some kind of legislative actions, three by amending conventions, and two by convening periodic councils of censors.[30] Variations of these mechanisms found their way into national documents.

The Second Continental Congress and the Writing of the Articles

The Second Continental Congress derived its authority from its claim to represent colonial interests whose delegates attended, rather than from a written constitution, but it sought such authority by drafting the Articles of Confederation under which its legitimacy would be more fully recognized. Proposed and debated in Congress in 1777, the document required unanimous state consent and did not fully go into effect until Maryland, which had waited for the large states to give up their western land claims, ratified in 1781. Richard Henry Lee had introduced the resolution for preparing a plan of confederation on June 7, 1776, the same day that he introduced resolutions for drawing up a declaration of independence and seeking foreign allies.[31] Congress was accustomed to operating according to committees, and it assigned much of the initial drafting of the Articles to John Dickinson, the gifted "penman of the Revolution."[32] Congress did debate the Articles, but perhaps largely because it had many other matters, including the Revolution, to which it had to attend, these debates were far more limited than those in which the Constitutional Convention would later engage.

It was not until mid-November 1777 that the Continental Congress sent the Articles of Confederation to the states for approval. Rather than focusing on the difficulty of drawing up the Articles while it was also legislating, the Congress chose to stress the arduousness of accommodating divergent state interests. In a circular letter accompanying the Articles, Congress thus observed, "This business, equally intricate and important, has in its progress been attended with uncommon embarrassments and delay, which the most anxious solicitude and persevering diligence could not prevent. To form a permanent union, accommodated to the opinion and wishes of the delegates of so many States differing in habits, produce, commerce, and internal police, was found to be a work which nothing but time and reflection, conspiring with a disposition to conciliate, could mature and accomplish."[33]

Although the Second Continental Congress shared some similarities with an Article V convention, which the current Constitution authorizes, there were many differences. Thus, the Congress that drafted the Articles, like the Congress that it proposed under the Articles, was unicameral rather than bicameral, and it represented states equally rather than, as with the current House of Representatives, according to population. As a newly created institution, the future of Congress was far less secure than that of the current body. Indeed, as Benjamin Franklin observed after a colleague said they should hang together after signing the Declaration of Independence ("Yes, we must, indeed, all hang together, or most assuredly we shall all hang separately") the British considered its leaders to be traitors.[34]

Because there was no independent executive and no national judiciary under the Second Continental Congress, no national body could have checked national legislative excesses. As James Madison observed, state governments, which exercised primary power, often exhibited excesses of their own.[35] Moreover, what body of limiting precedents largely stemmed from Great Britain, the nation the Congress was opposing.

Although some states had drafted new constitutions, the Second Continental Congress had far fewer precedents to examine for formulating republican government when it was drafting the Articles of Confederation than it would have in 1787 or than it would have today. Great Britain had relied on an unwritten constitution consisting largely of long-standing legal conventions. Before 1787 no national governments were federal, no national courts had exercised judicial review, and relatively few, if any, were headed by elected presidents who combined the functions of head of government and head of state.

The Congress under the Articles of Confederation exercised limited powers in a system that still treated the states as sovereign entities. As Article II of the document proclaimed: "Each state retains its sovereignty, freedom, and independence, and every Power, Jurisdiction and right, which is not, by this confederation expressly delegated to the United States, in Congress assembled."[36] Consistent with such state sovereignty, Article XIII, the final article, provided that "this Articles of this confederation shall be inviolably observed by every state and the union shall be perpetual; nor shall any alteration at any time hereafter be made in any of them; unless such alteration be agreed to in a congress of the united states, and be afterwards confirmed by the legislatures of every state."[37] The Articles had thus provided for a formal amending process, but its unanimity requirement proved to be too difficult.

The Congress under the Articles and Proposed Amendments

Congress began considering amendments to the Articles of Confederation even before the document formally went into effect. After George Washington was forced to cancel a military campaign to recapture New York when Congress failed to receive adequate funds that it had requisitioned from the states, a 1780 convention meeting in Hartford, Connecticut, proposed an amendment that would have enabled Congress to use force to collect such revenues. For a time supported, but later repudiated by James Madison (who preferred to enable the national government to act directly on individuals rather than states), Congress never submitted this proposal to the states.[38]

On February 7, 1781, even before the Articles went into effect, the Second Continental Congress had proposed an amendment granting itself the power to enact an import tax of 5 percent on most incoming goods. Ratification of the Articles within the next month meant that this amendment would require unanimous state ratification. All the states except Rhode Island ratified the amendment by the fall of 1782,[39] but much to the consternation of James Madison and other supporters, Virginia rescinded its ratification in December, and the measure did not become part of the Articles.

Congressional committees issued a number of reports in March and August 1781 related to amendments, but they did not propose another set of amendments until April 18, 1783. Reflecting the precarious state of finances, these would have granted Congress power to collect tariffs for twenty-five years. They would have apportioned additional taxes among the states largely according to population, amended with the infamous provision, which the U.S. Constitution later used, to count slaves as three-fifths of a person. The states did not ratify this revenue amendment. On April 30, 1784, Congress proposed yet another amendment that would have granted it power to regulate foreign commerce for the next fifteen years, but the states did not ratify it either.[40]

Frustrations with this process and the need to resolve outstanding issues between them led Maryland and Virginia to send delegates to a meeting at George Washington's house at Mt. Vernon in March 1785 to discuss common issues of navigation and trade.[41] These states, in turn, issued a call for commissioners to meet: "To take into consideration the trade of the United States; to examine the relative situations and trade of the said States; to consider how far a uniform system in their commercial regulations may be necessary to their common interest and there permanent harmony; and to report to the several States, such an act relative to this great object, as, when unanimously ratified by them, will enable the United States in Congress, effectually to provide for the same."[42] Delegates subsequently met in Annapolis, Maryland, in September 1786 to discuss such issues.[43]

The Constitutional Convention and the Amending Process

Although only five state delegations attended the Annapolis Convention,[44] leading members, including Alexander Hamilton, James Madison, and John Dickinson, used this meeting to call for a constitutional convention "for the sole and express purpose of revising the Articles of Confederation and reporting to Congress and the several legislatures such alterations and provisions therein as shall, when agree to in Congress and confirmed by the states render the federal constitution adequate to the exigencies of Government and the preservation of the Union."[45] The call for the convention was aided by fears generated by a taxpayers' uprising in Massachusetts that winter known as Shay's Rebellion.[46]

On February 21, 1787, Congress accordingly adopted a resolution of support: "*Resolved* that in the opinion of Congress it is expedient that on the second Monday in May next a Convention of delegates who shall have been appointed by the several states be held at Philadelphia for the sole and express purpose of revising the Articles of Confederation and reporting to Congress and the several legislatures such alterations and provisions therein as shall, when agreed to in Congress and confirmed by the states render the federal constitution adequate to the exigencies of Government and the preservation of the Union."[47] Twelve states eventually chose seventy-four delegates, fifty-five of whom met in Philadelphia in the summer of 1787.

Although the Annapolis Convention and Congress had called for revising the Articles, delegates from Virginia, the most populous state, had concluded that the Articles were so flawed that a new start was needed. They introduced a plan that occupied most of the discussion during the first two weeks of the convention. Largely the brainchild of James Madison, who had spent months analyzing the flaws of both the Articles of Confederation and other republics throughout world history,[48] this Virginia Plan called for creating three branches of the national government rather than one, for dividing the legislature into two houses, each of which would be represented according to population (and/or wealth) rather than representing states equally, establishing a Council of Revision, granting Congress a veto of state legislation, and proposing many more innovations.[49]

In about two weeks, William Paterson of New Jersey introduced an alternate plan that, while incorporating a number of aspects of the Virginia Plan, would have retained a strengthened unicameral congress that would have continued to represent states equally. Although the delegates soon voted to proceed with the Virginia Plan, the issue of state representation quickly reemerged during Convention debates. Delegates did not resolve this issue until mid-July, when delegates agreed to apportion the House of Representatives according to population (with slaves counting as three-fifths of a person and each state guaranteed at least one vote) and to represent states within the Senate equally. Other compromises involved the issue of slavery, the mode of presidential and judicial selection, and a host of lesser issues. The delegates proposed a Constitution of about five thousand words, consisting of a preamble and seven distinct articles, some with multiple sections.

The U.S. Constitution

The opening paragraph, or Preamble, which was largely the work of Gouverneur Morris of Pennsylvania, began by referring to "We the People." It articulated the broad purposes—including the creation of "a more perfect union"—principles for which the delegates to the convention had been striving. It was followed by seven divisions generally marked by Roman numerals, known as articles, most of which had multiple sections.

The first three articles illustrated the principles of separation of powers and checks and balances by dividing national powers among three separate branches. The first article outlined the powers of a bicameral Congress elected by voters (the House of Representatives) for two years and by state legislatures for six years (the Senate). The Constitution vested Congress with enumerated powers to legislate (especially with respect to taxes and spending), subject to a limited presidential veto, as well as specific limitations, like prohibitions against ex post facto laws and bills of attainder (Section 9), most of which also applied to the states (Section 10). Article II described a unitary president, chosen for four-year terms through an indirect system of election known as the Electoral College, and serving as commander-in-chief of the armed forces. Article III established the Supreme Court as the pinnacle of the judicial system with members appointed during good behavior by the president with the advice and consent of the Senate. The court's powers would come to include that of invalidating unconstitutional legislation.

Article IV described the relations between and among the states and the national government, which shared sovereignty (the principle of federalism). Article V outlined the constitutional amending process, and Article VI dealt with miscellaneous matters, including the supremacy of the federal Constitution and its laws. Article VII specified how the new document would be ratified. The document was followed by the signatures of thirty-nine delegates from twelve states. As indicated in chapter 2, this document has subsequently been amended twenty-seven times.

Madison's Assessment

Although the Philadelphia Convention did not produce a perfect document, the longevity of the Constitution it produced, as well as the widespread veneration for it,[50] suggests that it has been relatively successful. In assessing the likely success or failure of future conventions to amend or rewrite the Constitution, it is appropriate to assess the factors that led to the success of the Convention in Philadelphia that drafted the current document.

Even before the states ratified the Constitution, James Madison, who was attempting to head off a second convention, was acknowledging in Federalist No. 49 that "the danger of disturbing the public tranquility by interesting too strongly the public passions is a still more serious objection against a frequent reference of constitutional questions to the decision of the whole society."[51] He further offered his own assessment of why he thought both state and national conventions had succeeded: "We are to recollect that all the existing constitutions were formed in the midst of a danger which repressed the passions most unfriendly to order and concord; of an enthusiastic confidence of the people in their patriot leaders, which stifled the ordinary diversity of opinions on great national questions; of a universal ardor for new and opposite forms, produced by a universal resentment and indignation against the ancient government; and whilst no spirit of party connected with the changes to be made, or the abuses to be reformed, could mingle its leaven in the operation."[52]

Why Did the Constitutional Convention of 1787 Succeed?

These and other factors bear further articulation and examination. Although the discussion that follows focuses specifically on the advantages and disadvantages that those who assembled in Philadelphia in 1787 faced, Madison's comments indicate that there are two overarching questions that anyone who favors one or more amendments should face. The first is whether the perceived advantage of the proposal or proposals will be outweighed by the destabilizing utilization of the powers used to implement them. The second is whether the mechanism chosen is more likely to appeal chiefly to reason or to passion. As much as possible, affective considerations, like veneration and patriotism, need to be in the service of the common good.

External Environment Prior to the Convention

In writing about politics in *The Prince*, Niccolo Machiavelli distinguished between virtue and fortune. Some of the factors that influenced the success of the convention had to do less with the leaders, the rules, and the organization of that body (what Machiavelli would have called virtue) and more with the time and circumstances in which it took place (or fortune).

A Widespread Perception of Crisis

Scholars generally agree that although the Articles of Confederation succeeded in winning the American Revolution and in serving as a bridge to the new government, the system was an overall failure.[53] The unicameral Congress, in which each state had a single vote, was far less representative of the population than the current Congress. It required too many supermajorities (most key matters required the consent of nine states, and amendments required approval by all thirteen), and had inadequate powers. Congress did not, for example, have a monopoly on coining money, and it exercised no control over interstate commerce. Congress unduly depended on states for revenues and for military forces and could not operate directly on individual citizens, being in a position to request without being able to persuade or coerce the states. The government could not pay its debts, and inflation was rampant. The Articles had no independent executive, and foreign governments gave it little respect. Shay's Rebellion called into question the nation's ability to protect states against internal disorders and added a sense of real urgency that had been lacking since the Revolutionary War had ended, and the existing amendment process, through which changes might ideally have been initiated, had proven to be too difficult.

Although scholars generally portray the creation of the Constitution as a reaction to internal threats, it is important to remember that the Articles also faced threats from European powers that controlled neighboring territories.[54] England had won former French territories to the North, and the Spanish and French posed possible threats from the South and West. What is generally regarded as the most hotheaded proposal at the convention actually focused on the possibility that small states might seek foreign allies against the large ones.[55] State delegations that might have otherwise considered walking out of the Convention realized that doing so would have left them in a potentially precarious situation.

A Relative Lack of Entrenched Institutions

Commentators on early American politics have often noted that, at the time of the writing of the Constitution, the United States lacked an established church, an established aristocracy, or a monarchy, conditions that were common in European nations.[56] The nation's most prominent military leader had no intention of taking over the government by force, and there was widespread sentiment against a standing army. Existing American national institutions were also more malleable because they were still in their infancy.

Scholars continue to regard the period from 1775 through 1789 as a critical time in U.S. history. At the onset of the American Revolution, Thomas Paine had identified the cause of America as that of the world.[57] The Declaration of Independence broadened the Founders' appeal beyond the rights of Englishmen to those of all humankind. The American triumph against Britain seemed to be a classic case of David defeating Goliath. Although Congress rejected early suggestions by Franklin and Jefferson to depict Americans as the new Israel in revolt against the Pharaoh, the Great Seal of the United States proclaimed that the Constitution instituted "A New Order of the Ages."[58] Anything seemed possible.

Many of the leaders of the Revolution, including George Washington, viewed what they perceived to be the national decline under the Articles of Confederation with alarm but still had a sense of possibility that the Revolution had opened. It was not unusual to tie the idea of government to the idea of experimentation (one of the reasons that Jefferson had favored periodic constitutional change), and experiments with state constitutions provided models for the national level. In part because the Articles limited members to serving three consecutive one-year terms, members of Congress were not as entrenched as they are today. There was no independent executive or judiciary. States had relatively weak governors and fairly large legislatures. Moreover, because the Articles had been proposed by a Congress and ratified by state legislatures, rather than being proposed by a national convention and ratified by the people in conventions, it did not have the popular authority of the current document.

States did, of course, exercise primary sovereignty under the Articles of Confederation, and some prominent state leaders (Virginia's Patrick Henry, for example), seemed cognizant that they could lose power under the new system. However, the very dispersal of sovereignty under the Articles made unified opposition to the proposed new Constitution difficult. Further lacking a unified national party system, resistance to proposed changes would largely be a state rather than a local affair.

The Absence of National Political Parties

One of the most notable background features of the Constitutional Convention may have been the absence of national political parties. Madison thus observed that the Constitution was formed "whilst no spirit of party connected with the changes to be made, or the abuses to be reformed, could mingle its leaven in the operation."[59] There were numerous geographical divisions, including those among the North (or Northeast), South, and West, the last of which was not yet organized into the states and thus relatively unrepresented at the convention. There were also differing philosophical emphases, with some delegates leaning in a more republican, some in a more classical liberal, and others toward a more aristocratic system. Still, there was not yet a national party umbrella, or set of umbrellas, with which most of the delegates would have identified.

The dispute over ratification of the Constitution led, of course, to divisions between Federalists, who supported the document, and Antifederalists, who opposed it, but while there were parallels, Federalists (who included both Hamilton and Madison) subsequently found themselves in both the Federalist and Republican camps. Once states adopted the Constitution, however, both sides accepted its validity, although their interpretations of the document varied significantly. It seems highly doubtful that the Constitutional Convention could have succeeded had delegates arrived with strong party attachments, or had they been playing to outside party constituencies. Indeed, the window of opportunity, which may have depended in large part on nonpartisanship, for writing the Constitution may have been rather limited.[60]

Internal Dynamics of the Convention

A favorable external environment provided a good opportunity but did not by itself guarantee the success of the convention. Many features of this convocation further facilitated success.

Extraordinary Leadership

There is general agreement that the nation was blessed with extraordinary leadership first during the Continental Congresses (the second of which had proposed both the Declaration of Independence and chosen George Washington as commanding general), the Articles of Confederation, and again during the Constitutional Convention. Although scholars often identify James Madison as the "father" of the Constitution, he was surrounded by such extraordinary men as Roger Sherman and Oliver Ellsworth of Connecticut, Nathaniel Gorham and Rufus King of Massachusetts, Alexander Hamilton of New York, John Dickinson of Delaware, William Paterson of New Jersey, Gouverneur Morris and James Wilson of Pennsylvania, George Mason of Virginia, and Charles Cotesworth Pinckney of South Carolina.[61] The delegates had a wealth of experience in both state and national offices and, in some cases, with state constitution writing.

Madison believed that the Founding period had witnessed "an enthusiastic confidence of the people in their patriotic leaders, which stifled the ordinary diversity of opinions on great national questions."[62] Moreover, Simon J. Gilhooley has shown that Federalist advocates of the Constitution relied on the reputation of the authors to argue for constitutional ratification.[63]

Two men at the convention had intercontinental reputations. George Washington, in his prime at the age of 55, had successfully led the American Revolution and gained fame as an American Cincinnatus when he yielded his military powers back to Congress. He not only agreed to preside over the convention, but his apparent willingness to assume the duties of the new chief executive strongly influenced the development of that institution at that body.[64] Benjamin Franklin, who was, at the age of 81, the oldest member of the convention, had established himself as a printer, inventor, and diplomat, known for his wit, wisdom, and cosmopolitanism. Washington's and Franklin's willingness to attend the convention and to lend their prestige to the ratification of the Constitution, while risky to their own reputations,[65] was essential to its positive reception. One could probably count on one's hands (perhaps on one) the number of successors who have garnered the same kind of respect, and deference, of these two leaders, and especially of Washington.

Democratic Accountability

Eighteenth-century ideas of democracy did not require that women, African-Americans (many of whom were legally enslaved), or 18-year-olds exercise voting rights, hold public offices, or otherwise exercise equal rights. Most states permitted chattel slavery. Moreover, the Framers often sought to refine or filter public will through a number of representative mechanisms.[66] In the case of the delegates to the Constitutional Convention, as with most conventions that had come before,[67] members of elected state legislatures appointed delegates rather than holding elections for such seats.

Although Antifederalists would criticize the delegates for exceeding their mandate and for bypassing the amending procedures under the Articles of Confederation, they do not appear to have criticized their mode of selection, which accorded with the primacy that the Articles gave to state institutions. Moreover, convention debates are notable not only for debates among delegations from different states but within delegations from the same state. This suggests that state legislatures themselves attempted to provide balance by representing diverse points of view. Delegates further sought to increase the perceived ties between their deliberations and the popular will by providing for ratification in special conventions held within the states. Although the Constitution was formulated out of the public eye, it was very publicly debated throughout the states.

Rules That Enhanced Deliberation

One of the first actions that the delegates to the Constitutional Convention took was to appoint a committee to draw up rules to govern the convention. George Wythe, a law professor at the College of William and Mary who was only the second such professor in the English-speaking World (the first was England's William Blackstone),[68] chaired this committee before returning home to comfort a dying wife.

Such rules can be described as "a blend of orderly procedures and good manners."[69] Consistent with rules under the existing Articles of Confederation, each state had an equal vote, and delegations voted by states, with a majority of the delegation required in order to cast the state vote. Rules required a minimum of seven states for a quorum and a majority of states on all votes, expected members to rise when speaking, specified that delegates who had not spoken got to speak before those who had already done so, prohibited the recording of votes under individual names, allowed for revotes, provided for the selection of committee members by ballots, and so forth.[70] The most controversial, but arguably important rule (discussed later in this chapter) prohibited publication of the proceedings.

A Willingness to Compromise

One of the most remarkable aspects of the Constitutional Convention, which rules undoubtedly enhanced, was not the absence of controversy but the relative success of the delegates in dealing with it. In analyzing the convention by focusing on civility, Derek A. Webb observed that the convention: "was marked, first, by an unusual degree of civic friendship fostered through ground rules of parliamentary procedure that facilitate respect, listening, and open-mindedness, initial gestures of respect and deference, and extensive social interaction among the delegates leading up to and during the Convention."[71] Personal interactions were undoubtedly fostered by the relatively small size of the convention, in which the average attendance would be about 40 percent of the size of today's U.S. Senate.

The most divisive and passionately argued issue at the convention involved state representation. Smaller, less-populous states wanted to retain their equal representation under the Articles of Confederation, and the more populous states insisted that such equal representation for entities with different populations contradicted democratic theory. Although the rhetoric was often heated, the delegates ultimately resolved this dispute through the Great, or Connecticut, Compromise. It provided for representation according to population in the House of Representatives and for equal state representation within the U.S. Senate and sealed this by preventing any state from being deprived of its equal representation in the Senate without its consent.

The convention compromised other issues as well. States were split between those, concentrated in the South, that permitted, and some of which depended heavily on, slavery and those, largely in the North, where the institution was in decline. Despite highly moralistic arguments, especially from delegates who opposed perpetuation of the institution, the delegates, who assiduously avoided mentioning slavery by name in the document they were formulating, adopted compromises to deal with slave representation for purposes of taxation and representation, congressional control over slave importation, and the return of fugitive slaves.[72]

The delegates considered numerous proposals for selecting the chief executive ranging from selection by Congress (the original Virginia Plan) to direct election. They compromised by inventing the Electoral College.[73] Other controversies centered on term lengths; whether to impose term limits; the process of selecting, confirming, and removing judges; the majorities required to ratify amendments; the process of adopting constitutional amendments; and the like. Remarkably, while some delegates were disaffected enough to return home (and others had already done so for more practical reasons), 42 of 55 delegates stayed to the final day, and 39 of these (one by proxy) agreed to sign the document.

Good Drafting

One secret to the continuing success of the U.S. Constitution was the manner in which it successfully blended institutional structures with specific grants of power and prohibitions. In notes that he took while serving on the Committee of Detail at the Constitutional Convention, Edmund Randolph observed that in drafting a constitution, it was important:

1. To insert essential principles only, lest the operations of government should be clogged by rendering those provisions permanent and unalterable, which ought to be accommodated to times and events, and
2. To use simple and precise language, and general propositions, according to the example of the (several) constitutions of the several states (For the construction of a constitution of necessity differs from that of law.)[74]

Both the committee and the convention as a whole largely adhered to these standards. Mark Graber thus observes that "The United States seems to incorporate the appropriate mix of detail and elasticity," which he believes have contributed to its "long shelf life."[75]

Secrecy

One of the first rules that delegates adopted at the beginning of the convention provided that its proceedings would be secret, and they adhered to this rule very faithfully. Given the result of the Federalist/Antifederalist debate that followed, it is possible that day-to-day coverage might have served the salutary purpose of persuading the delegates to add a bill of rights before leaving the convention, and thus hastening ratification. However, it seems far likelier that debates could have led to street demonstrations, to greater political posturing on the part of the participants, and to far greater attention to their own state constituencies. Many who might have accepted the final product might also have rejected the specific compromises that got it to that point. In an article comparing the Constitutional Convention of 1787 to the French Constituent Assembly of 1789, Jon Elster points out that the former was secret whereas the second was not. He followed this observation by observing that "Many of the debates at the Federal Convention were of high quality: remarkably free from cant and remarkably grounded in rational argument. By contrast, the discussions of the Assemblée Constituante were heavily tainted by rhetoric, demagoguery and overbidding."[76]

A recent report by the American Political Science Association's Task Force on Negotiating Agreement in Politics suggests that members of Congress have far greater flexibility, and express far more willingness to compromise behind closed doors than they do when they expect their actions to appear on the nightly news.[77] Significantly, historians often trace the first report of logrolling in Congress—involving assumption of state debts and the location of the nation's capital—to a private dinner meeting between Alexander Hamilton and James Madison at the house of Thomas Jefferson rather than to the floor of Congress.[78] Many of the convention delegates roomed and dined together, and they undoubtedly took mutual consolation in sharing the experience of deliberating through a long hot summer. Most attended knowing that their "investment" of time could prove completely fruitless unless they worked together to bring ratification of the document to fruition.

Postconvention Factors
Media Support

Many observers of the ratification debates have commented on the role that newspapers and pamphlets played in favoring the document.[79] Constitutional supporters tended to be concentrated in cities on the Eastern seaboard where most of the periodicals were located and where methods of transportation and communication were faster whereas Antifederalists were more concentrated in the hinterlands where such media were not as pervasive. Federalists took advantage of this during the early ratification debates by pushing through as many state ratifications as they could in areas of media strength and were able to capitalize positively on the inertia that this generated.

Those who had attended the convention had an additional advantage in that they had spent a summer together and arguably understood the document better than most of their opponents who had to wait to examine it until the convention adjourned. Those who had attended faithfully would have already heard many of the arguments that opponents raised about provisions that were more controversial. This advantage was likely accentuated by shared experiences of those who had served together in Congress.

Superior Argumentation

In recent years, scholars have directed renewed attention to the arguments of the Antifederalists and have given them increased respect.[80] Many Antifederalist essays raised legitimate constitutional concerns that continue to this day.[81] However, no Antifederalist writing is in the same league as the Federalist Papers. Moreover, whatever tactical advantages the Federalists brought with them, they still ultimately had to persuade state conventions to ratify. Although some states ratified quickly, others did so only after extensive debates. In Virginia, this required Federalists to respond to the florid rhetoric of Patrick Henry. In New York, it meant battling back the forces of Governor George Clinton. In Massachusetts, it involved flattering John Hancock. In Maryland, it meant countering Luther Martin.[82]

Much of the Federalist success in getting the Constitution ratified stemmed ultimately from better arguments. As any number of modern critics emphasize, the new Constitution hardly rose to modern standards of egalitarian democracy, particularly with respect to the institution of slavery and with respect to equal state representation in the Senate, but it apportioned representation much more democratically than had the Articles of Confederation and provided a national forum for legislation. The new Constitution would not prevent all abuses of power, but it divided the most powerful legislative branch into two houses, and it posed Congress against two coordinate branches that made such abuse much less likely. The Constitution resisted calls to advantage the original thirteen states and instead provided for a way for new states to enter the union as equals, and the system of representation provided a way for republican government to extend over an area the size of the United States. Moreover, with broader authority, the new national government attracted the kind of talents (perhaps most evident in the first five presidents) that were likely to enhance the nation's success. It gave states representation within the nation's highest counsels, and it further provided the basis for soft power mechanisms, like judicial review, that would prevent most issues from having to be resolved by force of arms.

A Positive Solution

Historians and political scientists have often analyzed how meanings changed as a result of convention debates. One such change involved the word federalism. When the convention met, individuals commonly used the term "federal," or "foederal," to designate a government, like that under the Articles of Confederation, that modern political scientists designate as a "confederal" government. Perhaps seeking to minimize the scope of changes that the Constitution had initiated, its defenders chose the term Federalists to describe themselves.[83] By further casting their opponents as Antifederalists, Federalists managed to convey that they had a positive solution to fairly obvious problems in the existing government while their opponents knew what they opposed—the new Constitution—without necessarily knowing what they favored.

As Federalists presented the choice to the American people, it was between a relatively young government that was clearly not working and that seemed unsusceptible to amendments, and a government that might work, and the flaws of which stood a more reasonable chance of being altered by amendments. Some Antifederalists favored yet a second convention, but other than possibly proposing a bill of rights (which Congress showed its willingness to do on its own), it was unclear what it would propose to do. By contrast, Federalists had a plan at hand.

Serendipitous Factors

When she wrote about the Constitutional Convention, Catherine Drinker Bowen referred to the "miracle" of Philadelphia.[84] Other individuals continue to believe that the hand of Providence was at work at the convention. Whatever explanation one offers, the success of the convention and the ratification of the Constitution, like many other important historical events, reflected elements of contingency.

Without Shay's Rebellion, it is doubtful that twelve states would have sent delegations. Had George Washington stuck to his original intention to sit the convention out, the Constitution might not have succeeded in being either formulated or ratified. An unwillingness on the part of Federalists to compromise on the Bill of Rights during the ratification debates or on the part of the Antifederalists to accept the legitimacy of the new government might have left the Constitution stillborn, as might a few more Antifederalist votes in the ratifying conventions in Massachusetts, Virginia, or New York. As frustrating as it can be for social scientists, the essentials for successful constitutional writing will vary with the times.

Nonserendipitous Factors

Many factors converged in favor of constitutional ratification, but the convention's success in 1787 would have been even more likely had it not faced several significant obstacles. From a purely legal standpoint, the Constitutional Convention of 1787 was not an Article V convention (and was not completely legal)[85] because the Articles of Confederation did not specifically provide for it. Delegates might have had even greater chances of success if they had been operating under the express authority of a constitutional provision that both provided for the calling of such a convention and that mandated approval by state conventions. Similarly, delegates might have been able to arrive at the Great Compromise far more quickly (or might have not realized the necessity for compromise) had states been voting at the convention or in the Congress under the Articles of Confederation according to population rather than equally.

The delegates' hands would likely have been further strengthened had all thirteen states participated, and had all the delegates signed the document. The presence of additional luminaries such as John Adams, Thomas Jefferson, and Patrick Henry might have furthered deliberation (or increased dissension) and enhanced the collective reputation of the convention.[86] Compromise would have been far easier had the former colonies been more homogeneous, and especially had the southern states already formulated plans to put slavery on a course of ultimate extinction. Had delegates added a bill of rights during the convention, rather than promising to do so during ratification debates, this would likely have helped to speed ratification. An even greater external threat might have made delegates more willing to compromise.

The Value of the Paradigm

The key is to recognize that although the Convention of 1787 met at a propitious time and had much going for it, neither it nor similar bodies are likely to be constructed perfectly or to meet at perfect times any more than is a Congress that proposes amendments or the states that ratify them. Fortunately, no amending body requires a set of perfect circumstances in order for it to be effective.

Still, the deliberations of the Convention of 1787, like the ratification debates that followed in the states, remain somewhat paradigmatic. They provide an affirmative answer to Alexander Hamilton's question "whether societies of men are really capable or not of establishing good government from reflection and choice?" rather than "accident and force."[87]

Lessons from the Convention

If it is overly optimistic to expect that all conventions will rise to the standards that the Founders set in 1787, it is also overly pessimistic to believe that their heirs cannot, with proper rules in place, exercise similar displays of responsible public spiritedness. As the following chapter demonstrates, the Framers of the Constitution did not want to multiply further conventions, but they thought that it was essential to the survival of the Constitution to create mechanisms for changing, or if necessary, even legally rewriting the document should further contingencies so require. The American people arguably further the Founders' legacy less by absolute veneration of the language of the Constitution that they drafted than by a willingness to exercise their same belief in progress when pursued in a deliberative fashion consisting with the institutions that they bequeathed.

The Establishment of the Amending Provisions in Article V and the Ratification Provisions in Article VII

As chapter 1 described, although most delegates probably gathered in Philadelphia to revise the Articles of Confederation, they soon decided to consider a new plan. In drafting the U.S. Constitution, delegates to the Constitutional Convention of 1787 drew from their amending experiences at the state level and under the Articles of Confederation. These influenced their decisions both with respect to the kinds of procedures that provided for future amendments in Article V and with regard to how to ratify the new Constitution in Article VII. Moreover, many scholars who have concentrated on the former have largely ignored the latter and have consequently failed to get a complete picture of the Framers' view of the amending mechanisms.

Debates over the Amending Process at the Constitutional Convention of 1787

The Constitutional Convention, which was initially set to convene on May 14, did not muster a quorum until May 25, 1787. The Virginia Plan, which Governor Edmund Randolph introduced on May 28, set the agenda for the opening weeks of the convention. In fairly sparse terms, it had proposed "that provision ought to be made for the amendment of the Articles of Union whensoever it shall seem necessary, and that the assent of the National legislature ought not to be required thereto."[1] This proposal leaves just a bit of a mystery since the primary obstacle to amendments under the Articles was the requirement for state unanimity rather than congressional proposal, but the authors may have designed the provision chiefly to allay fears that the proposed strengthened Congress might become oppressive. Moreover, the primary purpose of including an amending provision within the Virginia Plan likely had less to do with outlining an expected final procedure than with serving as a reminder, or placeholder, for a more detailed solution to follow.[2]

The delegates began discussing the amending provision on June 5. Although convention notes indicate that Charles Pinckney of South Carolina "doubted the propriety or necessity of it,"[3] he was likely not objecting to the propriety of an amending process per se but to the Virginia Plan's statement excluding Congress from it.[4] Thus, after citing experience at the state level, Elbridge Gerry of Massachusetts observed that "the novelty & difficulty of the experiment requires periodical revision. The prospect of such a revision would also give intermediate stability to the Govt. Nothing had yet happened in the States where this provision existed to proves [sic] its impropriety."[5] Perhaps with the American Revolution in mind, Gerry was thus observing that a constitution subject to reasonable constitutional change was much more likely to last than one that required revolutionary changes.

Speaking on June 1, in response to some unnamed delegates who doubted either the need for an amending provision or the necessity of excluding congressional consent to such amendments, George Mason of Virginia undoubtedly articulated the views of many delegates when he added, "The plan now to be formed will certainly be defective, as the Confederation has been found on trial to be. Amendments therefore will be necessary, and it will be better to provide for them, in an easy, regular and Constitutional way than to trust to chance and violence." With his characteristic republican fear of national institutions, Mason further observed, "It would be improper to require the consent of the Natl. Legislature, because they may abuse their power, and refuse their consent on that very account."[6]

Perhaps because it began with a resolution proposing that the Articles of Confederation "ought to be revised, corrected & enlarged, as to render the federal Constitution adequate to the exigencies of Government, & the preservation of the Union,"[7] the New Jersey (or small-state) Plan that William Paterson introduced at the convention on June 15 did not contain an amending clause. It seems most likely that it would have left the method of congressional proposal and unanimous state confirmation under the Articles in place. Although the New Jersey Plan influenced the adoption of the Great Compromise that equally represented states in the Senate, few, if any, delegates appeared wedded to the amending mechanism under the Articles, and delegates soon resumed discussion of the Virginia Plan.

After proposing on June 29 that states should be equally represented in the Senate, Oliver Ellsworth of Connecticut said that he would not "be surprised (although we made the general government the most perfect in our opinion,) that it should hereafter require amendment—But at present this is as far as I possibly can go—If this convention only chalk out lines of a good government we shall do well." Arguing against admitting such "inconsistent principles in framing a system of government," Madison focused on the difficulties of amending

previous constitutions: "The difficulty of getting its defects amended are great
and sometimes insurmountable. The Virginia state government was the first
which was made, and though its defects are evident to every person, we cannot
get it amended. The Dutch have made four several [sic] attempts to amend their
system without success. The few alterations made in it were by tumult and faction and for the worse."[8] Madison further highlighted the need for substantial
rather than piecemeal change by adding that "if the old fabric of the confederation must be the ground-work of the new, we must fail."[9]

On July 23, after voting without dissent to affirm a provision stating "that provision ought to be made for future amendments of the articles of Union," delegates opined about how this provision might relate to one requiring members
of the national government to swear an oath that they would support the Constitution. After James Wilson expressed fear that such oaths "might too much
trammel the Members of the Existing Govt in case future alterations would be
necessary," Nathaniel Gorham responded that "the oath could only require fidelity to the existing Constitution. A constitutional alteration of the Constitution,
could never be regarded as a breach of the Constitution, or of any oath to support it."[10] Delegates must have agreed since they recommended the oath without
a dissenting state.[11]

Despite all the debate, when the Committee of Detail was formed on July
24, the delegates had actually decided on little with respect to the actual amending mechanism. The only resolution the committee considered with respect to
constitutional amendments provided "That Provision ought to be made for the
Amendment of the Articles of Union, whensoever it shall seem necessary." After
considering this resolution and the debates that members had heard on the topic,
the committee reported on August 6 the provision of Article V that is today so
subject to controversy. The language provided that "this Constitution ought to
be amended whenever such Amendment shall become necessary; and on the
Application of the Legislatures of two thirds of the States in the Union, the Legislature of the United States shall call a Convention for that purpose." This motion prevailed over a suggestion by Gouverneur Morris of New York "that the
Legislature should be left at liberty to call a Convention, whenever they please."[12]

Perhaps inadvertently, the proposal by the Committee of Detail appeared to
make convention action final. Just a week prior to the end of the convention,
Gerry, who strongly favored states' rights, thus objected that if the Constitution
were paramount to state constitutions, "two thirds of the States may obtain a
Convention, a majority of which can bind the Union to innovations that may
subvert the State-Constitutions altogether."[13]

Expressing a different perspective, which put greater faith in national than
in state institutions, and that saw "no greater evil in subjecting the people of the

U.S. to the major voice than the people of a particular State," Alexander Hamilton, who had been born abroad, said that experience under the Articles of Confederation demonstrated that "an easier mode" for introducing amendments was needed. He was suspicious of state legislatures and thought that Congress should be able to propose amendments on its own: "It was equally desirable now that an easy mode should be established for supplying defects which will probably appear in the new System. The mode proposed was not adequate. The State Legislatures will not apply for alterations but with a view to increase their own powers—The National Legislature will be the first to perceive and will be the most sensible to the necessity of amendments, and ought also to be empowered, whenever two thirds of each branch should concur to call a Convention—There could be no danger in giving this power, as the people would finally decide in the case."[14]

Madison had additional concerns. Almost as if he could foresee much of the subsequent controversy that has enveloped Article V conventions, Madison wondered about the phrase "call a Convention for the purpose." He questioned, "How was a Convention to be formed? By what rule decide? What the force of its acts?"[15]

Roger Sherman was a strong defender of states' rights from Connecticut, and had been an early advocate of the formula for state representation that was eventually incorporated into the Great Compromise. He arguably encompassed the concerns of both Gerry and Hamilton by suggesting that "the Legislature may propose amendments to the several States for their approbation, but no amendments shall be binding until consented to by the several States." If, as it appears, Sherman anticipated perpetuating the same unanimity that the Articles of Confederation required, fellow delegates overruled him when they voted first for a provision requiring ratification by two-thirds of the states and then by the current three-fourths majority.[16] Such votes confirm what Professor Melissa Schwartzberg, who favors successive votes, rather than supermajority ones, for enacting constitutional changes, calls "the arbitrary selection of the supermajority amendment threshold."[17]

Seemingly still determined to bypass a convention mechanism, Madison proposed, and Hamilton seconded, a motion that provided that "the Legislature of the U—S—whenever two thirds of both Houses shall deem necessary, or on the application of two thirds of the Legislatures of the several States, shall propose amendments to this Constitution, which shall be valid to all intents and purposes as part thereof, when the same shall have been ratified by three fourths at least of the Legislatures of the several States, or by Convention in three fourths thereof, as one or the other mode or ratification may be proposed by the Legislature of the U.S."[18] Delegates subsequently qualified this provision by an entrenchment clause limiting congressional powers over slave importation for the next twenty years.[19]

Two days before delegates signed the Constitution, the proposed amending clause provided:

> The Congress, whenever two thirds of both Houses shall deem necessary, or on the application of two thirds of the Legislatures of the several States shall propose amendments to this Constitution, which shall propose amendments to this Constitution, which shall be valid to all intents and purposes as part thereof, when the same shall have been ratified by three fourths at least of the Legislatures of the several States, or by Conventions in three fourths thereof, as the one or the other mode of ratification may be proposed by the Congress: Provided that no amendment which may be made prior to the year 1808 shall in any manner affect the [1 & 4 clauses in the 9.] section of Article I.[20]

As a representative from a small state, Sherman renewed concerns that Gerry had expressed earlier that "three fourths of the States might be brought to do things fatal to particular States, as abolishing them altogether or depriving them of their equality in the Senate" and proposed prohibiting any state from being "affected in its external police, or deprived of its equality in the Senate." Mason feared that the proposed amending process was "exceptional & dangerous."[21] His explanation rested on the distinction that he drew between the *government*, as represented in Congress, and the *people*.[22] As he explained: "As the proposing of amendments is in both the modes to depend, in the first immediately, and in the second, ultimately, on Congress, no amendments of the proper kind would ever be obtained by the people, if the Government should become oppressive, as he verily believed would be the case."[23] In a note he had added to his copy of the draft constitution, Mason had further observed that "by this article Congress only have the power of proposing amendments at any future time to this constitution and should it prove ever so oppressive, the whole people of America can't make, or even propose alterations to it; a doctrine utterly subversive of the fundamental principles of the rights and liberties of the people."[24]

Gouverneur Morris subsequently introduced an amendment, which Gerry seconded, to alter the revised process to "require a Convention on application of ⅔ of the St[ate]s."[25] Consistent with earlier concerns, Madison seemed to damn this proposal with faint praise and with concerns over its practical application: "Mr. Madison did not see why Congress would not be as much bound to propose amendments applied for by two thirds of the States as to call a Convention on the like application. He saw no objection however against providing for a Convention for the purpose of amendments, except only that difficulties might arise as to the form, the quorum &c which in Constitutional regulations ought to be as much as possible avoided."[26] Despite such reservations, delegates accepted the motion requiring Congress to call a convention at the request of the states.[27]

Delegates further rejected a proposal by Sherman to allow Congress to decide on an ad hoc basis the majorities by which states should ratify amendments, and they defeated a proposal by Gerry to delete the state convention method of ratification. Delegates further first rejected, and then accepted, a motion that Sherman made, and which Gouverneur Morris reintroduced, permanently to secure the Great Compromise by guaranteeing that states could not be deprived of their equal representation in the Senate without their consent.[28] Madison, who had been among the strongest opponents of the compromise, observed, "This motion being dictated by the circulating murmurs of the small States was agreed to without debate, no one opposing it or on the question saying no."[29]

Article V of the Constitution

The final result was Article V of the U.S. Constitution, which fell just before the last two articles respectively dealing with miscellaneous matters, including the supremacy of the new Constitution and its laws, and the provision providing for its ratification by state conventions. In its entirety, Article V reads as follows:

> The Congress, whenever two thirds of both Houses shall deem it necessary, shall propose Amendments to this Constitution or, on the Application of the Legislatures of two thirds of the several States, shall call a Convention for proposing amendments, which, in either Case, shall be valid to all Intents and Purposes, as Part of this Constitution, when ratified by the Legislatures of three fourths of the several States, or by Conventions in three fourths thereof, as the one or the other Mode of Ratification may be proposed by the Congress; Provided that no Amendment which may be made prior to the Year One thousand eight hundred and eight shall in any Manner affect the first and fourth Clauses in the Ninth Section of the first Article; and that No State, without its Consent, shall be deprived of its equal Suffrage in the Senate.[30]

Whereas the Preamble to the Constitution invokes "We the People," Article V subsumes such people in three distinct institutions, namely, a bicameral Congress (which delegates to the convention expected to be the most representative of the three branches of the national government), state legislatures (which they expected to have a similar role in the states), and state conventions. Article V provides for two methods for proposing constitutional amendments and two methods for ratifying them. Each combination of methods for amending the document requires the consent of two institutions or sets of institutions.

Congress, which the Article mentions first, can take the initiative and propose amendments by two-thirds majorities of both houses,[31] whenever its members "deem it necessary."[32] Similarly, Congress "shall" convene a convention for the purpose of proposing such amendments when it receives petitions from two-thirds of the state legislatures. Once either Congress or a convention proposes such amendments, Article V authorizes Congress to specify in each case whether three-fourths of the states would ratify them through their legislatures or through special conventions called for this purpose.[33]

Whereas the U.S. House and Senate respectively cast their votes in a single sitting, states that call for an Article V convention or states that ratify amendments do so separately and in no prescribed or predictable order. Moreover, whereas the Constitution specifies the overall majorities in Congress to propose amendments and the percentage of states needed to ratify them, states currently decide on their own by what majorities they will ratify them. All the states but Nebraska currently have bicameral legislatures, so, like the decision to propose amendments in Congress, state calls for a convention, and state legislative ratifications of amendments, involve not one, but two, separate votes.

The Federalist Defense and Early Experience

No defense of the Constitution is more widely known, or widely accepted as an interpretation of the Constitution, than *The Federalist*. In this series of newspaper articles that were compiled into a book, Publius (the collective pen name for Alexander Hamilton, James Madison, and John Jay) added further insights into the amending process in arguing for constitutional ratification. Because these essays were published at the time, rather than remaining secret for many years like convention deliberations, they may be even more important in illuminating the understandings of those who ratified the Constitution than the convention debates themselves.[34]

Madison's Analysis

In Federalist No. 39, Madison defended the process for including both state and federal institutions by observing that "it is neither wholly federal nor wholly national."[35] As he explained:

> Were it wholly national, the supreme and ultimate authority would reside in the *majority* of the people of the Union; and this authority would be competent at all times, like that of a majority of every national society to alter or abolish its established government. Were it wholly federal, on the other hand, the concurrence of each State in the Union would be essential to every alteration that would be binding on all. The mode provided by the plan of the convention is not founded on either of these principles. In requiring more than a majority, and particularly in computing the proportion by *States*, not by *citizens*, it departs from the national and advances towards the *federal* character; in rendering the concurrence of less than the whole number of States sufficient, it loses again the *federal* and partakes of the *national* character.[36]

In Federalist No. 43, Madison further praised the Article V amending process by arguing that it would be neither too easy nor too difficult. He also highlighted how its federal character vested equal power in both Congress and the state legislatures: "It guards equally against that extreme facility, which would render the Constitution too mutable; and that extreme difficulty, which might perpetuate its discovered faults. It, moreover, equally enables the general and the State governments to originate the amendment of errors, as they may be pointed out by the experience on one side, or on the other."[37]

In an apparent diversion that he appears to have designed to forestall those who favored calling a second convention to propose amendments before the Constitution was ratified,[38] Madison continued in Federalist No. 49 by opposing a provision that Thomas Jefferson had proposed for the Virginia Constitution. Jefferson's proposal would have permitted two-thirds of the members of any two branches of government to call a convention to rewrite the document. Madison was aware of the democratic appeal of calling periodic conventions: "As the people are the only legitimate fountain of power, and it is from them that the constitutional charter, under which the several branches of government hold their power, is derived, it seems strictly consonant to the republican theory to recur to the same original authority, not only whenever it may be necessary to enlarge, diminish, or new-model the powers of government, but also whenever any one of the departments may commit encroachments on the chartered authorities of the other."[39]

Although Madison raised a number of objections, his chief concern was that such a mechanism would prove to be destabilizing: "As every appeal to the people would carry an implication of some defect in the government, frequent appeals would, in a great measure, deprive the government of that veneration which time bestows on every thing, and without which perhaps the wisest and freest government would not possess the requisite stability."[40] Observing that a "nation of philosophers" might support a constitution through reason alone, Madison argued that "the most rational government will not find it a superfluous advantage to have the prejudices of the community on its side." By contrast, he feared that Jefferson's proposal could never expect to "turn on the true merits of the question." As he explained: "It would inevitably be connected with the spirit of pre-existing parties, or of parties springing out of the question itself. It would be connected with persons of distinguished character and extensive influence in the community. It would be pronounced by the very men who had been agents in, or opponents of, the measures to which the decision would relate. The *passions*, therefore, not the *reason*, of the public would sit in judgment."[41]

Madison launched similar critiques in Federalist No. 50 against the provisions in the constitution of Pennsylvania for periodic meetings of the Council of Cen-

sors to review the operations of the constitution.[42] Notably, however, Madison
also observed in Federalist No. 49 "that a constitutional road to the decision
of the people ought to be marked out and kept open, for certain great and extraordinary occasions."[43] This suggests that he was already viewing the method
of congressional proposal and state ratification as the norm and the Article V
convention mechanism as an exception, chiefly for rewriting rather than amending constitutions.[44]

Madison thus further illumined convention debates by suggesting that however salutary amendments could be, excessive recurrences to the process could
undermine the reverence for the document, which was designed to provide national stability.[45] The new constitution would not only organize government,
but over the course of time it would also signal the public that things were on
proper course.

Hamilton's Analysis

When examining *The Federalist*, it is common to focus on Madison's comments
on the amending process,[46] as well as on his opposition to a second convention,[47]
a position that George Washington shared.[48] Alexander Hamilton, however, al-
luded to the amending process in two of his essays. In Federalist No. 78, where
he defended the institution of judicial review, Hamilton thus observed: "Until
the people have by some solemn and authoritative act, annulled or changed the
established form, it is binding upon themselves collectively, as well as individually; and no presumption or even knowledge of their sentiments, can warrant
their representatives in a departure from it prior to such an act."[49]

More importantly in the final Federalist essay,[50] Alexander Hamilton attempted to bolster Madison's arguments for the amending process by arguing
that although the new Constitution was not perfect, it was good. He touted
ratification of the document as a way out of "the precarious state of our national
affairs" and as an alternative "to the jeopardy of successive experiments in the
chimerical pursuit of a perfect plan."[51] Taking a cue from Benjamin Franklin's
venerable closing speech at the Constitutional Convention,[52] Hamilton focused
on the difficulty of complete constitutional revision: "I never expect to see a perfect work from imperfect man. The result of the deliberations of all collective
bodies must necessarily be a compound, as well of the errors and prejudices as
of the good sense and wisdom of the individuals of whom they are composed.
The compacts which are to embrace thirteen distinct States in a common bond
of amity and union must as necessarily be a compromise of as many dissimilar
interest and inclinations. How can perfection spring from such materials?" He
further suggested, again with a view toward distinguishing the Convention of
1787 from others that might attempt to refine its work, the "utter improbabil-

ity of assembling a new convention under circumstances in any degree so favorable to a happy issue as those in which the late convention met, deliberated, and concluded."[53] Hamilton argued that whereas modifying the Constitution before ratification would require unanimous consent of the states, once states adopted the document, they could amend it through Article V, which would require the consent of only three-fourths of them.[54]

In what is the most conclusive evidence that Hamilton in particular and the Framers in general favored allowing states to call limited constitutional conventions, Hamilton further compared the difficulty of designing a new document involving "a great variety of particulars in which thirteen independent States are to be accommodated in their interests or opinions of interests,"[55] with the relative ease of adopting a single amendment or amendments. He thus explained: "But every amendment to the Constitution, if once established, would be a single proposition, and might be brought forward singly. There would then be no necessity for management or compromise in relation to any other point—no giving nor taking. The will of the requisite number would at once bring the matter to a decisive issue. And consequently, whenever nine, or rather ten States, were united in the desire of a particular amendment, that amendment must infallibly take place."[56]

Acknowledging that some opponents of the new Constitution feared that "the persons delegated to the administration of the national government will always be disinclined to yield up any portion of the authority of which they were once possessed,"[57] Hamilton, whose nationalism was well known, first argued against the general proposition but then observed that Congress would have no discretion as to whether it called an Article V convention.[58] He explained that

> the national rulers, whenever nine States concur, will have no option upon the subject. By the fifth article of the plan, the Congress will be *obliged* "on the application of the legislatures of two thirds of the States [which at present amount to nine], to call a convention for proposing amendments which *shall be valid*, to all intents and purposes, as part of the Constitution, when ratified by the legislatures of three fourths of the states, or by conventions in three fourths thereof." The words of this article are peremptory. The Congress "*shall* call a convention." Nothing in this particular is left to the discretion of that body.[59]

Perhaps the most notable, and overlooked, aspect of this quotation (arguably the "smoking gun" with respect to the Founders' view of the nature of such conventions) is that Hamilton was arguing that an Article V convention would be meeting on behalf of what he had just described as "the desire of a particular amendment."[60] That is, it would be a *limited* convention designed to formulate a particular change, rather than a general convention to rewrite the Constitution that had already been formulated. Although due consideration should be given to the fact that *The Federalist* was a work of advocacy, it would have been overly ingenious indeed had Hamilton failed to mention that, by the way, states that desired a single amendment or series of amendments would necessarily have to call for another unlimited convention that could reconsider the entire document. Moreover, such an unlimited convention was the very kind of convention that he was opposing in this essay![61]

Hamilton ended the essay by repeating his opposition to "attempts to amend, prior to the establishment of the Constitution." Citing an essay by the English philosopher David Hume, "The Rise of Arts and Sciences," Hamilton reiterated the difficulty of balancing "a large state or society."[62] Further pointing to the "awful spectacle" of "A NATION, without a NATIONAL GOVERNMENT" and to the fact that seven states had already ratified the document,[63] Hamilton pleaded with readers to approve the work of the convention and set the new government in motion before seeking amendments rather than taking the imprudent course of seeking to make the document perfect before approving it.

Antifederalist Arguments

Professor Kurt T. Lash, on whom I have relied for a number of quotations from the ratifying conventions, has observed that "Article V aroused little controversy in the state ratification conventions,"[64] where Federalists chiefly used the existence of the process to argue that any defects discovered in the new system could be rectified. Thus, at the North Carolina convention James Iredell, who would serve as a Supreme Court Justice, observed that Article V would permit the Constitution to be "altered with as much regularity, and as little confusion, as any act of Assembly; not, indeed, quite so easily, which would be extremely impolitic; but it is a most happy circumstance, that there is a remedy in the system itself for its own fallibility, so that alterations can without difficulty be made, agreeable to the general sense of the people."[65] At the Virginia convention, Patrick Henry did question the effectiveness of the mechanism by arguing that "four of the smallest states, that do not collectively contain one tenth part of the population of the United States, may obstruct the most salutary and necessary amendments,"[66] but delegates undoubtedly realized that under the Articles of Confederation a single state, representing even fewer people, had the same power.

George Nicholas argued at the Virginia Convention that "there might have been danger" had the Constitution left amendments completely in the hands of Congress, but pointed to the Article V convention option. In an argument that seems very similar to that of Hamilton in Federalist No. 85, Nicholas observed that delegates to such a convention "will have their deliberations confined to a few points; no local interest to diver their attention; nothing but the necessary alterations. . . . No experiments to devise; the general and fundamental regulations being already laid down."[67]

Madison's Advocacy of the Bill of Rights

After the Constitution went into effect, Madison, who had authored many of the Federalist essays, was also caught up in the debates over the desirability of a bill of rights. Initially tepid toward the idea that "parchment barriers" could control popular passions to secure such liberties, Madison was won over either by the arguments of Jefferson,[68] or, more likely, by the desire to head off the possibility of a second convention that he feared might largely undo the work of the first.[69] He took the chief responsibility for shepherding the Bill of Rights through the first Congress.[70] Both Congress's action and state ratifications within two years appeared to confirm that he and other Federalist supporters of the Constitution had been correct in arguing that the amending process was an effective means of bringing about desired constitutional changes. Madison clearly sought to seize the initiative from the states, and the method of congressional proposal and subsequent state ratification has remained the norm.

Themes That Emerged from the Debate over Article V

Several distinct themes emerge from the convention debates and the arguments of those supporting the new document. First, the delegates showed continuity with their revolutionary past by continuing to reject parliamentary sovereignty. They did so by insisting on replacing the Articles of Confederation with another *written* constitution, by assembling as a convention rather than waiting for Congress to propose a new constitution on its own, and by distinguishing the amending process from the ordinary legislative process. Second, the delegates were aware of their own fallibility and of the need to provide for future contingencies. Although a few delegates were unsure whether the Constitution needed to delineate the details of a formal amending process, most desired a method of orderly constitutional change that would forestall the need of future violence like that which they had witnessed during the Revolutionary War. Third, and related to the Founders' desire for "republican" government, Article V "embraces deliberative action by representative bodies, rather than direct action by citizens";[71] the convention mechanism is as close as Article V comes to providing for a referendum.

Fourth, a significant number of delegates, perhaps best represented by George Mason, did not completely trust the initiation of future amendments to Congress, in part because they were not fully sure what to expect from this body, which they expected to gain renewed power because of its proximity to the people. Some delegates, Hamilton among them, did not fully trust granting this power to the states either, because they feared they would use the process simply to increase their own powers. As in constructing three branches of government, the delegates were wary of identifying *any* branch of government or any level of government directly with the people. Wayne D. Moore notes that they believed "that any particular governing institution only partially represented the people" and that they recognized that "the people had multiple constitutional identities: as individuals, as members of political associations, as members of the states, and at least upon the founding of the U.S. Constitution as members of the United States."[72] Sanford Levinson further observes that the delegates specifically distinguished between "the people of the States" and "the *legislatures* of the respective states," to whom they did not entrust the task of ratifying the Constitution.[73] Just as the delegates provided a method to bypass state legislatures by allowing Congress to specify ratification by convention, so too they provided a way for the people or the states largely to bypass Congress through the Article V convention mechanism.

Fifth, although they provided an alternative whereby states could request that Congress call a convention, the delegates did not go into detail about how a convention to propose amendments would work. In the words of William A. Platz, the language of Article V on this matter was "lamentably vague."[74] This could suggest that they thought such procedures were clearly established, that they did not anticipate that the convention method of proposing amendments would be used as frequently, or that they did not expect such action for routine changes but only when a new constitution was needed. Whatever the reason, the lack of details with respect to such conventions sowed the seeds for future ambiguities.

Sixth, consistent with their conception of the Constitution as fundamental law, the Framers required supermajorities in both houses of Congress or of the state legislatures to propose and another supermajority at the state level to ratify amendments. They did this to help ensure full deliberation and debate about any future changes. Seventh, the Framers added a federal dimension to the amending process by involving both state and national institutions in most amending pathways—even the Article V convention process, which was intended as an alternate path to congressional proposal, requires Congress to call the convention and to specify how states will ratify its recommendations.[75]

Eighth, the delegates distinguished between individual state conventions designed to ratify the Constitution and amendments proposed by Congress and general conventions, like the one that proposed the Constitution or like some conventions that Congress might convene at the request of the states to propose amendments. Probably because some delegates feared that a second convention might undo their own work, delegates as a whole seemed far more comfortable with conventions designed to ratify the Constitution versus those to actually propose them. Consistent with this preference, delegates were in the ironic position of arguing that a general convention had been necessary to remedy the defects of the Articles of Confederation but that amendments to the new document should be offered in a piecemeal fashion. This, in turn, depended on the argument that the delegates to Philadelphia had gotten the essential principles and structures right and that future changes, at least those in the immediate future, would involve mere tinkering. Ninth, in the final Federalist essay, while arguing against another general convention, Hamilton argued that if Congress did not offer desired amendments to perfect the new document once it was ratified, states would be able to call limited conventions that would propose desired amendments.

For purposes of this book, the greatest ambiguity that emerged from the convention debate is the relationship between the state legislatures, which have the power to propose a convention, and the delegates who will represent the states in an Article V convention. At a time when it was common for state legislatures to appoint delegates to interstate conventions, the delegates to the Constitutional Convention of 1787 may not have anticipated much difference, but one can certainly imagine a case in which the opinions of state legislatures might differ significantly from opinions within a state delegation to an Article V convention. If state legislative opinion reflects true sentiments within a state, legislatures should have relative confidence that delegates chosen for a convention will share their views. If legislatures do not have this confidence, they should probably refrain from calling a convention rather than attempting to bind delegates by oaths and/or tightly prescribed agendas.

Debates at the Constitutional Convention over Ratification of the U.S. Constitution

The Framers' views of constitutional amendments are inextricably related to, and can be enhanced by, proper understandings of corresponding understandings of how they provided for the new Constitution to be ratified. Such an understanding is especially important in putting the Founders' attitude toward constitutional conventions into perspective.

Although the Articles of Confederation required state legislatures to ratify amendments unanimously, the delegates to the Constitutional Convention had not only exceeded their initial authority to revise the Articles of Confederation but had also proposed a new document that they specified would go into effect when nine or more states ratified. When the Virginia delegates had introduced their initial sweeping provisions to the convention, they had also provided that any amendments "ought at a proper time, or times, after the approbation of Congress to be submitted to an assembly or assemblies of Representatives, recommended by the several Legislatures to be expressly chosen by the people, to consider & decide thereon."[76] After Connecticut's Roger Sherman suggested on June 5 that the convention should follow the procedures under the Articles of Confederation for state legislative ratification of convention proposals, Madison argued that it was "indispensable that the new Constitution should be ratified in the most unexceptionable form, and by the supreme authority of the people themselves."[77] This indicates that Madison was, at least in this case, more comfortable equating the people with conventions than with their state legislatures.

Rufus King of Massachusetts saw advantages in having unicameral conventions rather than bicameral legislatures ratify the document. He pointed out that state legislatures might be naturally biased against the suggested reforms since they would be losing power. James Wilson of Pennsylvania further hoped to prevent a few states from blocking action on a new Constitution, and Charles Pinckney of South Carolina suggested that ratification by nine states might be adequate to initiate a new government among ratifying states.[78]

On June 20 Sherman's Connecticut colleague Oliver Ellsworth said that he favored allowing "the plan of the Convention to go forth as an amendment to the articles of Confederation, since under this idea the authority of the Legislatures could ratify it. If they are unwilling, the people will be so too." Indeed, Ellsworth had less faith in state conventions than in existing state legislatures: "He did not like these conventions. They were better fitted to pull down than to build up Constitutions."[79]

Virginia's George Mason renewed arguments on ratifying the Constitution in debates on July 23, the same day the convention voted without dissent to accept a fairly generic amending provision providing "that provision ought to be made for future amendments of the articles of Union." Mason observed that the people were the source of all governmental power. Referring to the Constitution that the convention was writing, he claimed that "the Legislatures have no power to ratify it." He explained: "They are the mere creatures of the State Constitutions, and cannot be greater than their creators. And he knew of no power in any of the Constitutions, he knew there was no power in some of them, that could be competent to this object. Whither then must we resort? To the people with whom all powers remains that has not been given up in the Constitutions derived from them. It was of great moment he observed that this doctrine should be cherished as the basis of free Government." Since one state legislature could not bind another, a future legislature might seek to repudiate the actions of an earlier one. Moreover, with a view to the fact that state legislatures had formulated a number of state constitutions, including Virginia's, Mason questioned whether some existing state legislatures were sufficiently "derived from the clear & undisputed authority of the people."[80]

Fellow Virginian Edmund Randolph, who was popular enough within his own state to have been elected as governor, observed that delegates anticipated that many state and local leaders would oppose the new Constitution. He thought that it was therefore essential to bypass existing state power structures:

> Whose opposition will be most likely to be excited agst. the System? That of the local demogagues who will be degraded by it from the importance they now hold. These will spare no efforts to impede that progress in the popular mind which will be necessary to the adoption of the plan, and which every member will find to have taken place in his own, if he will compare his present opinions with those brought with him into the Convention. It is of great importance therefore that the consideration of this subject should be transferred from the Legislatures where this class of men, have their full influence to a field in which their efforts can be less mischievous. It is moreover worthy of consideration that some of the States are more averse to any changes in their Constitution, and will not take the requisite steps, unless expressly called upon to refer the question to the people.[81]

By contrast, Elbridge Gerry of Massachusetts, who feared direct action by the people like that of Shay's Rebellion, which had occurred within his own state, favored legislative approval over what he anticipated might be less-regularized convention proceedings. He explained: "Great confusion, he was confident would result from a recurrence to the people. They would never agree on any thing. He could not see any ground to suppose that the people will do what their rulers will not. The rulers will either conform to, or influence the sense of the people."[82]

On the same day, Nathaniel Gorham of Massachusetts countered by extolling the superiority of the convention ratification mechanism. All together, he offered five arguments. The first focused on the previously cited difficulty of getting entrenched institutions like the state legislatures to give up their powers: "Men chosen by the people for the particular purpose, will discuss the subject more candidly than members of the Legislature who are to lose the power which is to be given up to the Genl. Govt." Second, he pointed out that it would be easier to get ratification through unicameral conventions than through bicameral legislatures. Third, he argued that existing state legislatures excluded "many of the ablest men," among whom he counted "members of the Clergy who are generally friends to good Government," and whom he apparently anticipated would be eligible to serve as convention delegates. Fourth, he argued that "the Legislatures will be interrupted with a variety of little business, by artfully pressing which, designing men will find means to delay from year to year, if not to frustrate altogether the national system."[83] His fifth and final argument focused more on the reason not to require unanimous state consent—as strict adherence to the amending provision of the Articles of Confederation would have man-dated—than on arguing for the merits of convention over legislative ratification.

Although he continued to favor state legislative ratification, Oliver Ellsworth observed a change in thinking among his contemporaries that modern scholars have documented with respect to equating popular will with the deliberation of conventions.[84] As he explained that "a new sett [*sic*] of ideas seemed to have crept in since the articles of Confederation were established. Conventions of the people, or with power derived expressly from the people, were not then thought of. The Legislatures were considered as competent."[85]

Although much of the discussion necessarily centered on the respective like-lihood of ratification by one or the other mechanism, some focused on which body was likely to be the wiser group of men. Although believing that either state conventions or state legislatures had power to ratify the Constitution, Hugh Williamson of North Carolina argued "that Conventions were to be preferred as more likely to be composed of the ablest men in the States." Rufus King of Massachusetts, who also thought that either state legislators or state conventions had authority to ratify, argued that conventions were "the most certain means of obviating all disputes & doubts concerning the legitimacy of the New Constitu-tion; as well as the most likely means of drawing forth the best men in the States to decide on it."[86]

King added an interesting wrinkle to the argument by observing that some state legislators might think that their oaths to support the existing constitution might hinder them from ratifying another.[87] Ever the theoretician, Madison fur-ther argued that states ratified leagues and treaties, but that the people should ratify a new constitution. He observed that "comparing the two modes in point of expediency he thought all the considerations which recommended this Con-vention in preference to Congress for proposing the reform were in favor of State Conventions in preference to the Legislatures for examining and adopting it." After rejecting both Ellsworth's motion for legislative ratification and a motion by Gouverneur Morris to send the Constitution "to one general Convention, chosen & authorized by the people to consider, amend, & establish the same[88] (a proposal that arguably capitalized on Madison's own praise for the Philadelphia body), the delegates accepted the arguments in favor of individual state conven-tion ratification.

The delegates renewed debate on the subject on August 30 as they examined the wisdom of a proposal (then labeled Article XXI) that "the ratifications of the Conventions of States shall be sufficient for organizing this Constitution."[89] Wilson proposed allowing a majority of seven state ratifications to launch the new Constitution. Gouverneur Morris suggested that the number might vary depending on whether the ratifying states were or were not contiguous. Sherman thought that fellow delegates should require a minimum of ten states, while Randolph favored nine and Wilson suggested eight. Madison feared that any number less than ten would result in putting the document "in force over the whole body of the people. tho' less than a majority of them should ratify it." Wilson had a handy analogy: "As the Constitution stands, the States only which ratify can be bound. We must . . . in this case go to the original powers of Society, The House on fire must be extinguished, without a scrupulous regard to ordinary rights."[90] Pierce Butler of South Carolina suggested ratification by nine states and Daniel Carroll of Maryland by thirteen.

Debate on the subject resumed the following day. After Carroll said that the constitution of his state provided exclusive mechanisms for changing the Constitution, Gouverneur Morris moved to allow states to ratify the Constitution however they wanted. King repeated his conviction that "Conventions alone, which will avoid all the obstacles from the complicated formation of the Legislatures, will succeed, and if not positively required by the plan, its enemies will oppose that mode." Madison again reiterated the argument that state legislators might be disinclined to give up further powers. He further addressed Carroll's concerns by observing that "the people were in fact, the fountain of all power, and by resorting to them, all difficulties were got over. They could alter constitutions as they pleased. It was a principle in the Bill of Rights that first principles might be resorted to."[91]

Luther Martin of Maryland highlighted potential divergence between state legislatures and state conventions when he expressed the fear of "the danger of commotions from a resort to the people & to first principles in which the Governments might be on one side & the people on the other." Likely reflecting his own increasingly negative view, he did not anticipate that either body would be likely to ratify the new Constitution in his state. King saw little difficulty. He noted, "The State [Massachusetts] must have contemplated a recurrence to first principles before they sent deputies to this Convention."[92]

After rejecting proposals to set the number at thirteen, ten, or seven (with these containing a majority of the population), delegates further decided that ratification in nine of the states would be sufficient for ratification among those so agreeing.[93] This was three-fourths of the twelve states that had sent delegates to Philadelphia and was consistent with the provision in Article V that requires three-fourths of the states to ratify amendments.

On August 31 the delegates further discussed whether the convention would need to submit the proposed Constitution to Congress for ratification. Gouverneur Morris and Pinckney proposed that the convention should send the document to Congress for it to send to the states without requiring its own "approbation" (perhaps much as Congress might today send a proposal requested by two-thirds of the states to a convention?). Eight of eleven state delegations voting agreed. Addressing the issue of timing, Gouverneur Morris further suggested that states should call ratifying conventions speedily "to prevent enemies to the plan, from giving it the go by." Luther Martin, who opposed the new document's nationalism, countered that the people "would not ratify it unless hurried into it by surprise," and Gerry, with an eye to the amending provision in the Articles of Confederation, denied the propriety of ratifying the Constitution without unanimous state consent.[94]

As constitutional proponents argued for ratification by conventions within each of the states, delegates with reservations about the convention's work were beginning to advocate what George Mason called "another general Convention." Perhaps to show that another convention might go even further toward a consolidated government than the present one, Morris responded that "he had long wished for another Convention, that will have the firmness to provide a vigorous Government, which we are afraid to do." Governor Randolph clearly sided with Mason in hoping that "the State Conventions should be at liberty to propose amendments to be submitted to another General Convention which may reject or incorporate them, as shall be judged proper." The convention then voted to ask Congress to ask states to call ratifying conventions.[95]

On September 10 delegates reconsidered whether the convention should send the Constitution to Congress for its assent before sending it to state conventions. Gerry, who would join the Antifederalist camp, feared that excluding Congress would give "just umbrage to that body," and, perhaps unexpectedly, Alexander Hamilton agreed. In an observation reminiscent of those related to congressional oaths, Thomas Fitzsimmons of Pennsylvania thought that delegates had struck the provision for congressional approval "in order to save Congress from the necessity of an Act inconsistent with the Articles of Confederation under which they held their authority."[96]

Announcing that he might have to dissent from the plan as a whole, Randolph wanted state conventions to "be at liberty to offer amendments to the plan,—and that these should be submitted to a second General Convention, with full power to settle the Constitution finally."[97] After James Wilson opposed such a "reconsideration" of the convention's work, delegates continued to debate the desirability of submitting the convention's work to Congress for its approval, and Hamilton proposed a motion to do so, seconded by Gerry. Wilson questioned the prudence of such a move: "After spending four or five months in the laborious & arduous task of forming a Government for our Country, we are ourselves at the close throwing insuperable obstacles in the way of its success."[98] Hamilton withdrew his motion after it was postponed, and the convention agreed to confirm ratification by state conventions.

On September 15 Randolph renewed his plea for allowing state conventions to propose amendments to the proposed Constitution, "which would be decided on by another General Convention." Pointing out that "this Constitution had been formed without the knowledge or idea of the people," Mason further argued that "a second Convention will know more of the sense of the people, and be able to provide a system more consonant to it. It was improper to say to the people, take this or nothing."[99]

By contrast, Charles Pinckney of South Carolina thought that "nothing but confusion & contrariety could spring from the experiment [offered by Randolph and Mason]." Perhaps anticipating subsequent reluctance to employ the General Convention mechanism, he observed that "Conventions are serious things, and ought not to be repeated." Although Gerry also restated the hope "for a second general convention,"[100] Pinckney's argument carried the day.

In a clear indication that the delegates realized that their plan went far beyond a mere amendment of the Articles, delegates further provided that the new government would take effect only among the states that chose to ratify.[101] Realistically, however, even ratification of three-fourths of the states would have been insufficient had the larger states like Virginia or Pennsylvania failed to ratify. Once eleven states, including these powerhouses, ratified, they exerted tremendous pressure on the other two (North Carolina and Rhode Island) to do so as well.

Article VII of the Constitution

Article VII is both the last and the shortest of the Constitution's articles. It provides in full that "the Ratification of the Conventions of nine States, shall be sufficient for the Establishment of this Constitution between the States so ratifying the Same." The signatures of thirty-nine delegates from twelve states who signed the document on September 17, 1787, immediately followed.

Wayne D. Moore explains that "Article VII of the U.S. Constitution delineated a hybrid super-majoritarian/unanimity requirement." He further explains, "The Constitution would not go into effect unless and until it was approved by conventions representing nine of the initial 13 states (i.e., more than a simple majority, less than unanimity). But it would bind only those ratifying."[102]

The Federalist Defense of Article VII

In addition to justifying the amending process in Article V, the Framers had to defend the convention's decision to bypass the requirements under the Articles of Confederation for congressional approval and for state legislative ratification of all amendments. Some of these arguments were intertwined with those for Article V, and some were separate.

In attempting to show in Federalist No. 39 that the new Constitution was "republican," or representative, in nature, James Madison looked first at the foundation of the new government. Attempting to argue that the new government blended elements previously associated with both consolidated and confederal governments and was therefore both partly national and partly federal, Madison relied on what he hoped would be support for the convention method of ratification: "The Constitution is to be founded on the assent and ratification of the people of America, given by deputies elected for the special purpose; but ... this assent and ratification is to be given by the people, not as individuals composing one entire nation, but as composing the distinct and independent States to which they respectively belong. It is to be the assent and ratification of the several States, derived from the supreme authority in each State—the authority of the people themselves." Although this suggested that ratification was a "national" act, Madison said that it was federal. This character was demonstrated by the fact that ratification "is to result neither from the decision of a majority of the people of the Union, nor from that of a majority of the States. It must result from the unanimous assent of the several States that are parties to it."[103]

In Federalist No. 40, Madison tackled a question, connected to the wisdom of both Article V and Article VII, as to the authority of the convention to propose a new Constitution. He acknowledged that the convention had bypassed the formal requirements for amending the Articles of Confederation. Madison further argued that halfway reforms would not have accomplished the ends for which the Annapolis Convention and Congress had called the convention, namely that of "rendering the constitution *adequate to the exigencies of government and the preservation of the Union.*"[104]

In justifying the provision allowing the new Constitution to go into effect without unanimous approval of the existing states, Madison rather cagily played on sentiments against Rhode Island, which had not sent delegates to the convention, by focusing on the possibility of opposition by a single state rather than by four. He pointed to "the absurdity of subjecting the fate of twelve States to the perverseness or corruption of a thirteenth." He further observed that the actions of the convention "were merely advisory and recommendatory" and that the proposed Constitution "is to be of no more consequence than the paper on which it is written, unless it be stamped with the approbation of those to whom it is addressed."[105]

Further elevating the importance of substance over form, Madison cited the Declaration of Independence as to the right of the people to "'abolish or alter their governments as to them shall seem most likely to effect their safety and happiness,' since it is impossible for the people spontaneously and universally to move in concert towards their object; and it is therefore essential that such changes be instituted by some informal and unauthorized propositions, made by some patriotic and respectable citizen or number of citizens."[106] Madison proceeded to defend the convention method in general by reminding his readers that those who wrote the Constitution "must have recollected that it was by this irregular and assumed privilege of proposing to the people plans for their safety and happiness that the States were first united against the danger with which they were threatened by their ancient government; that committees and congresses were formed for concentrating their efforts and defending their rights; and that *conventions* were *elected in the several States* for establishing the constitutions under which they are now governed." Madison tried to convince readers that the approval by "the people themselves" would "blot out antecedent errors and irregularities."[107]

Immediately after arguing in Federalist No. 43 that the proposed amending process in Article V would strike a mean between the extremes of extreme mutability and extreme difficulty that equally enabled both Congress and the states to initiate change, Madison further sought to justify Article VII by noting that it recognized that "the express authority of the people alone could give due validity to the Constitution." He further inquired as to how the Articles could be superseded without unanimous state consent and what the relationship would be between states that ratified the proposed Constitution and those that did not. In answering the first question, Madison found himself recurring, in language that echoed that of the Declaration of Independence, to a litany of answers including "the absolute necessity of the case; to the great principle of self-preservation; to the transcendent law of nature and of nature's God, which declares that the safety and happiness of society are the objects at which all political institutions aim and to which all such institutions must be sacrificed." He further observed that one of the weaknesses of the Articles was "that in many of the States it had received no higher sanction than a mere legislative ratification," and he suggested that, as a treaty or compact, breaches on the part of one party "absolves the others, and authorized them, if they please, to pronounce the compact violated and void." In answering the second question, Madison animadverted that ratifying and nonratifying states would retain their "moral relations" if not their "political" ones while anticipating "a speedy triumph over the obstacles to reunion."[108] As discussed earlier, in Federalist No. 85 Hamilton further advocated ratification of the Constitution prior to the proposal of further amendments.

Themes That Emerged from the Debate over Article VII

As in the debates over Article V, several distinct themes emerged from the debates over Article VII. First, delegates believed that necessity sometimes trumped absolute constitutional propriety. When delegates faced a constitution that they did not believe adequately provided for change, they were prepared to bypass some of its provisions, if they could muster sufficient public approval to do so. In the case of the Constitution, they were willing to substitute consent on the part of nine or more state conventions for the unanimous consent of existing state legislatures required for constitutional amendments under the Articles of Confederation.

Second, the delegates believed that, at least in the case at hand, consent offered through state conventions would give the new Constitution greater legitimacy than acting through existing state legislatures. They followed such legitimizing arguments with additional arguments relative to the bias of existing legislators, who would be giving up some power under the new system; to the fact that state legislators were simultaneously doing other tasks and could therefore be diverted from the issue at hand; and to the possibility that conventions might draw from expertise that then-existing rules excluded from legislative counsels. However, their primary argument centered on the belief that convention delegates, who would be elected specifically to approve or disapprove of the new Constitution, would convey greater legitimacy to the new document than mere state legislative approval.

Third, delegates were committed enough to the idea of popular sovereignty that they did not believe that any state, or the people therein, should be bound to a constitution that they did not approve. Although the delegates allowed for a minimum of nine states to begin a new government among themselves, they did not provide the means whereby these nine states could force others to join without their consent.

Fourth, and somewhat ironically, even as they met in convention, provided for convention approval of their work, and included a convention mechanism for proposing amendments within Article V, delegates expressed continuing reservations about conventions in general. Thus, Oliver Ellsworth thought that conventions "were better fitted to pull down than to build up Constitutions," and Pinckney thought that "Conventions are serious things, and ought not to be repeated."[109]

Fifth, and largely as a consequence, the Framers tried to negotiate a path wherein they would allow a set of state conventions to decide on ratification of the Constitution without thereby entrusting them with power to propose new amendments that would open up the possibility of yet another general convention. If called prior to constitutional ratification, such a convention would not have been bound by Article V and might thus have undone the work of the first. In a letter to Edward Everett dated August 28, 1830, Madison candidly observed:

When the Constitution was adopted as a whole, it is certain that there were many parts which if separately proposed, would have been promptly rejected. It is far from impossible, that every part of the Constitution might be rejected by a majority, and yet, taken together as a whole be unanimously accepted. Free constitutions will rarely if ever be formed without reciprocal concessions; without articles conditioned on & balancing each other. Is there a constitution of a single State out of the 24 that wd. bear the experiment of having its component parts submitted to the people & separately decided on.[110]

Sixth, by specifying that states would ratify the new Constitution by conventions rather than through existing state legislatures, the Framers recognized that the interests of the two bodies could differ and that the people might articulate their interests differently in the two sets of institutions.

Sorting through these diverse themes, delegates had the delicate task of justifying the work of their own extraconstitutional convention, which actually proposed a new Constitution rather than merely recommending amendments, while seeking to rein in the role of future conventions to that of confirming their own good work or proposing amendments to an existing constitutional structure. However much the Framers had sought to domesticate the convention mechanism by specifically providing for it within the new document in a way that the Articles of Confederation had not, they continued to fear another *extraconstitutional* convention that might undo the work that they had accomplished in the summer of 1787 even before the new Constitution went into effect. This concern is arguably reflected in modern concerns about a "runaway" convention. Ironically, the delegates' own departure from the amending script under the Articles of Confederation may have sown the seeds for fears that future conventions might do likewise, albeit with the possibility of less salutary effects.

Rewriting or Replacing a Constitution

Historically, conventions have served three primary governmental purposes. One, best embodied in the Constitutional Convention of 1787, is the task of rewriting a constitution and proposing a substitute. Another, to date exclusively exercised at the state level, is that of proposing a singular amendment or a set of piecemeal amendments. A third, embodied in Article V, and exercised in the case of the Twenty-First Amendment, involves ratifying a constitution or constitutional amendment.

The language of Article V provides that "Congress . . . on the Application of the Legislatures of two thirds of the several States, shall call a Convention for proposing Amendments." This suggests that the Framers largely anticipated using a constitutional convention to propose needed amendments that Congress refused to propose on its own. Since they made no other constitutional provision for rewriting the Constitution, however, should the need for such a rewriting occur, the Article V convention process would also appear to be the most appropriate way to do so.[111]

The History of Constitutional
Amendments in the United States

Although members of Congress have introduced about twelve thousand amending resolutions (most concentrating on a far smaller number of subjects) in U.S. history, the necessary two-thirds majorities have proposed only thirty-three amendments since the Constitution went into effect in 1789, and the states have ratified twenty-seven of these.[1] Each has followed the path of congressional proposal and state ratification. Like the experience of the Constitutional Convention of 1787, the history of proposing and ratifying constitutional amendments is also relevant to thinking about the components of successful constitutional change. Because there are numerous solid treatments of the history of such amendments,[2] this chapter will only present a broad overview of the subject, which is designed to give an idea of the breadth and depth of existing constitutional reforms.

The Bill of Rights Helps Ease
Concerns about the New Constitution

Congress proposed the first ten amendments as a group (originally of twelve). These proposals grew from concerns for protecting individual rights against the new national government that the debates in the states on ratification of the U.S. Constitution had generated. Despite Federalist assurances that the enumeration of powers would limit the powers of Congress, Antifederalists, who were already alert to the possibility that Congress would make liberal use of its implied powers, wanted specific assurances that the new Congress would not trample individual rights. Although they refused to condition state ratification of the Constitution upon the adoption of specific amendments, Federalists agreed that ratifying states could propose amendments for congressional consideration,[3] and, as a member of the House of Representatives, James Madison took the responsibility of compiling, articulating, and shepherding these amendments through the very first Congress.

Madison, who had expressed concerns about the mechanics of Article V conventions in Philadelphia and who feared holding another convention that might undo the work of the first, effectively established the mechanism of congressional proposal and state ratification, rather than the constitutional convention mechanism, as the default method for adding an individual amendment or series of amendments to the Constitution when he introduced the Bill of Rights within Congress. Subsequent leaders approved. When Chief Justice John Marshall wrote his famous opinion in *Marbury v. Madison* (1803), which legitimized judicial review of federal legislation, he followed his observation that the people "have an original right to establish for their future government, such principles as, in their opinion, shall most conduce to their own happiness," with the observation that "the exercise of this original right is a very great exertion, nor can it, nor ought it, to be frequently repeated."[4]

In proposing the Bill of Rights, Madison did not completely carry the day. After telling fellow members of Congress that "the State Governments are as liable to attack these invaluable privileges as the General Government is, and therefore ought to be cautiously guarded against," he had proposed that "No State shall violate the equal rights of conscience, or the freedom of the press, or the trial by jury in criminal cases," but Congress did not propose this amendment.[5] Moreover, he had favored inserting amendments into the text of the existing Constitution so that their impact on existing provisions would be clearer.[6] Roger Sherman was among those who favored adding amendments to the end of the document, lest it appear that George Washington and other signers had agreed to proposals that could not rightly be attributed to them. Ironically, the adoption of Sherman's strategy arguably enhanced the status of the Bill of Rights, especially in modern times, and has certainly made it easier for citizens and scholars to trace subsequent amendments than Madison's strategy would have.

Many Americans are probably as familiar with the Bill of Rights as with any other part of the Constitution. The First (and arguably most important) Amendment prohibited Congress from establishing a religion or prohibiting the free exercise thereof. It also guaranteed the related rights of free speech, free press, peaceable assembly, and petition. All of these are essential not only to personal development but to the proper functioning of republican government and, indeed, to the very process of generating ideas for constitutional change.[7]

The Second Amendment protected the controversial right to bear arms. Lawyers and scholars continue to debate whether this is primarily a personal or a collective right, but recent Supreme Court decisions have upheld the former view.[8] With a view back to British abuses at the time of the Revolutionary War, the Third Amendment further prohibited governments from quartering soldiers in private homes during peacetime without the owners' consent or in times of war other than through legally designated procedures. The Fourth Amendment prohibited "unreasonable searches and seizures" by barring general warrants, like those under which the colonists had suffered under British rule, that did not describe with particularity "the place to be searched, and the persons or things to be seized."[9] With a few notable exceptions, the Supreme Court has enforced this amendment, first against the national government,[10] and later against the states,[11] through the exclusionary rule, which prevents the government from using evidence that it has attained illegally.

The Fifth Amendment contains the provision prohibiting the government from depriving individuals of their rights to "life, liberty, or property, without due process of law." The amendment included protections for individuals accused of crimes, including a guarantee for grand jury indictment, a prohibition against double jeopardy, and a provision against compulsory self-incrimination. In what Akhil Reed Amar believes is a case of "clever bundling,"[12] the amendment also prohibited governmental takings of private property for public use without just compensation, a provision arguably undercut by the judicial acceptance of liberal interpretations of the public use clause.[13]

The Sixth and Seventh Amendments spelled out trial rights. These included the right to trials by petit juries (those that determine guilt or innocence), the right of defendants to be informed of the charges against them, the right of compulsory process in obtaining witnesses, and the assistance of counsel, which the Supreme Court had ruled includes free governmental provision of legal services to the indigent.[14] Moving from the trial stage to punishments, the Eighth Amendment further prohibited excessive fines and bail as well as "cruel and unusual punishments."[15]

The two most ambiguous amendments deal with concerns that it was easier for the Founders to articulate than to settle. One such issue, which the Ninth Amendment addresses, involves whether the rights listed in the Bill of Rights were exhaustive.[16] Although the amendment indicated that they were not, it did little to delineate what such other rights might be or who would enforce them. A second concern, which the Tenth Amendment addressed, affirmed that the individual states retained certain reserved powers, often referred to as police powers, again without specifically enumerating what they are. Both amendments are arguably more useful as guides to constitutional interpretation than as protections of specific rights.

Further Expansion of the Scope of the Bill of Rights

The First Amendment specifically directed its initial prohibitions against Congress ("Congress shall make no law . . ."). Chief Justice John Marshall's unanimous decision in *Barron v. Baltimore* (1833) later reaffirmed that the amendments limited acts of national, rather than state legislation.[17] Only after the Fourteenth

Amendment (1868) extended due process rights to state citizens did U.S. courts begin to apply what the justices considered to be the most fundamental provisions of the Bill of Rights to the states (those implicit in "due process of law"), a list that now includes almost all of them.[18]

Since Federalists and Antifederalists both agreed that they did not want a government that could threaten individual liberties, the requisite number of states ratified ten of the twelve amendments that Congress proposed within a two-year period. The two proposals that failed dealt with structural matters. One of these, which states finally ratified as the Twenty-Seventh Amendment in 1992, delayed the implementation of congressional pay raises until after intervening elections. The other dealt with the size of the U.S. House of Representatives. As discussed earlier, Madison was especially anxious to avoid a second convention that might reverse the work of the first, and Congress both took the initiative in proposing the amendments and specifying that states would ratify through their legislatures rather than through conventions called specifically for this purpose. The fact that states so quickly ratified most of the proposed amendments seemed to verify Madison's defense of the amending process in Federalist No. 43 as being neither too easy nor too difficult.

An Early Positive Assessment by Nathaniel Chipman

One of the earliest post-ratification explanations and assessments of the U.S. Constitution is a book by Nathaniel Chipman (1752–1843), then a judge for the U.S. District Court in Vermont (and later a professor of law at Middlebury College), entitled *Sketches of the Principles of Government.*[19] Published within two years of the ratification of the Bill of Rights, Chipman's assessment of the amending process is one of the most positive in U.S. history. Basing his theory of the origins of government on humankind's capacity for progress, Chipman lauded the constitutional amending process in Article V as a way of overcoming the inertia of previous systems (especially that of Great Britain), in which "an opinion of the present perfection of government, and a dread of encouraging a spirit of innovation, the bane of a well regulated society, have concurred to prevent any regular plan of fundamental reformation in government, and to continue, as unalterably perfect, those institutions, which were adapted only to the weakness, ignorance, and barbarous manners of an infant people."[20] His sentiments on the strengths of the amending process were similar to those that Madison had commended in *The Federalist.* Chipman thus observed:

> It is calculated to admit amendments, corresponding with the progress of the
> citizens in social improvements, and political science. The idea of incorporating,
> in the constitution itself, a plan of reformation, which, without encouraging a

spirit of innovation, the parent of anarchy and final despotism, might enable the
people, with deliberation, and more mature experience, to correct what should
be, at any time, found wrong in the form, principles, or operation of the government, was first adopted, in practice, in some of the individual states of the
confederacy. It had been found, not only practicable and safe in the exercise, but
its happy effect in ameliorating the fundamental principles of the government,
had, in several instances, been fully evinced.[21]

With a view to the ratification of the Bill of Rights, Chipman observed:

In virtue of the power vested in Congress, and reserved to the people and the
states, by this article, several important amendments have already been adopted
in the federal constitution; and we have reason to believe, that whatever, on
experience, shall be found deficient in principle, will be added; whatever shall
be found dangerous to the rights of the people or the states, or impracticable
in operation, will be retrenched and corrected. The wisdom, which formed it,
aided and matured by experience, may, not only extend its principles, with the
progress of social improvements, but carry it to a greater degree of practical perfection than any thing, which has yet been known in government.[22]

Although Chipman did not comment separately on the Article V convention
mechanism, his reference to "the power vested in Congress, and reserved to the
people and the states, by this article [Article V]"[23] suggests that, like Madison,
Chipman anticipated that the amending process would work both to protect
congressional and state interests.

The Eleventh and Twelfth Amendments Address
Perceived Constitutional Defects

The Eleventh Amendment demonstrated the power of amendments to restore
widespread constitutional understandings. Despite assurances of state sovereign
immunity that Federalists offered during the Federalist/Antifederalist debates,
the Supreme Court, which had relied more strongly on the actual language of Article III of the Constitution, had ruled in *Chisholm v. Georgia* (1793) that states,
which were often unwilling or unable to pay debts they had incurred during the
Revolution, could be sued by citizens of other states or countries without their
consent.[24] Two years later, the Eleventh Amendment restored what appears to
have been the Framers' original understanding and showed that states remained
alert to the exercise of centralized power under the new system.[25]

Although this development did much to clarify that Supreme Court decisions were subject to the ultimate will of the people, in some ways this example
was anomalous since one of the primary methods by which the Constitution
has been adapted to new circumstances through much of U.S. history has been

through judicial decisions, some of which have overturned earlier understandings. In a classic study of the subject, Clement Vose has observed that the process by which the U.S. Supreme Court has overruled the Court's previous decisions has been "the most distinctive and dramatic technique of constitutional change in this [the twentieth] century."[26]

The Twelfth Amendment, adopted in 1803, showed how the amending process could deal with unforeseen issues in constitutional procedures. It addressed problems that stemmed from the largely unanticipated development of the American party system.[27] By requiring that electors cast separate votes for president and vice president (rather than, as in the original Constitution, casting two votes for president), the Twelfth Amendment made it highly unlikely that a president and vice president would be elected from different parties, as John Adams (a Federalist) and Thomas Jefferson (a Jeffersonian Republican) had done in the election of 1796. It also significantly decreased the chances that candidates from the same party would tie, as Thomas Jefferson and Aaron Burr had done in the election of 1800 when all Democratic-Republican delegates cast both their votes for both party candidates. Although the latter result had allowed Federalists within the House of Representatives to meddle in, without ultimately foiling, the results, such Federalists undoubtedly understood that they could just as easily become the victims of this system in the next election.

A Period of Amending Drought

Although the nation struggled for the next six decades with issues relative to slavery, regional differences prevented the national amending process from successfully addressing them. This period from 1803 to 1865 was, in fact, the longest such amending drought in U.S. history. As the next chapter documents, it was also a period during which extra-constitutional meetings assumed more importance than Article V mechanisms and in which a number of scholars accordingly began questioning the effectiveness of the formal amending provisions.

The Civil War ultimately resolved issues that seemed beyond simple constitutional remedy. The Union victory opened the way for three of the nation's most consequential amendments. The chapter that follows details some of the highlights of this period, which included a number of extralegal and illegal conventions.

The Postbellum Amendments

Although Abraham Lincoln had long proclaimed that the nation could not long endure "half slave and half free,"[28] it had done so during the course of its first four score and seven years. Because he justified it as a war measure, Lincoln's Emancipation Proclamation freeing slaves applied only behind rebel lines.[29] By the war's end, the toll in blood was repaid not simply with the preservation of the Union (Lincoln's initial paramount goal), but with emancipation of the slaves, which abolitionists had been advocating for decades.

The Thirteenth Amendment, which states ratified in the same year that the war ended, abolished involuntary servitude except as punishment for a crime, and it did so without compensating slave owners. The two amendments that followed provided guarantees of equal rights to the freedmen.[30] The Fourteenth Amendment (1868) overturned the notorious decision in *Dred Scott v. Sandford* (1857)[31] by declaring that all persons born or naturalized in the United States were U.S. citizens and by guaranteeing all citizens their privileges and immunities,[32] due process, and equal protection.[33] It also answered a number of other questions that the Civil War had generated. Section 2, which Congress never enforced, thus permitted Congress to reduce representation for states that restricted voting rights. Section 3 disabled some former rebels from participating in the new government unless and until they were pardoned. Section 4 affirmed the good faith of the United States while repudiating Confederate debts, and section 5 vested enforcement powers in Congress. The Fifteenth Amendment (1870) prohibited discrimination in voting with respect to race or national origin.

All three of these postbellum amendments included clauses vesting Congress with special enforcement powers.[34] In many cases, it took until the 1960s before it fully exercised them, and the Supreme Court, which had initially issued very narrow interpretations of the amendments,[35] recognized its power to do so.[36]

Congress refused to recognize the legitimacy of southern governments that had attempted to secede from the Union until they ratified the Fourteenth Amendment. Still, there is no doubt but that all states are currently committed to the principles (albeit not always to individual interpretations) of equal protection and due process that this amendment embodies.[37] This somewhat calls into question the attention that some scholars, most notably Bruce Ackerman,[38] have devoted to this and other amending anomalies.

The Progressive Era Amendments

Amid a rising chorus of scholarly complaints that the amending process was inadequate,[39] the nation went more than forty years until another round of amendments. They succeeded after decades of populist agitation and progressive reform, much of it at the state level. The Sixteenth Amendment (1913) overturned the Supreme Court decision in *Pollock v. Farmers' Loan and Trust* II (1895) and affirmed the constitutionality of the national income tax.[40] This created a significant revenue stream for the national government as well as the possibility of using taxes to redistribute income. That same year, the Seventeenth Amendment (prompted in large part by state calls for an Article V convention) democratized the Constitution by providing for direct election of senators but arguably in the process weakened the role of states, as states, within Congress.[41] The Eighteenth Amendment (1919), which responded to a social movement that had gained in strength over the previous several decades, and especially during World War I, mandated national alcoholic prohibition.[42] The Nineteenth Amendment (1920) effectively doubled the voting population by fulfilling the dream of the delegates to the Seneca Falls Convention (1848) by prohibiting discrimination in voting on the basis of sex.[43]

Although the implementation of three of these amendments went smoothly, there was rising opposition to the Eighteenth Amendment, which was widely flouted and which contributed to the rise of organized crime, whose members were willing to supply the product that the amendment had legally banned. The states ratified the Twenty-First Amendment to repeal Prohibition in 1933, shortly after the election of Franklin D. Roosevelt. It remains the only amendment that ever repealed another and the only amendment that states ratified, as specified by Congress, through state ratifying conventions.[44] Although the Twenty-First Amendment repealed one Progressive Era reform, earlier that year states ratified the Twentieth Amendment, which affirmed another such reform by moving inaugurations forward, thereby shortening the lame-duck terms (when elected officials remained in office until their successors took office) of exiting presidents and members of Congress.

From 1951 to the Present

Just as he had returned military power to Congress at the end of the Revolution, so too, George Washington retired from the presidency after his second four-year term of office. Adams was not reelected, and Thomas Jefferson continued Washington's precedent, which scholars widely regarded as part of America's unwritten constitution, until Franklin Roosevelt was elected to his third and fourth terms during World War II.[45] In 1951 states ratified an amendment, reestablishing the two-term precedent, which had particular resonance among Republicans who had witnessed five successive presidential wins by Democrats.[46] This amendment is one of only a few (the Sixteenth and Seventeenth are others) that continue to be the subject of persistent repeal proposals, in part because it limited rather than expanded popular power, and in part because it may have inadvertently undercut the powers of second-term lame-duck presidents.

Ten years later, the Twenty-Third Amendment provided that the District of Columbia, which was otherwise unrepresented in presidential elections because it was not a state with representatives in Congress, would cast votes in the Electoral College equal to that of the smallest state (three). The Twenty-Fourth Amendment, which states ratified in the same year that Congress adopted the Civil Rights Act of 1964 limiting discrimination in places of public accommodation, prohibited use of a poll tax—a head tax required to vote that significantly reduced voting among racial minorities and the poor—in primary or general elections. Three years later the nation, which had witnessed a recent presidential assassination and a number of presidential health scares in an age where presidents had their fingers on the nuclear trigger, provided greater clarity to deal with cases of presidential disability through the Twenty-Fifth Amendment. On a related matter, this amendment also filled another constitutional gap by providing for filling vice-presidential vacancies.[47]

Aware both of rising educational levels and of the sacrifices that young people were making on the battlefields of Vietnam, in 1971 the nation followed by partially reversing the effects of the Supreme Court decision in *Oregon v. Mitchell* (1972).[48] The Twenty-Sixth Amendment provided that states could not discriminate against voters who were eighteen years or older. Previously, most states had drawn the line at twenty-one.

The only amendment the nation has adopted since then is the Twenty-Seventh Amendment (1992), which limits raises for new members of Congress until after intervening elections. Congress originally proposed this amendment in 1789 as part of the Bill of Rights, and Gregory Watson, an aide to a Texas state legislator, successfully revived interest in it after a series of congressional scandals.[49] Seeming to cast doubt on prior statements (most notably in *Dillon v. Gloss*) proclaiming that amendments must reflect a contemporary consensus,[50] in point of fact, proponents observed that states had continued to ratify the amendment since it was proposed, and no state had ever attempted to rescind its ratification.

Failed Amendments

Thousands of proposals have died in committee or have secured less than the support of two-thirds of both houses, but two amendments successfully ran this gauntlet in the nineteenth century that the states did not ratify. One was an elusive amendment, usually called the Reed Amendment, which Congress proposed in 1810. It would have put further teeth in the emoluments clause of Article I, Section 9 by stripping citizenship from any American who accepted foreign titles of nobility.[51] The amendment, generated by fears connected to foreign influence, failed. Similarly, prodded in part by the Peace Convention of 1861,[52] Congress proposed the Corwin Amendment in the same year. It would have perpetually guaranteed slavery in those states that wanted to retain it.[53] Instead of ratifying this amendment, states engaged in a war that settled the issue.

Congress subsequently proposed three additional amendments in the twentieth century that failed. In 1924 it proposed a child labor amendment, which some southern states competing for industries opposed. Changes in judicial decision-making that allowed Congress to use existing constitutional powers to legislate on the subject also undermined arguments for the necessity of such an amendment.[54]

In 1972 Congress proposed an Equal Rights Amendment for women. Even after a controversial decision by Congress extending the original seven-year ratification deadline, which it had included in the authorizing resolution rather than in the text,[55] a sufficient number of states failed to ratify. Opponents raised two somewhat contradictory, albeit ultimately effective, arguments. One contended that the amendment was no longer needed because of Supreme Court decisions that were increasingly applying the equal protection clause of the Fourteenth Amendment to women's issues.[56] The second, not unlike modern arguments against a "runaway" Article V convention,[57] raised fears that the amendment would undermine the right to privacy, might require women to serve in combat, and could give undue interpretative leeway to the judiciary, which opponents accused of already being too activist.[58] A final amendment, which Congress proposed in 1978, to grant voting congressional representation to the District of Columbia, failed chiefly because the district was so solidly Democratic that Republican state legislatures had a clear disincentive to adopt it, and perhaps in part because it would appear to have further distorted the ratio between voters and representatives within Congress.[59]

Near-Miss Calls for Article V Conventions

Although the earliest state petitions requested general conventions, ever since Nebraska petitioned for a convention to propose the direct election of senators in 1893, petitions for such limited conventions have "become the norm."[60] As Russell Caplan has so ably documented, the twentieth century witnessed three movements for Article V conventions that came close to rallying two-thirds of the states. Caplan records that thirty-one states, a single state shy of the two-thirds majority, had petitioned for a convention to mandate direct election of senators by 1912.[61] Caplan is not as sure as other scholars that this drive was the cause of Senate approval—he notes that an increasing number of senators who voted on the measure had been selected in states that had agreed to accept the popular-vote winner.[62] In either case, the outcome certainly suggested that if Congress acts expeditiously to take action on its own, it might therefore take the steam out of the convention option.

The U.S. Supreme Court decisions on legislative apportionment, most notably *Baker v. Carr*,[63] *Reynolds v. Sims*,[64] and *Wesberry v. Sanders*,[65] prompted a similar movement to call a convention in the 1960s. Republican Senate minority leader Everett McKinley Dirksen of Illinois took the lead in encouraging state petitions and is believed to have reached thirty-three, one short of the required three-fourths, at the time of his unexpected death in 1969.[66] According to Russell Caplan, Dirksen "planned to keep the campaign quiet until the final state had submitted applications, and then make a dramatic announcement that the requirements for an article V convention had been fulfilled."[67]

One obstacle to the campaign may have been that it elicited calls by the Council of State Governments not simply to overrule *Baker v. Carr*, but also to allow two-thirds of the state legislatures to propose identically worded resolutions that would bypass the convention mechanism, and create a "Court of the Union" consisting of state supreme court justices with the power to reverse U.S. Supreme Court decisions. Contemporary scholars widely criticized these proposals.[68] For example, Professor William Swindler of the College of William and Mary said they were a throwback to the Articles of Confederation,[69] Professor Charles Black of Yale said they were "a threatened disaster,"[70] and Professor Alpheus T. Mason at Princeton called them the "'Disunion' Amendments."[71] A journalist further published a story in the popular magazine *Look* under the title "Seventeen States Vote to Destroy Democracy as We Know It."[72]

Fears of a runaway convention also put a damper on the call for an Article V convention. Caplan observes: "Three states rescinded their applications, at least partially out of fear that a convention might be uncontrollable. A principal reason for North Carolina's retraction, according to one legislator, was the prospect of a nationally televised convention attracting unsavory characters and "some degree of violence."[73]

Caplan further notes that Republicans, who were initially most concerned about the implications of the apportionment decision (which generally shifted power from rural to urban interests) for federalism, found that they were winning races "in newly redrawn suburban districts." He further observes that one of the reasons that Senator Sam Ervin introduced the Federal Constitutional Convention Act in 1967 was "to allay fears of a 'runaway' assembly."[74]

Proposals for a convention to propose a balanced budget amendment garnered thirty-two state applications in the 1970s and 1980s.[75] In turn, the Senate votes in 1994 and again in 1997 were but a single vote from that necessary to send such an amendment to the states for ratification. Passage of the Gramm-Rudman-Hollins Law may have prevented others.

Throughout the efforts, individuals continued to ask whether a convention to write a balanced budget might backfire. Caplan observes that, although he favored a balanced budget amendment, Arizona senator Barry Goldwater in his

1964 presidential campaign expressed fears that "if we hold a constitutional convention, every group in this country—majority, minority, middle-of-the-road, left, right, up, down—is going to get its two bits in and we are going to wind up with a Constitution that will be so far different from the one we have lived under for 200 years that I doubt that the Republic could continue."[76] Lest it be thought that Goldwater's view represented only those from the far right, Caplan observed that, in seeking reelection to the presidency, Jimmy Carter expressed fears that a convention would be "extremely dangerous" and "completely uncontrollable."[77] As to the specific issue of the balanced budget amendment, experts continue to question whether such mechanisms would be effective and how they would be enforced, but thirty-four states already have budget-balancing provisions in their own constitutions.[78]

Although three issues have come the closest to prompting conventions, states have petitioned for conventions on many other subjects. Petitions for limited conventions have called for amendments that would have affected or established the selection and tenure of federal judges, the right to life (had abortion been illegal, there might well have been petitions for a convention to provide for reproductive choice), revenue sharing, federal preemption of state laws, federal taxing power, the line-item veto, the coercive use of federal funds, school prayers, federal debt limits, revision of the Article V amending process, presidential electors, and the validity of the Fourteenth Amendment. Others have involved a call for world federal government, restrictions on unfunded federal mandates, antipolygamy proposals, treaty making, state control over public education, repeal of the Sixteenth Amendment, antitrust concerns, school assignment, sedition laws, limiting presidential tenure, school funding, and congressional term limits.[79]

Lessons from Amending History

Examining the history of constitutional amendments in the United States is a bit like looking at a python that has swallowed a number of prey in somewhat irregular intervals. More often than not, amendments have been adopted in groups or clusters. The first ten amendments were almost an extension of the original constitution and reaffirmed that the national government would not exercise powers that its authors never claimed to have given it. The adoption of these amendments served to prevent the Federalist/Antifederalist divide from becoming permanent, although it did not prevent the subsequent emergence of the Federalist and Democratic-Republican parties.

The Eleventh and Twelfth Amendments were adopted relatively contemporaneously but largely remedied unanticipated interpretations or consequences that cut across party lines. The Eleventh Amendment is particularly important in that it was the first that overturned a Supreme Court decision, thus arguably vindicating the idea that the people exercise their sovereignty through the amending process. The Thirteenth through Fifteenth Amendments all resulted from the North's military successes in the Civil War but furthered ideals that the nation had espoused in the Declaration of Independence.

The Sixteenth through Nineteenth Amendments were largely attributable to democratizing emphasis of the Progressive Era, although the example of the Eighteenth Amendment serves as a prudent warning that some behaviors may be largely beyond the realm of effective constitutional proscription. The nation adopted four amendments between 1961 and 1971, a time of civil rights successes, war, and great social tumult. States ratified four amendments (the Eleventh, Fourteenth, Sixteenth, and Twenty-Sixth) that repudiated Supreme Court decisions relatively quickly after the Supreme Court made them.

To date, the nation has demonstrated a clear preference for using the model of congressional proposal and state ratification that the first Congress initiated with the introduction of the Bill of Rights, but this may partly result from historical accident. As observed earlier, Madison was very fearful of calling a second convention—which would in fact *not* have been an Article V convention but one like that which had met in Philadelphia in 1787 under the Articles of Confederation—before the work of the first was ratified. When, in relatively short order, a convention rewrote the Constitution and Congress proposed and states ratified twelve discrete amendments, it was logical to associate the former with wholesale constitutional change and the latter with individual reforms. Most subsequent calls for conventions appear to have been far more motivated by the desire to prod congressional action for individual amendments than by hopes to rewrite the document. Whether out of conviction or as a matter of strategy, opponents have in turn played on fears of a "runaway" convention as a way of discouraging changes that they oppose. Once adopted, amendments are likely to remain, although Congress may not always enforce them.

Predictors of Success

It is almost tautological to observe that amendments that require two-thirds majorities of both houses of Congress and ratification by three-fourths of the states require a high degree of national consensus. This often involves decades of percolating public opinion that cannot be limited to a narrow geographical region. Successful amendments have the support of popular political movements like abolitionism, women's suffrage, progressivism, or the modern civil rights movement.

Amendments are often associated with individual leadership. James Madison largely shepherded the Bill of Rights through the first Congress, Abraham Lincoln laid the groundwork for emancipation of the slaves, Senator George Norris of Nebraska was a key force behind the lame-duck amendment, Senator Birch Bayh of Indiana was a key proponent of the Twenty-Fifth, and Gregory Watson largely led the renewed campaign for ratification of the Twenty-Seventh Amendment. Veneration for the current document generally generates sufficient inertia to resist amendments with largely symbolic significance, although there are cases (the post–Civil War amendments) where the amendments seem more like markers for changes that have already been brought about than the actual initiators of such change.[80] Despite fears that amendments could undermine or diminish civil liberties, the nation repealed the only amendment that has arguably done so (the Eighteenth, which mandated national alcoholic prohibition), and amendments have liberalized voting requirements, allowed voter participation in elections for U.S. senators, and made the Electoral College more democratic.

Portents of Failure

Amendments that chiefly appeal to members of one party are rarely incorporated into the Constitution unless this party clearly dominates or the nation has been subject to a cataclysmic event, like the Civil War. Americans undoubtedly recognize that there are many social problems—teen pregnancy, drug abuse, violence, poverty, and unemployment—that may not be amenable to strictly constitutional solutions. To date at least, Americans have largely settled on articulating negative rights and rejecting the kinds of political and social guarantees that are common in many twentieth-century constitutions.[81] Perhaps in part because of the experience of Prohibition, Americans are wary of unintended consequences, and opponents of amendments can sometimes tap into these fears in order to oppose amendments (like the Equal Rights Amendment) that might otherwise seem fairly unproblematic.

Assessing the Amending Process

The amending process is particularly frustrating to individuals who favor major changes in the Constitution, because its supermajority requirements advantage status quo arrangements by emphasizing deliberation and consensus.[82] Constitutional language is generally flexible enough to allow judicial interpretations to adapt the Constitution to changing circumstances, but there are some issues that can only be changed by amendments, consensus for which may be lacking. This arguably creates incentives for short cuts that do not require the same degree of national consensus. As the next chapter will describe, extra-constitutional conventions were particularly evident during the nineteenth century.

CHAPTER 4

The Late Eighteenth Century and Nineteenth Century Provide a Rival Set of Convention Precedents

As chapter 3 demonstrated, although the early experience with both amendments and conventions was largely positive, one of the first tasks of the Federalists was that of deflecting the call for another general convention that they feared might undo the work of the first. Moreover, the time between the ratification of the Twelfth Amendment in 1804 and the Thirteenth Amendment in 1865 (especially the latter part), during which the nation did not adopt any amendments, was traumatic enough that it bears separate examination.

This period was, of course, a time of rising sectional division. This was fueled first by differences of opinion between southern and western forces, which largely favored war with Great Britain, and New England states, which suffered disproportionate economic burdens generated by embargoes on commerce and war during this conflict, which they viewed far more negatively. The North/South divide was further highlighted from 1828 to 1832 over the legitimacy of tariffs on incoming manufactured goods that in the process of encouraging nascent American industries more harshly affected southern rather than northern interests. Finally, the nation witnessed the disputes over slavery and states' rights that eventuated in the Civil War.

The first chapter of this book described how the convention mechanism began as a somewhat irregular gathering, often during revolutionary periods, that over time became domesticated as a constitutional institution. Although Article V thus provided convention mechanisms both to propose amendments and to ratify them, it did not specifically prohibit other gatherings. Throughout early U.S. history, states and other actors sometimes used other, less prescribed conventions, often without explicit constitutional safeguards and sometimes with dubious constitutional justifications. They raised concerns that reflect developments elsewhere in the world as well.

The French Revolutionary Experience

Just as American Revolutionaries received support from the French, so too did those who participated in the French Revolution that began in 1789 with the storming of the Bastille draw some of their inspiration from American revolutionary success. Disputes as to whether America should back Great Britain, support France, or remain neutral between them was a major bone of contention between Federalists and Democratic-Republicans in the early republic. Although the latter were initially far more supportive of the revolutionaries than were the former, most Americans undoubtedly came to view their own more conservative revolution, which concentrated on achieving independence rather than remaking society in its entirety, as preferable to how events transpired in France.

From 1792 to 1795 this revolution was guided by a national convention, or assembly, that in many ways resembled the first and second Continental Congresses within the United States. The outcomes of the two revolutions were, however, quite different. The French National Convention was caught between two opposing factions known as the Montagnards and the Girondins.[1] Moreover, the revolution led not only to state terror against aristocrats and other alleged enemies of France but also to foreign wars that so riled American public opinion and the rise of the dictatorship of Napoleon Bonaparte. It is likely that these results tarnished the convention mechanism in many American minds.

The Hartford Convention

Although states' rights sentiments ultimately became most closely identified with the South and the cause of slavery, neither was the only sectional interest in the early republic. From December 14, 1814, to January 5, 1815, the legislatures of five northern states, whose commerce had suffered through a series of embargoes and a war with Great Britain, chose twenty-six representatives who met together at the Hartford Convention to address common interests and propose constitutional change, including the possibility of disunion.[2] Although the convention rejected the latter option, it proposed a number of constitutional reforms. These included eliminating the three-fifths clause (which resulted in increased congressional representation for slave-holding states), requiring a two-thirds majority to admit new states (thus making the admission of new slave states less likely), limiting Congress's power to impose embargoes, raising the majority in Congress required to declare war, restricting naturalized citizens from serving in Congress, and limiting the president to one term.[3]

As delegates from Hartford were arriving at the nation's capital, its residents were celebrating the American victory at the Battle of New Orleans and the news that the United States and Great Britain had signed a treaty ending the War of 1812. The Federalist Party, which was closely associated with the Hartford Convention, in turn, soon disintegrated, but the memory of the convention undoubtedly lingered. Even though the Hartford Convention was not an Article V convention, it may, by negative association, have tainted the idea of resorting to this mechanism.[4]

John C. Calhoun and the Nullification Crisis

The most important southern spokesperson to emerge from the South out of the next two controversies was John C. Calhoun of South Carolina, a one-time vice president and U.S. senator, who was a major interpreter (mis-interpreter might be more accurate) of the amending process.[5] Calhoun is best known for his defense of slavery as a positive good for both masters and slaves (earlier southern leaders had understood the institution of slavery as a necessary evil) and for his theory of concurrent majorities, which emphasized the need to protect minority interests. Calhoun was especially concerned about protecting the interest of slave owners by providing them with a veto over numerical majorities. There was much that he therefore admired in the supermajorities that Article V required for amending the Constitution. In his *Discourse on the Constitution and Government of the United States*, Calhoun accordingly heaped great praise on the mechanism:

> It is, when properly understood, the *vis medicatrix* [healing power] of the system;—its great repairing, healing, and conservative power;—intended to remedy its disorders, in whatever cause or causes originating; whether in the original errors or defects of the constitution itself,—or the operation of time and change of circumstances, or in conflict between its parts,—including those between the co-ordinate governments. By it alone, can the equilibrium of the various powers and divisions of the system be preserved; as by it alone, can the stronger be preserved from encroaching on, and finally absorbing the weaker.[6]

In time, however, Calhoun began to fear that northern states might employ this process to limit or abolish slavery. He further tried, as it were, to turn constitutional presumptions on their head, by requiring three-fourths or more of the states to affirm disputed exercises of federal powers, anytime one or more states challenged them. As he wrote:

> It is, then, more hostile to the nature and genius of our system to assume powers not delegated, than to resume those that are; and less hostile that a State, sustained by one fourth of her co-States, should prevent the exercise of power really intended to be granted, than that the General Government should assume the exercise of powers not intended to be delegated.[7]

Over time, Calhoun became an advocate of using a convention for what he called "great emergencies."[8] He further recommended: "The States ought to be convened in a general Convention—the most august of all assemblies—rep-

resenting the united sovereignty of the confederated States, and having power
and authority to correct every error, and to repair every dilapidation or injury,
whether caused by time or accident, or the conflicting movements of the bodies
which compose the system."[9] It appears that Calhoun anticipated that a convention could address a single subject, and that the work of such a convention would
go into effect without state ratification. In surveying petitions for constitutional
conventions, William R. Pullen thus observed that Calhoun apparently anticipated that its power would be "much broader than that actually set forth in the
exact language of the amending article."[10]

Consistent with such an understanding, in the winter of 1832–33, the South
Carolina legislature adopted resolutions saying that it was "expedient that a convention of the States be called as early as practicable to consider and determine
such questions of disputed powers as have arisen between the States of the Confederacy and the General Government."[11] The most fascinating aspect of this call
is that the Georgia and Alabama legislatures responded to South Carolina by
calling specifically for an Article V convention, while the Delaware legislature
not only questioned the expediency of a convention but also specifically distinguished "a convention of the people" under Article V from a "convention of the
States" as called by South Carolina.[12] In time, rising southern fears that northern
states would employ the amending process to destroy slavery, and the southern
conviction that states could not only nullify federal laws but actually secede from
the Union, led to the Civil War.

National Nominating Conventions

In the early years under the new Constitution, party caucuses within Congress
nominated presidential candidates. Beginning with the Anti-Mason Party in
1831, just as most states had shifted from having legislatures write and ratify constitutions to having conventions do so, parties began using national nominating conventions to select their presidential and vice-presidential candidates and
to draft party platforms.[13] The choice of this mechanism, which was a natural
growth of the Jacksonian Era in American politics, undoubtedly reflected the
idea that such conventions would be more democratic than the prior method of
selection.

The development of party primaries, which began in the Progressive Era but
gained prominence in the 1960s, has taken most of the suspense out of modern
conventions, which with their increasing size are more like ratification than deliberative bodies.[14] However, early conventions were full of suspense and sometimes veered off the expected trail with the nomination of so-called "dark-horse"
candidates.[15] As party bodies, which sometimes took positions with respect to

proposed amendments, such conventions did not, of course, have any formal authority to propose amendments or rewrite the Constitution. Still, it is likely that the popular mind began to associate the raucous pageantry of such events with both partisanship and with surprise candidates. Neither of these elements would have been likely to appeal to those who were seeking regularized methods of constitutional change. Seeking a suitable analogy to a "runaway convention," Phyllis Schlafly, whose Eagle Forum is unalterably opposed to convening Article V conventions, recently asked readers to "imagine Democratic and Republican conventions meeting in the same hall and trying to agree on constitutional changes."[16]

Dorr's Rebellion

An examination of Dorr's Rebellion, like reflections on national nominating conventions, provides a further opportunity to observe that not all events leading up to the Civil War focused on purely sectional issues or slavery. One of the more dramatic events, which led to an important Supreme Court decision, occurred in Rhode Island. It illustrates the difficulty of a constitution, in this case a variation of its original charter, that does not specifically provide for constitutional change. As other states liberalized and democratized their constitutions,[17] many in the 1820s and 1830s,[18] Rhode Island had resisted such changes and retained a property qualification for voting that largely disenfranchised immigrants until attorney Thomas Wilson Dorr called a People's Convention that met on October 4, 1841, and proposed a liberalized constitution. That November the state legislature proposed its own Freemen's Constitution, which voters rejected.

Although the people (some newly enfranchised) voted to accept Dorr's document in a referendum, the existing charter government refused to acknowledge its existence, and the two sides nearly came to blows before President John Tyler's expressed willingness to use military force to support the charter government largely led to the demise of Dorr's forces, one of whom sued over what was alleged to be an illegal entry into his house by agents of the charter government. The Supreme Court ruled in *Luther v. Borden* (1849) that the issue of which government was legitimate was a "political question" for the elected branches to resolve.[19] In the interim, the state had voted to accept yet another constitution, which did embody many of the aims of the Dorr forces. Although this could be viewed as at least a partial success, it seems likely that public association of a rebellious government with a convention mechanism (even though it was a state affair, rather than an Article V creation) might have led to further reservations about the revolutionary potential of convention mechanisms in general, especially among those who were in power.

The Seneca Falls Convention

One of the most important conventions of the nineteenth century was the Seneca Falls Convention that convened at the Wesleyan Methodist Chapel in Seneca Falls, New York, on July 19, 1848. Chiefly organized by Elizabeth Cady Stanton and Lucretia Mott, it was attended by more than three hundred people and resulted in a Declaration of Sentiments—patterned after the U.S. Declaration of Independence—that outlined women's grievances and petitioned for woman suffrage.

Carrie Chapman Catt later observed that the convention initiated "56 campaigns of state referenda, 480 campaigns to convince state legislatures to submit suffrage amendments to voters, 47 campaigns attempting to get state constitutional conventions to write woman suffrage into state constitutions, and 19 campaigns with 10 successive Congresses."[20] In time, of course, the call for woman suffrage resulted in the adoption in 1920 of the Nineteenth Amendment, which is today a national source of pride and a precursor to further gains with respect to gender equality.

In the short run, however, the convention may have been far more important for what many observers believed to be its radicalism. In their account of the event, Virginia Bernard and Elizabeth Fox-Genovese observed that Stanton's husband decided not to attend. Moreover, "Judge Daniel Cady, Elizabeth's father, reportedly rushed to Seneca Falls fearing for his daughter's sanity. Her older sister Tryphena Bayard wept over Elizabeth's involvement in such a radical cause, but her younger sister, Harriet Eaton, attended the convention and signed its Declaration of Sentiments, though she later rescinded her signature at the urging of her husband."[21] Although it bears pointing out that this was not an Article V convention, it might again have tainted such a convention by association.

The Nashville Convention

Just as New England states had aired their grievances and consulted about possible solutions in Hartford during the War of 1812, so too southern states, with John C. Calhoun's blessing, held their own nine-day meeting, which began on June 3, 1850, when 176 delegates (including 101 from Tennessee) from nine southern states met at the McKendree Methodist Church in Nashville.[22] Although South Carolina had generated much of the sentiment for the convention, a bipartisan convention that had met in Jackson, Mississippi, the year before had actually issued the call for it.

Although secession was among the options discussed, as in the earlier Hartford Convention, cooler heads prevailed, and the convention introduced eighteen resolutions, most of which related to issues that the Compromise of 1850 subsequently resolved, at least temporarily.[23] Largely because of that meeting, interest in a second session called for November declined. Still, seven states sent more than fifty delegates to this second meeting, which was also held in Nashville. As in the case of the Hartford Convention, neither of the Nashville meetings had been called under the authority of Article V, but both might have furthered the idea that conventions were not altogether to be trusted.

The Nashville Convention contributed to Southern nationalism. It also spawned a number of state conventions to debate its recommendations. These may well have formed the template for later state conventions that called for secession.

The Kansas Conventions

As controversy increased over the issue of slavery, attention increasingly shifted to the constitutionality of expanding into or restricting slavery within the territories. Abraham Lincoln and the Republican Party opposed such expansion. By contrast, the 1857 decision in *Dred Scott v. Sandford* declaring that Congress had no right to restrict such expansion is commonly regarded as a major catalyst to the Civil War.[24]

Nowhere was this conflict more intense than in Kansas, where pro- and antislavery forces (including those led by John Brown, who would later lead another revolt in what is today Harper's Ferry, West Virginia) engaged in open warfare.[25] From 1855 to 1858 Kansas held a series of conventions, most of which John Jameson has demonstrated to have been illegal.[26] Eventually, Congress rejected the proslavery LeCompton Constitution that one of these conventions had proposed, but the precedents probably soured many on conventions in general while setting a further precedent for the extra-constitutional secession conventions that would follow in a number of southern states.

Abraham Lincoln and the Civil War

Just before the Civil War, there was a flurry of activity directed at amending the Constitution to avoid the impending conflict. Taking note of this activity in his First Inaugural Address, Abraham Lincoln observed: "This country, with its institutions, belongs to the people who instituted it. Whenever they shall grow weary of the existing Government, they can exercise their *constitutional* right of amending it or *revolutionary* right to dismember or overthrow it. While I make no recommendation of amendments, I fully recognize the rightful authority of the people over the whole subject, to be exercised in either of the modes prescribed in the instrument itself; and I should, under existing circumstances, favor rather than oppose a fair opportunity being offered the people to act upon it."[27]

Undoubtedly aware that southern states were considering calling only for a convention of states from that region to dismember the Union, Lincoln expressed a willingness to call a general convention of all of the states to save it,[28] while expressing what he believed to be its advantages in proposing amendments when compared to state legislatures. "I will venture to add that to me the convention mode seems preferable, in that it allows amendment to originate with the people themselves, instead of only permitting them to take or reject propositions originated by others, not especially chosen for the purpose, and which might not be precisely such as they would wish either to accept or refuse."[29] Lincoln, who later favored the method of congressional proposal and state ratification for the Thirteenth Amendment's abolishing of slavery, thus anticipated both that a convention would represent the popular will and that it would have at least some flexibility in formulating amendments, although his words were certainly consistent with the idea that the states might establish the general subject matter of the convention.

Antebellum State Conventions

Instead of such an Article V convention, states—beginning with South Carolina, which issued its call on Christmas Eve of 1860—began calling conventions to secede from the Union.[30] Moreover, two other interstate conventions were held, neither of which followed Article V guidelines.

The Peace Convention

In February 1861, twenty-one of thirty-four states sent a total of 132 delegates to the Willard Hotel in Washington, D.C., for what became known as a Peace Convention, or Peace Conference. Each state attending sent five to eleven delegates. Two states were represented by their congressmen, twelve by representatives their state legislatures chose, and seven by representatives state governors selected.[31]

Former president John Tyler from Virginia, who was chosen to head the convention, was among those attending who critiqued the amending process. Perhaps drawing from Jefferson's earlier support of periodic conventions, Tyler thus observed that "our ancestors probably committed a blunder in not having fixed upon every fifth decade for a call of a General Convention to amend and reform the Constitution. On the contrary, they have made the difficulties next to insurmountable to accomplish amendments to an instrument which was perfect for five millions of people, but not wholly so as to thirty millions."[32]

The convention further created a committee, headed by James Guthrie of Kentucky, consisting of one delegate from each state. It reported seven propositions, which the convention proposed as a thirteenth amendment, which it wanted Congress to send to the states for approval by special conventions.[33] Instead, Congress proposed the so-called Corwin Amendment, which would have guaranteed the continuing existence of slavery in states whose governments wanted to keep it. It was superseded by another Thirteenth Amendment that put the final nails in the coffin of chattel slavery in America.

The Montgomery Convention

Forty-three delegates from six southern states that had already declared their independence in individual state conventions met at another convention in Montgomery, Alabama, on February 4, 1861. These delegates drafted a provisional constitution in four days. Needless to say, this was a classic revolutionary convention rather than an Article V convention.

Delegates to the Montgomery Convention significantly shortened the amending process by providing simply that "the Congress, by a vote of two-thirds may, at any time, alter or amend the Constitution."[34] This was a fairly problematic provision for a government based on states' rights since it omitted the provision for state proposal of amendments altogether. Congress exercised this power only once when it granted itself the authority to increase the number of judicial districts.[35] The provision was soon superseded when the provisional Confederal Congress rewrote it.

The Provisional Confederate Congress

Subsequently designating themselves as the Provisional Congress of the Confederate States of America, members of this convention appointed a committee of twelve to draft a more permanent document. The chair, Robert Barnwell Rhett Sr. of South Carolina, presented this to the Confederate Congress on February 28. Acting much as the Second Continental Congress had done earlier, it met as a congress in the morning and as a convention in the afternoon and evening. This group, joined by additional delegates, prepared the permanent constitution, which the convention adopted on March 11, 1861, and which eleven southern states eventually ratified.[36]

The convention that drafted the Confederate Constitution relied largely on the format of the existing U.S. Constitution. Although it introduced a number of innovations, like an acknowledgment of God, a single six-year presidential term, and a presidential line-item veto, most modifications emphasized state sovereignty and protected the institution of slavery. Because delegates did not anticipate that they would join, the convention did not face the need to placate free states, but it could do nothing to avert the determination of the U.S. president to preserve the Union through use of force. The threat of impending war and the desire to unite other southern states undoubtedly provided incentives for the convention to do its work quickly.

The Confederate Amending Provision

Article V of the Confederate Constitution created an amending mechanism, which the government never used during its existence. It provided for three or more individual state conventions to call a convention of all the Confederate states to consider proposals, which to become law would then require two-thirds of the states to approve. The specific language provided:

> Upon the demand of any three States, legally assembled in their several conventions, the Congress shall summon a Convention of all the States, to take into consideration such amendments to the Constitution as the said States shall concur in suggesting at the time when the said demand is made; and should any of the proposed amendments to the Constitution be agreed on by the said Convention—voting by States and the same be ratified by the legislatures of two-thirds thereof—as the one or the other mode of ratification may be proposed by the general Convention—they shall thenceforward form a part of this Constitution. But no State shall, without its consent, be deprived of its equal representation in the Senate.[37]

This provision is notable in a number of ways. First, and consistent with the constitution's emphasis on states' rights, it placed all of the power of initiating amendments in the states rather than following Article V of the U.S. Constitution and sharing this power with Congress.[38] Second, by using both the word "demand" and "shall," this provision appeared even more obligatory than the corresponding provision in the U.S. Constitution. Third, it allowed, indeed required, states that desired amendments to express themselves through the actions of conventions rather than state legislatures.[39] Fourth, and consistent with Calhoun's theory of concurrent majorities,[40] it lowered the bar to propose amendments from two-thirds majorities of both houses of Congress or of the state legislatures, to three state conventions, and it reduced the number of states required to ratify amendments from three-fourths to two-thirds. This was in accord with southern views, like those that John Tyler had expressed at the Peace Convention, that the Article V amending process in the U.S. Constitution had been too difficult. In explaining the Confederate Constitution to the people of Alabama, Robert H. Smith thus observed: "The restrictions thrown around amendments to the organic law by the Constitution of the United States proved to be a practical negation of the power to alter the instrument. . . . [W]ithout a concurrence of [two-thirds of each House or two-thirds of the state legislatures] no body could be assembled even to consider the complaints of members of the Union."[41] His claim may well have been mistaken, but Robert Barnwell Rhett later claimed that "if it had been part of the Constitution of the United States the vast discontent which preceded the war, and made it inevitable, would have been easily arrested and allayed; and the states in convention would have settled amicably their differences."[42] Similarly, Robert Smith of Alabama said, "The substituted provision imparts a wholesome flexibility to our Constitution and, at the same time, assures us against an assembling of the States for light or transient causes, or hopeless purposes, and the consultative body, when convened will be confined to action on propositions put forth by three States."[43]

The fifth, and most striking, provision of the amending mechanism proposed by the Confederate Constitution is the clause that refers to "such amendments to the Constitution as the States shall concur in suggesting at the time when the said demand is made." This provision would more clearly have limited consideration by the convention to the specific topics proposed by the states than does the current Article V of the U.S. Constitution.[44]

A full understanding of this change might go far toward clarifying nineteenth-century understandings of Article V of the U.S. Constitution. Like others before me, however,[45] I have not been able to ascertain whether the Confederate rewriters believed that they were allowing states to exercise the power of limiting deliberations of conventions that they had not previously exercised or been permitted to exercise, or whether they were simply clarifying what they believed to be existing constitutional understandings of the convention mechanism.[46] If they were doing the latter, I am further unsure why they might have thought such clarification was necessary—had southern legislatures feared proposing a constitution to ensconce slavery further for fear that the convention might seek instead to eliminate it?[47]

Amending Experiences under the Confederacy

In a development not unlike that which followed the adoption of the U.S. Constitution, South Carolina, which believed that the new document should have gone even further in protecting the institution of slavery, almost immediately adopted resolutions calling for another convention of Confederal states. South Carolina wanted such a convention to achieve a number of objectives, including replacing the three-fifths clause with full representation; prohibiting the admission of free states except by unanimous consent; repealing the ban on the slave trade; and forbidding Congress from incurring debt for any purpose other than war making. Although attention shifted instead to the ensuing war, the call manifested South Carolina's clear understanding of the power of the states to set the agenda.[48]

Although neither the conventions in which states declared that they were seceding from the Union, nor the Peace Convention designed to formulate a compromise, nor the convention that created the Confederate Constitution was an Article V convention, collectively they may have left a negative impression in the public memory about conventions in general. This may have been further accentuated when in 1864 a number of Southern states considered calling a convention of all the states, North and South, to consider a way to end the Civil War, presumably involving mutual concession rather than Northern victory.[49] Instead, Northern victories in Richmond brought the war to an end with Robert E. Lee's surrender at the Appomattox Courthouse, and the Confederate Constitution, and its provisions for constitutional change, largely faded from public memory.

Ratification of the Confederate Constitution

Whereas the Framers of the U.S. Constitution had required ratification of nine or more of the thirteen states in convention before the new document went into effect, the Confederate Constitution, which grew from individual assertions of state sovereignty, lowered the bar to five states and did not specify the mode of ratification. Once five states ratified the document, the Confederate Constitution provided for the provisional congress to make arrangements for election of the president and for a more permanent Congress. In the meantime, the same provisional congress/convention that had drawn up the new document continued to exercise its powers.

The Troubled Antebellum Legacy

Although delegates had met in Philadelphia in 1787 without specific constitutional sanction, they had proceeded in a highly deliberate manner and had sought to domesticate the convention mechanism by incorporating it into the new constitution. Leading delegates had left the Convention of 1787 with the hope of averting yet a second convention that might undo the work of the first. They succeeded in doing so largely because Congress took the lead in introducing the Bill of Rights, a procedure that has been followed ever since.

In the first four-score years of the republic, however, it was clear that Article V had not completely preempted the calling of other extra-constitutional conventions. Dorr's forces had used the convention mechanism to challenge the existing charter in Rhode Island. The Seneca Falls Convention had shocked public opinion by advocating woman's suffrage. The Hartford Convention, the Nashville Convention, and the Peace Conventions had all eventually pursued moderate courses, most of which had salutary effects, but at least two broached the subject of secession. Moreover, all these meetings arguably prepared the way for the revolutionary state conventions that emerged as southern states declared their independence from the Union and as delegates eventually met in Montgomery to form an entirely new constitution. Although Lincoln was among those who favored calling an Article V convention rather than going to war, it was clear that states might call conventions that did not conform to Article V guidelines and that many, like the threatened conventions, which the Bill of Rights had preempted, might have greater potential for rending the Union, or replacing the Constitution, than for healing and amending it.

One can only hypothesize about whether an Article V convention would have prevented war, but with the Union so evenly split between slave states and free states, and with attitudes increasingly hardening on both sides of the slavery issue during most of the antebellum period, it seems doubtful either that two-thirds of the states could have been mobilized to propose amendments to solve the controversy or that three-fourths of them could have been persuaded to ratify them. As it is, the greatest debates over the nature of the Union, most notably the Webster-Hayne debate, took place not in an assembly of states but in Congress,[50] where the outcomes (most notably the Missouri Compromise and the Compromise of 1850) were tentative compromises rather than permanent cures. In the absence of peaceful constitutional change to resolve the issue either of slavery or of states' rights, the nation went to war. It was, in turn, followed by another series of debates that resulted in the adoption of the Thirteenth through Fifteenth Amendments.[51] Proponents of change then held the upper hand because they had power both to reconstruct the states that had rebelled and to insist that they ratify the new amendments before their delegations were seated in Congress.

Although the Article V convention remained as a possibility, the conventions' associations with revolutionary change appeared to continue. Notably, toward the end of the nineteenth century, a resolution was introduced at the Iowa Populist State Convention of 1894 for "a mass convention of the American people to assemble in . . . Des Moines on the first Monday in December, 1894, to consider the necessary amendment of the fundamental law of the land."[52] Similarly, two popular novels of the day, Frederick Upham Adams's *President John Smith*, and Henry O. Morris's *Waiting for the Signal*, both written from populist perspectives, imagined ushering in new constitutions through conventions.[53] Although no Article V conventions were actually called, as the next chapter demonstrates, commentators continued to consider the option.

CHAPTER 5

A Survey of Early Commentary on Article V

In all the modern debates over the Article V convention mechanism, one issue has dominated all others: whether Article V requires states that want to amend the Constitution to call a general convention or whether states and/or Congress may limit a convention call to a particular amendment or subject area. That issue has, in turn, fueled fears of runaway conventions that opponents of conventions, as well as opponents of particular reforms, often employ to good effect.

The Context

Although Alexander Hamilton made a persuasive case in Federalist No. 85 that once they ratified the Constitution states had the power to call a limited convention to remedy perceived defects in the new Constitution, there is very little evidence that such Article V conventions were the subject of much discussion from this point throughout the rest of the next century. John Jameson's distinction between revolutionary conventions and constitutional conventions certainly comes relatively close, but it was directed to discussion of state conventions. I have found no evidence that opponents raised fears of unlimited Article V conventions until the beginning of the twentieth century, when states came close to calling such a convention to propose an amendment for the direct election of U.S. senators.[1]

There is a general scholarly consensus that at least until the years immediately preceding the Civil War, all the states that petitioned for conventions called for broad conventions rather than for conventions to propose particular amendments. This fact, however, is itself subject to interpretation. Especially in the very early years, where the precedent of 1787 dominated and when many individuals might still largely have viewed the new Constitution as an experiment, it might have made just as much sense to reconsider the document as a whole before it took firm root than to examine an individual provision or provisions. Congress showed relative sensitivity to early calls for individual amendments (as in the cases of the Bill of Rights and the Eleventh and Twelfth Amendments) so states may not have thought they needed to call for Article V conventions.

In his short story "Silver Blaze," Sir Arthur Conan Doyle once portrayed Sherlock Holmes as having solved a case by drawing a conclusion from the absence of a barking dog. In reviewing the literature on Article V conventions, we find not one but two dogs that have not barked in this case. If the first is the absence of state calls for single-issue conventions in the early years, the second is the apparent lack of arguments against single-issue conventions until the 1940s, and, more particularly, in the 1960s. One could, of course, hypothesize that the nation lost touch with a fairly obscure constitutional provision after 100 years, but at least in my mind, an argument that takes 150 years to hatch should be a bit suspect.

The key concern, of course, is that of a runaway convention, but this fear too needs closer examination. It seems clear that the Framers, who were wary of directly equating any single institution or set of institutions with sovereignty, intended to allow both Congress and the states to be able to initiate amendments. What is not clear, at least to me, is how the Founders assessed (or we should assess) the respective representativeness of state legislatures and state conventions and the relations between them.

In an ideal world (in which, however, Congress proved unresponsive to considered popular judgments), state legislatures would reflect popular sentiments in calling for an Article V convention and have confidence that delegates to an Article V convention would share these concerns. If state legislatures were, for example, convinced that their constituents wanted a balanced budget amendment and chiefly a balanced budget amendment, then they would have little cause to fear that if they called an Article V convention, their citizens would instead seek to establish a monarchy. Legislators may have had greater cause to expect similarly between their own concerns and those of a convention in 1787 when they were most likely to be picking the delegates, but one might still hope that state legislators would have their fingers close enough to the pulse of popular opinion within their states to be confident that if they desired a convention for one purpose and chiefly, if not exclusively, for this purpose, then so would their constituents.

It seems logical to believe that the Framers formulated the Article V convention in the knowledge that it would have been almost impossible to assemble state legislators from throughout the nation in a single assembly. It is less certain whether the Framers were also anticipating that because state legislators might themselves sometimes be unrepresentative that it might be prudent to have amending proposals emerge from a separate body. If they, in fact, anticipated that all conventions would be open conventions, then they might also have anticipated that state legislatures (at least those who knew that they were out of touch) would hesitate to expose their own distance from the people by calling for such an assembly. Although it may be impossible to know whether they specifically thought about this or not, the Constitution clearly requires that the work of any convention be ratified either by three-fourths of the state legislatures or by three-fourths of special ratifying conventions. This suggests that the Framers also recognized that an Article V convention might ultimately fail the test of representativeness and would itself need to be retrained.

Although it is common to move immediately from a discussion of the debates at the 1787 Convention and a review of *The Federalist* to an analysis of modern law review articles, it is wiser to mine major treatises written on the subject of constitutional amendments and constitutional conventions throughout U.S. history for insights that they might offer. That is the path that this chapter will follow. I caution, however, that the questions that motivated earlier thinkers are not always those that scholars ask today. Early commentators rarely give a yes or no answer to modern questions, and yet their perspectives can be vital to illuminating what the title of this book describes as "conventional wisdom" on the subject.

Thomas Jefferson Favored Periodic Conventions

Although it is common to associate the thought of Thomas Jefferson with that of his close friend James Madison, the amending process is one area in which they expressed long-standing, albeit civil, disagreements. An earlier chapter has already observed that in *The Federalist* Madison had opposed the idea that Jefferson had advanced for Virginia whereby two of three branches could call a convention to correct what they perceived to be breaches of the Constitution by the other branch. Moreover, during debates over ratification of the Constitution, Jefferson had initially joined the arguments of some Antifederalists in favoring calling a second convention to perfect the work of the first.[2]

Jefferson continued to express support for periodic conventions and—in a position with implications for modern balanced budget amendment proposals—for preventing one generation from incurring debt for future generations. In a letter to Madison dated September 6, 1789, Jefferson laid the foundation for such conventions on the principle "'that the earth belongs in usufruct to the living'; that the dead have neither powers nor rights over it."[3] Using actuarial tables, he had thus proposed that every law and every constitution should expire at the end of nineteen years. Although a more sober-minded Madison subjected this view to withering critique, Jefferson continued to advocate periodic conventions, chiefly at the state level, with apparent faith that the people would act wisely. Opposing those who "look at constitutions with sanctimonious reverence, and deem them like the arc [*sic*] of the covenant, too sacred to be touched,"[4] Jefferson argued in a letter to John Epes dated June 24, 1813, that "each generation is as independent as the one preceding, as that was of all which had gone before. It has then, like them, a right to choose for itself the form of government it believes most promotive of its own happiness; consequently, to accommodate to the circumstances in which it finds itself, that received from its predecessors; and it is for the peace and good of mankind that a solemn opportunity of doing this every nineteen or twenty years, should be provided by the constitution."[5]

Jefferson expressed a willingness to invoke Article V conventions during the election crisis of 1800. After electors evenly split their votes between Aaron Burr and him (both running as Democratic-Republicans), Jefferson declared that in the event that the House of Representatives could not settle the tie by inauguration, he would fight against Federalist threats to put the presidency into the hands of a non-elected official by calling for such a convention, which, he said, "gives them the horrors, as in the present democratical spirit of America, they fear they should lose some of the favorite morsels of the Constitution."[6] After likening the government without a president to a clock that had run down, Jefferson wrote in a letter to Dr. Joseph Priestly that "this peaceable & legitimate resource, to which we are in the habit of implicit obedience, superseding all appeal to force, and being always within our reach, shows a precious principle of self-preservation in our composition."[7]

James Madison Warmed to the Article V Convention Mechanism

Although James Madison defended both mechanisms for proposing amendments in *The Federalist*, scholars most frequently associate him with advocating and then using the congressional method of proposing amendments to bypass the possibility of a second constitutional convention that might undo the work of the first. Convinced at the Constitutional Convention that a much stronger national government was needed to overcome the weakness of the Articles of Confederation, he had advocated this. After the new government went into effect, Madison became a greater advocate of states' rights when he perceived that Alexander Hamilton and others were using the strengthened national government to foster the interests of commercial elites and when (as with the passage of the Alien and Sedition Acts) he believed that national assertions of authority were exceeding reasonable constitutional grants of power and endangering the civil rights and liberties that the Bill of Rights had sought to secure.[8]

Robert G. Natelson has argued that Madison accordingly became more sympathetic to the convention mechanism during this time. He cites Madison as observing in 1799 that "the Legislatures of the States have a right also to originate amendments to the Constitution, by a concurrence of two-thirds of the whole number, in applications to Congress for this purpose."[9] Describing such a mechanism as "strictly within the limits of the Constitution," Madison went on to say that the states "might have represented to their respective Senators in Congress their wish that two-thirds thereof would propose an explanatory amendment to the Constitution; or two-thirds of themselves, if such had been their option, might, by an application to Congress, have obtained a Convention for the same object."[10] Madison became similarly troubled over nullification. In a letter to Edward Everett that he penned opposing this doctrine, Madison indicated, "Should the provisions of the Constitution as here reviewed be found not to secure the Govt. & rights of the States agst. Usurpations & abuses on the part of the U.S. the final resort within the purview of the Constn. lies in an amendment of the Constn. according to a process applicable by the States."[11]

St. George Tucker Praised the Amending Process

St. George Tucker (1752–1827), who succeeded George Wythe as a law professor at the College of William and Mary, adapted the teachings of English legal commentator William Blackstone to the situation of America. In a five-volume set of his commentaries that he published in 1803, he included his "View of the Constitution of the United States." In describing the Article V process for congressional proposal and state approval, Tucker observed that the U.S. Constitution could "not be controlled, or altered without the express consent of the body politic of three fourths of the states in the union, or, of the people, of an equal number of the states." Further citing the method of congressional proposal and state ratification, Tucker said that "if congress should neglect to propose amendments in this way, when they may be deemed necessary, the concurrent sense of two thirds of the state legislatures may enforce congress to call a convention, the amendments proposed by which, when ratified by the conventions of three fourths of the states, become valid, as a part of the constitution." He continued by reflecting "on the peculiar happiness of the people of the United States, thus to possess the power of correcting whatever errors may have crept into the constitution, or may hereafter be discovered therein" without the danger of revolution.[12]

Later in this essay, Tucker again explained the two routes to amendments:

And this may be effected in two different modes: the first on recommendation from congress, whenever two thirds of both houses shall concur in the expediency of any amendment. The second, which secures to the states an influence in case congress should neglect to recommend such amendments, provides, that congress shall, on application from the legislatures of two thirds of the states, call a convention for proposing amendments; which in either case shall be valid to all intents and purposes as part of the constitution, when ratified by the legislatures of three fourths thereof, as the one or the other mode, of the ratification may be proposed by the congress.[13]

Tucker praised both mechanisms, with the latter serving chiefly as a guard against federal corruption: "Both of these provisions appear excellent. Of the utility and practicability of the former, we have already had most satisfactory experience. The latter will probably never be resorted to, unless the federal government should betray symptoms of corruption, which may render it expedient for the states to exert themselves in order to the application of some radical and effectual remedy. Nor can we too much applaud a constitution, which thus provides a safe, and peaceable remedy for its own defects, as they may from time to time be discovered."[14] Although Tucker went on to list more than a dozen proposed amendments that he favored,[15] he nonetheless praised the "obstacles and delays" in both sets of mechanisms as "a sufficient bar against light, or frequent innovations."[16] He thus expressed faith in both the method of congressional and convention initiation without specifically indicating whether he believed that the states or Congress could limit its agenda. He did, however, observe that the amending processes had been "found to be practicable without hazard, without tumult, and without the smallest interruption to the ordinary course of administering the government."[17]

Joseph Story Likened Article V to a Safety Valve

Joseph Story (1779–1845) was a part-time Harvard law professor and early justice of the U.S. Supreme Court. Although James Madison appointed him to the Court, Story usually allied with Chief Justice John Marshall. Story penned his influential *Commentaries on the Constitution of the United States* in the first half of the nineteenth century. He chiefly devoted his work to explaining the U.S. Constitution and its interpretation, rather than to discussing the convention mechanism, but he penned a positive appraisal of the amending process that seems indicative of early thinking on the subject.

Essentially following early positive appraisals of the amending process by its Federalist supporters, Story quoted the text of Article V in full and concluded that "little need to be said to persuade us, at once, of its utility and importance." After explaining that any constitution, especially one as novel as that for the United States, would require change, Story appears to have originated the "safety valve" analogy (particularly consistent with the invention and rise of the steam

engine) to describe the constitutional amending process as a way "to let off all
temporary effervescences and excitements; and the real effective instrument to
control and adjust the movements of the machinery, when out of order, or in
danger of self-destruction." He further argued that the process was arranged
both to protect "the stability of the government" and "the rights and liberties of
the people."[18]

Story heaped equal praise on initiating amendments "through the instrumentality of congress" and "at the instance of the states, through the instrumentality
of a convention." Consistent with the obligatory language of Article V, Story
observed, "The legislatures of two thirds of the states may require a convention
to be called, for the purpose of proposing amendments," but he quite reasonably
focused greater attention on the method that had been used to propose the first
twelve amendments that had been adopted in his own day. Overall, he thought
the amending process provided for needed changes while avoiding "the too hasty
exercise of the power, under temporary discontents or excitements." He observed
that "the mode, both of originating and ratifying amendments, (in either mode,
which the constitution directs,) must necessarily be attended with such obstacles
and delays, as must prove a sufficient bar against light or frequent innovations."[19]
Story did not specifically address whether states could call Article V conventions
for limited purposes.

Arthur J. Stansbury Omitted Mention
of the Article V Convention

It may seem a bit anomalous to include a survey of Arthur J. Stansbury's *Elementary Catechism on the Constitution of the United States* in this review: Stansbury
(1781–1865) was not a scholar in the same league with Tucker or Story, but a cler-
gyman and book illustrator.[20] However, his *Catechism*, first published in 1828,
not only adapted a familiar method of teaching religion to that of imparting information about the Constitution, but having been being specifically written for
schools, it likely reflected popular understandings of the document in his day.

What is fascinating about Stansbury's account, which was widely used and
has been reprinted numerous times, is that it acknowledged the need for allowing the people to change the document when "it is very clearly shown to be
the wish of the people," but it completely omitted the method whereby states
request Congress for a convention to propose amendments.[21] After the adoption of twelve amendments through the method of congressional proposal and
state ratification, Stansbury had, at least, completely lost sight of the convention
mechanism. In such circumstances, he was hardly in a position to speculate over
whether a convention would be limited or unlimited.

Smith v. Union Bank of Georgetown Recognized the Possibility of a Single-Issue Convention

One of Russell Caplan's contributions to the study of the Article V convention mechanism was to identify the Supreme Court decision in *Smith v. Union Bank of Georgetown* (1831) as affirming the possibility of a limited Article V convention.[22] The decision involved settling the debts of Samuel Robertson, a Maryland native, who had died intestate in Pennsylvania but owed debts in both Virginia and the District of Columbia. In deciding that the payment of such debts would be handled by Robertson's native state, where the estate was being administered, rather than by the jurisdictions in which he had property, Justice William Johnson, whom Thomas Jefferson had appointed to the Court, observed, in apparent answer to an argument by attorney Francis Scott Key, that "Whether it would or would not be politic to establish a different rule by a convention of the states under constitutional sanction is not a question for our consideration."[23]

Caplan saw this comment as indicating that Justice Johnson understood the possibility of "a convention on a single subject" to be "common and unremarkable knowledge."[24] However interpreted, the statement is obiter dicta, which was not directly relevant to the outcome of the case and thus of no real legal standing. Because Johnson further phrased the issue as that of the sovereign rights of the states,[25] which had been previously secured in part through the process of congressional proposal and state ratification in the case of the Eleventh Amendment, it is plausible to believe that the nullification controversy had rekindled reconsideration of the convention mechanism.

William Alexander Duer Rehashed Earlier Arguments

William Alexander Duer (1780–1858), a former judge of the New York Supreme Court and president of Columbia College (now Columbia University), published his *Course of Lectures on the Constitutional Jurisprudence of the United States* in 1833 and again in 1856.[26] He discussed amendments in the context of "the power of Congress to 'propose amendments to the Constitution, and call conventions for the purpose.'"[27] Duer noted "that useful alterations would be suggested by experience," and that the process "guards equally against that extreme facility which would render the Constitution too mutable, and the extreme difficulty which might perpetuate its faults," without indicating that he was quoting directly from James Madison. Following Madison's arguments, after citing the actual language of Article V, Duer further argued that the process "equally enabled" both "the General and State Governments . . . to originate amendments."[28]

The most fascinating aspect of Duer's discussion is that it appears to merge the two methods of proposing amendments by mistakenly observing that "the previous and more numerous amendments [those in the Bill of Rights] were proposed by some of the States as conditions of their accession to the Constitution."[29] Rather than emphasizing that Congress seized the initiative in actually proposing the amendments to forestall states from calling another convention, Duer emphasized that the states took the original initiative by proposing amendments when they ratified the document.[30] Duer thus at least indirectly indicated that state proposals could result in congressional action even absent an Article V convention.

Sidney George Fisher Argued
for Congressional Sovereignty

Sidney George Fisher (1809–71) was a Philadelphia lawyer who authored *The Trial of the Constitution* during the Civil War.[31] Whereas Joseph Story had in an earlier day praised the amending process as a safety valve, Fisher, who saw the nation's failure to formulate a solution that would prevent the Civil War, believed that it had become "an iron fetter."[32] In contrast to early Americans who had sought to bind all branches of government through the articulation of specific rights, Fisher favored the parliamentary model. This would have permitted Congress to make whatever changes were necessary and allow the people to judge the expediency of such measures at election time.

Although Fisher devoted most of his attention to arguing for congressional sovereignty, he shed light on a number of issues connected to constitutional conventions, and he expressed strong opinions as to why he thought that Congress was a superior body to propose constitutional changes. Contrasting what he believed to have been centuries of successful constitutional change in Great Britain against the U.S. inability to make constitutional changes that might have avoided the Civil War, he believed that legislators were better positioned than convention delegates to do the right thing. Referring to members of the British Parliament, he observed that "'grave and learned men'—the best minds of the nation—are now pondering the necessity for further change, what that change shall be and how it can be safely and beneficially made. They anxiously consult the indications of popular sentiment, though they summon no conventions of the people. There is no necessity for these, as Parliament is intrusted already with the whole power of the people, and is responsible to them. The action of Parliament is therefore free; members are not delegates to register a foregone conclusion, but meet to deliberate, to compare opinions, to gain light and knowledge."[33] One curiosity of this passage is that Fisher appeared to think that members of conventions (was he thinking of ratifying conventions, or is this a possible indication that he did think that the states could set the agenda for such conventions?) were there simply to ratify preordained amendments rather than to propose them.

Another fascinating aspect of Fisher's presentation is that he specifically identified the English Parliament as "a 'convention to amend the Constitution.'" Moreover, Fisher incorrectly asserted, with reference to the Bill of Rights but in apparent ignorance of the Eleventh and Twelfth Amendments, that "the Constitution has indeed been once amended in a legal manner."[34]

Fisher further doubted that states would call conventions during times of tranquility. Moreover, if states called them during times of crises, he feared that they would be unduly infused with party spirit:

> Therefore, in quiet times, appropriate to the consideration of the principles of government, such topics cannot be discussed with any prospect of securing such action as the Constitution requires. To put its cumbrous machinery in motion, the people must be roused and as the most organic changes are generally connected with the interests of sections or of classes, the people are very likely to be roused by them, to be divided into parties and to be influenced by passion. They thus become a very unfit tribunal to decide such questions, which are not likely to be tried on their merits. The contest would be for victory, not for truth, wide field and ample opportunity would be given to the arts of demagogues, and how far the struggle would go, and what would be its result, no one at the beginning of it, could predict.[35]

It is unclear why Fisher believed a convention would be more partisan than Congress, and indeed, his follow-up argument on the point is arguably inconsistent: "Why might not the subject be safely committed to Congress, a body as much elected by the people as a convention, and therefore, as likely to represent their wishes? What is the difference between the power of the people delegated to Congress and the power of the same people reserved to themselves, except that the former is always ready to act when an emergency makes it necessary, and the latter cannot act without hindrances and delay."[36]

Having said that Congress would be in an equal position, Fisher then argued for its superiority:

> Congress is more amenable to the control of the people than the convention proposed by the Constitution is likely to be, because the former is a permanent branch of the Government, elected at short intervals, so that at every election it is subjected to the popular control. The convention is, indeed, to be chosen by the people, and its work to be submitted to them for ratification. That done, however, the control of the people, over the convention and over the subject

ceases. The amendment once made, however injurious it may prove is irrevo-
cable, except by another convention elected by the same difficult forms.[37]

It is important to remember that Fisher was directly comparing parliamentary
sovereignty (and not specifically the Article V process that involves Congress
and the states) with the Article V convention mechanism and that he was specifically advocating that Congress change the Constitution without following the
forms of Article V. Still, many of his arguments point to comparisons that I will
highlight in chapter 7 with respect to the comparative advantages and disadvantages of convention proposal versus congressional proposal.

In an appendix to the book that Fisher devoted chiefly to the Emancipation
Proclamation (he believed that Congress should be taking similar initiatives),
he again contrasted what he believed would be the advantages of congressional
deliberation versus deliberation in a convention. He elaborated:

> And now it is proposed to choose, in the midst of civil war, by a popular elec-
> tion, a National Convention to do the work of a National Government. That
> Convention must be elected by the same people who have already elected a
> Congress. It will, therefore, represent the passions and opinions that divide the
> people and which are already represented in Congress. It will be governed by the
> same leaders of parties, the same "politicians," who already direct public senti-
> ment and control public affairs, for none others can be elected because none
> others are known to the people. It will be wholly irresponsible, because its mem-
> bers, chosen for the occasion only, will not be influenced either by the hope
> of re-election or the fear of being turned out, and the people will thus have no
> means or opportunity of expressing their disapprobation of the conduct of the
> Convention.[38]

Ignoring the Article V requirement for subsequent state ratification of the convention's work, Fisher further portrayed convention delegates as less subject to
checks: "There will be no check whatever on its action, such as Congress is subjected to by its division into two houses, by the veto of the President, and by
the opinion of the Judiciary. Invested thus with the omnipotence of an English
Parliament, but without any of its restraining influences, internal or external, the
Convention, dressed in a brief authority, might play some fantastic tricks . . . and
very probably produce the anarchy it was intended to prevent." Even though he
was arguing for legislative sovereignty, Fisher went on to charge that "Conventions are ever prone to exceed their commission." Again ignoring the ratification
mechanism, Fisher claimed: "A Convention must, like Congress, be governed by
a majority, and that majority, in the present state of opinion, is more likely to be
extravagant, aggressive and tyrannical than a majority of Congress, whilst a mi-

nority would have no protection whatever, either from the President or from the people, for the people having given their whole power to the Convention, could not withdraw it, whereas the work of Congress is never done, and the people are always giving and withdrawing their power."[39]

Fisher wondered what would happen if the people were dissatisfied with one convention and called another, which "unless assembled by the forms provided in the Constitution," would be a body unknown to the law, and therefore without legal authority."[40] Moreover, if a second convention did follow constitutional forms, it would be submitted "to a popular vote, in the midst of war, with a wide field opened to agitators and demagogues to do their work of iniquity."[41] Again, however, Fisher was not arguing for the superiority of the Article V method for congressional proposal and state ratification but for what he believed would be the superiority of legislative sovereignty over either method.

Francis Lieber Advocated the Use of Article V

As indicated in chapter 3, the Civil War was followed neither by the calling of an Article V convention nor by the assertion of legislative sovereignty but by the adoption of three amendments through the process of congressional proposal and state ratification. Francis Lieber (1798 or 1800 to 1872) was a German-born scholar of history and political science who transferred from South Carolina College in Columbia (today's University of South Carolina) to Columbia College in New York on the eve of the Civil War, and he advocated proposals that closely resembled those that became the Thirteenth through Fifteenth Amendments. Unlike Fisher, Lieber rejected the idea that Congress needed to adopt such amendments apart from Article V processes by suggesting that it was possible to take a reverent attitude toward America's Founders while still recognizing the need for additional constitutional changes.[42]

Anticipating organic views of the Constitution, Lieber tied the need for change to life itself: "All laws must change in the course of time—whether they form the framework of a people's polity, or are strictly municipal laws, or constitute the laws of nations . . . for living men banded more or less closely, in communities, and the condition of life is change—change for the better or for the worse. So long as life lasts so long is there change. Cessation of organic change is death." Although Lieber agreed with Fisher that a system using parliamentary sovereignty was "far easier," he also thought that "on that account" it was "also occasionally more dangerous." At one point Lieber said that "a far better instrument might be devised, if men of the stamp of the Framers, with their boldness and their circumspection, and with the addition of all our experience, could meet in a constitutional convention, and revise the whole fundamental law,"[43] but he proceeded to propose a series of seven amendments, which appear to have exerted at least some influence on the three that Congress proposed and the states ratified.

Timothy Farrar Feared a General Convention Would Only Be Called to Destroy Government

Daniel Webster's law partner, Timothy Farrar (1788–1874), published his *Manual of the Constitution of the United States* in 1867. He treated constitutional amendments in a chapter that he devoted to special legislative powers, which he respectively identified as those of proposing amendments, calling a convention at the request of the states, or prescribing the means of ratification of amendments. Observing that the Constitution did not specify "in what proportion; when, how, and by whom [delegates would be] chosen or appointed; where and when assembled; and how organized, governed, and restricted," he concluded that Congress would have to make such determinations because there was "no other" collective authority to do so.[44]

Farrar doubted that the Article V convention mechanism would ever be used. He observed:

> A simultaneous movement, by twenty-five or more different State legislatures, each composed of at least two distinct and independent bodies of men, in favor of a general convention of the people for proposing alterations of the fundamental law, without limit and without landmark, is a measure not likely to be resorted to for any other purpose than to destroy the government. Whenever so large a proportion of the American people become imbued with that purpose, it is safe to predict that they will march to their object by a more direct route than by procuring an amendment of the Constitution in this circuitous manner.[45]

Although he referred at the end of this passage to "an amendment," Farrar appears to be suggesting that states would only be likely to use the Article V convention mechanism for a complete rewrite of the document. Moreover, he thought that they would be more likely to do this by other (presumably extra-constitutional) means, perhaps revolution. It seems likely that Farrrar's views were shaped more by the conventions that had led to disunion than by any analysis of the intentions of the Founders.

Christopher G. Tiedeman Emphasized the Unwritten Constitution

The view that the Constitution should change organically, rather than through either of the paths that Article V outlined, however, continued, most notably in the works of Christopher G. Tiedeman (1857–1903), a professor of law at the University of Missouri who published *The Unwritten Constitution of the United States* in 1890.[46] Whereas Fisher had opposed judicial review as an obstacle to legislative sovereignty, Tiedeman praised the Court for preventing the Fourteenth Amendment from having "its full literal effect."[47] In words that arguably encouraged the role that the Supreme Court would exemplify in its decision in *Lochner v. New York* (1905),[48] in which it struck down a New York law regulating the hours of bakers, Tiedeman praised the Court for averting "evil consequences by keeping the operation of the amendment within the limits which they felt assured would have been imposed by the people, if their judgment had not been blinded with passion, and which in their cooler moment they would ratify."[49]

John J. Jameson Distinguished Constitutional Conventions from Their Revolutionary Counterparts

The most extensive early work devoted to the operation of constitutional conventions was Judge John J. Jameson's classic *Treatise on Constitutional Conventions*, which he originally published in 1867. It was followed by three other editions, the last of which was published in 1887. Jameson (1824–90) largely devoted this book to distinguishing constitutional conventions from their revolutionary forebears, and from what he considered to be some of the rogue conventions that had developed at about the time of the Civil War.

Whereas revolutionary conventions often exercised complete powers of government, including that of legislating, Jameson thought that constitutional conventions were subordinate to the legislature and other bodies that called them rather than sovereign. As he explained early in his book, a convention "is subaltern,—it is evoked by the side and at the call of a government preexisting and intended to survive it, for the purpose of administering its special needs. It never supplants the existing organization. It never governs. Though called to look into and recommend improvements in the fundamental laws, it *enacts* neither them nor the statute law; and it performs no act of administration."[50]

Jameson favored reserving conventions for what he described as "extraordinary maladies requiring a fundamental change in the Constitution, not to those constantly recurring put petty disorders which demand the interposition of the ordinary legislature."[51] Curiously, although he reviewed hundreds of state conventions, Jameson did not specifically discuss whether states can limit the kind of conventions that they call under Article V. However, his view that conventions are subaltern to existing governmental bodies suggested that either Congress, the states, or both had such power.

Charles Borgeaud Affirmed Limits
on Constitutional Convention

Charles Borgeaud of Switzerland authored a comparative study of the amending process that was published in English in 1895. One of the most notable aspects of the book may be that in discussing the United States, it focused chiefly on constitutional revision at the state level, where Borgeaud focused on the tie between constitutional change and the will of the people. After including the text of Article V of the U.S. Constitution, Borgeaud observed that "Congress has never availed itself of the clause which gives it the right to prescribe the election of conventions, through which the popular verdict might be obtained,"[52] showing that, as did American observers, he largely equated the convention mechanism with the people themselves.

In dealing with state counterparts, Borgeaud observed that most states had distinguished the process of introducing a single amendment or amendments, which they often accomplished through initial legislative action, from complete constitutional revisions, which conventions often initiated. Borgeaud was adamant that the convention "is not sovereign." He explained, "It is merely a committee on the constitution, charged with the preparation of an instrument to which the approval of the people can alone give the force of supreme law."[53] He further associated the doctrine of convention sovereignty with the secessionist states. Although his focus was on state conventions, his reasoning would appear largely applicable to the Article V convention mechanism:

> In the United States, the constitutional convention acts within the limits of its mandate. The legislature is the permanent representative of the people. The convention is a special committee of delegates. These delegates may have received, in general terms, the command to revise the constitution. In this case they are free to submit to the electors whatever plan they may deem fit, provided this plan contains nothing contrary to the provisions of the Federal constitution. But they may also have been given the special task of revising only certain parts of the constitution. In this case, they are bound absolutely by the act of the legislature, which has specified the points toward which their activity may be directed, and in consideration of which the people have conferred upon them their mandate. Their full power extends to this point and no further.[54]

Further referring to the powers of a convention as "delegated" powers, Borgeaud sided with Judge Jameson in believing that its powers were subordinated to the institution that called them.[55]

A. Caperton Braxton and Thomas Cooley
Repeat Jameson's Arguments

Jameson's distinctions became part of the warp and woof of American law. Citing, and perhaps quoting, from a South Carolina opinion by Justice O'Neil in *McDaniel v. McMeekin*,[56] A. Caperton Braxton (1862–1914), an attorney who served as a member of the Virginia Constitutional Convention of 1901–2, painted a very stark contrast:

> The Constitutional Convention is normal, the Revolutionary Convention is abnormal; the one is a child of law and order, the other, of violence and anarchy; the former is the companion of Peace, the latter the concomitant of War; the one is the fruit of political health, the other of political disease; the one evidences the growth and development of government, the other its overthrow; the former is the legitimate offspring of existing government, the latter a dispossessing intruder. The Constitutional Convention co-exists with the former government, which continues to perform its functions, by virtue of the old Constitution and laws, until the new Constitution is adopted; the *Revolutionary* convention is the Government itself, the co-existence with which of any other government is impossible. The Constitutional Convention repairs and improves the Government. The Revolutionary Convention rebuilds it *de novo* after it has been pulled down and destroyed.

Braxton continued: "One body exists as a lawful institution, the other exists because there is no law; the one necessarily recognizes the governmental system which gave it birth and by which it is bound, the other recognizes no institution and is a law unto itself. One is legitimate, the other illegitimate; one exists *de jure*, the other *de facto*. The one depends for its support upon the laws and existing institutions, the other upon its physical power to maintain itself."[57]

In combating the notion that a convention must be sovereign, Braxton asked: "But are the People, by the mere act of calling a Convention, obliged to confer upon it all of their powers? Surely not. Upon what principle, for what reason, or by what analogy, can it be contended that the people cannot constitute a limited, as well as a general, agency—that they cannot employ an agent or appoint a representative to do a particular service for them, without surrendering to such agent or representative *all* of their powers and functions?"[58]

Braxton concluded that a constitutional convention was safe. Although he was specifically addressing a convention at the state level, his logic would apply to the federal level as well:

> Viewed in this light, the Constitutional Convention, instead of being a menace to liberty, a dangerous experiment with a body of vast, vague, unknown and unlimited powers, will be seen to be just as regular, legitimate and normal a body

as the Legislature; that its powers and functions are just as well defined and as
strictly limited; that the alteration or reconstruction of a Constitution need,
and should, involve no more resort to revolution, or a "state of nature" (even in
theory), and be fraught with no more danger to the Commonwealth, than the
enactment of an ordinary statute; and that the change from the old to a new
Constitution should involve no more irregularity or breach in the smooth and
peaceful continuity of Government, than the change of executives.[59]

Thomas Cooley (1824–98) was an important legal commentator and justice
on the Supreme Court of Michigan. He did not go quite so far (Braxton's description arguably undercut the foundation of the U.S. Constitution, which had
emerged from an extralegal body), but otherwise he accepted Jameson's argument when Cooley observed that "the constitutional convention is the representative of sovereignty only in a very qualified sense, and for the specific purpose,
and with the restricted authority to put in proper form the question of amendment upon which the people are to pass; but the changes in the fundamental law
of the States must be enacted by the people themselves."[60]

Israel Ward Andrews Disfavored Conventions

In 1887 Israel Ward Andrews (1815–88), president of Marietta College, chiefly
designed his *Manual of the Constitution of the United States* as a textbook. This
was republished in 1900. In examining the constitutional amending process, Andrews noted that two-thirds of the states had yet to call for an Article V convention. He further observed that "it is fortunate for the country that a convention
has never been called for the purpose of proposing amendments. The organic
law of a people should be framed with great care and altered with the utmost
caution. A body of men convened for the purpose of suggesting alterations in the
Constitution would be likely to magnify their office in proposing many amendments."[61] Although he expressed concern that delegates would seek to magnify
their powers, Andrews did not specifically address why members of Congress
would not have the same incentives or whether state legislatures or Congress
could limit the agenda of such a convention.

James Bryce Explained the Lack of Article V Conventions

James Bryce (1838–1922), an English academic, Liberal member of Parliament,
and ambassador to the United States from 1907 to 1913, first printed his classic
The American Commonwealth in 1888. Like Alexis de Tocqueville's *Democracy
in America*, Bryce's book remains one of the greatest works on American government that a foreign observer has written. One of Bryce's central distinctions

was between a flexible constitution like that of Great Britain, where Parliament exercised sovereignty, and a rigid constitution like that of the United States, which Congress cannot change by ordinary legislative means.[62] This distinction furthered arguments by earlier critics that the U.S. amending process was too difficult.

In *The American Commonwealth*, Bryce provided a thorough analysis of Article V, in which he distinguished between both the two methods of proposing and the two methods of ratifying amendments. Bryce offered two reasons to explain why the United States had yet to use the Article V convention method. First, in an argument that suggests that many people might still have primarily associated the method of congressional proposal as the method for minor changes and conventions for complete rewritings, he observed that "it has never been desired to remodel the whole Constitution, but only to make changes or additions on special points." Second, he noted that "the procedure by National and State conventions might be slower, and would involve controversy over electing those bodies."[63]

One of Bryce's most astute observations, which could well be applied to conventions, focused on the connection between proposed amendments and partisan politics. Observing that most constitutional changes were likely to advantage one party over another, Bryce identified what novelist Joseph Heller would call a kind of Catch-22: "If a measure of reform is pressing, it becomes a matter of party contention, and excites passion. If it is not pressing, neither party, having other and nearer aims, cares to take it up and push it through. In America, a party amendment to the Constitution can very seldom be carried. A non-party amendment falls into the category of those things which, because they are everybody's business, are the business of nobody."[64]

In examining whether Americans might favor making the process of amendment easier, Bryce further explained the American reluctance to change the Constitution, summarizing their views as follows:

> A swift and easy method would not only weaken the sense of security which the rigid Constitution now gives, but would increase the troubles of current politics by stimulating a majority in Congress to frequently submit amendments to the States. The habit of mending would turn into the habit of tinkering. There would be too little distinction between changes in the ordinary statute law, which require the agreement of majorities in the two Houses and the President, and changes in the more solemnly enacted fundamental law. And the rights of the States, upon which congressional legislation cannot now directly encroach, would be endangered.[65]

Bryce went on to argue that Americans most typically resorted instead to flexible interpretations of the Constitution.

John W. Burgess Saw Conventions as a Way to Overcome Inertia

Often identified as the father of American political science, John Burgess (1844–1931), a professor of history, political science, and international law at Columbia College who was born in Tennessee, was among those who echoed Sidney George Fisher's view that the amending process was too difficult. In contrasting his views with those of Joseph Story, Burgess thus observed: "When I reflect that, while our natural conditions and relations have been requiring a gradual strengthening and extension of the powers of the central government, not a single step has been taken in this direction through the process of amendment prescribed in that article, except as the result of civil war, I am bound to conclude that the organization of the sovereign power within the constitution has failed to accomplish the purpose for which it was constructed."[66] Rather than advocating a convention, Burgess favored allowing two successive joint sessions of Congress to propose amendments that would be subject to ratification by state legislatures meeting in joint assemblies. Like Fisher, Burgess was willing to depart from the Framers' strict intentions on the subject.[67]

Burgess believed that the Constitutional Convention of 1787 had created the sovereign state and that another convention might change it in the future. In looking at Article V, Burgess observed that: "Article V provides, in the first place, for an organization apparently very nearly corresponding with the original organization back of the constitution, *viz*; a convention for proposing amendments, and conventions of the people resident within the several commonwealths for ratifying the same. According to the letter of the law, however, the general convention is only an initiating body, and three-fourths majority of the separate conventions in the real constituent."[68] Unlike some earlier commentators, he thus stressed that states would have to approve any recommendations of an Article V convention. Burgess further opined that:

> It is probable that another convention, representing in a single body the whole people of the United States, upon a truthful basis of representation, would have such a moral power as to carry its resolves through the separate conventions unchanged, unless some absorbing sectional interest should control the conventions in more than one-fourth of the commonwealths. In such a case the national convention might be able to propose and cause to be applied a different method of ratification from that provided in the existing constitution, as did the convention of 1787; but this would be revolution again, as that was, and not existing law.[69]

Burgess appears to have been thinking of an Article V convention solely in terms of rewriting the existing document rather than in offering individual amendments. Thus, he did not address the specific issue of whether states could limit a convention. Indeed, Burgess appeared to have been under the mistaken impression that state ratifying conventions might seek to alter (rather than simply reject) suggested changes that an Article V convention proposed to them.

Woodrow Wilson Critiqued the Amending Process

Few if any political scientists have had a greater influence on U.S. history than Woodrow Wilson (1856–1924), the Johns Hopkins–educated scholar who went on to head Princeton University, serve as New Jersey governor, and become president of the United States from 1913 to 1921, which included the critical years of American participation in World War I. As Christopher Wolfe has demonstrated, Wilson's thought appears to have changed from his first book, *Congressional Government*, where he stressed what he believed to be the inflexibility of the written Constitution (and his own preference for British-style cabinet government), to his later work in *Constitutional Government in the United States*, where he put greater emphasis on the role of the judiciary and the presidency in adapting the Constitution to new circumstances.[70]

Believing that the system of separation of powers that the Founders had established was based on an outdated Whig Newtonian, model of checks and balances, Wilson came to favor a more organic Darwinian approach. Wilson thus observed, "The trouble with the [Whig Newtonian] theory is that government is not a machine, but a living thing. It falls, not under the theory of the university, but under the theory of organic life. It is accountable to Darwin, not to Newton."[71] Similarly, he said, "The Constitution cannot be regarded as a mere legal document, to be read as a will or a contract would be. It must, of the necessity of the case, be a vehicle of life."[72]

As noted earlier, Wilson thought the chief mechanism for change was the Supreme Court. After observing that "The character of the process of constitutional adaptation depends first of all upon the wise or unwise choice of statesmen, but ultimately and chiefly upon the opinion and purpose of the Court,"[73] Wilson went on to observe that "The chief instrumentality by which the law of the Constitution has been extended to cover the facts of national development has of course been judicial interpretation,—the decisions of the courts. The process of formal amendment of the Constitution was made so difficult by the provisions of the Constitution itself that it has seldom been feasible to use it; and the difficulty of formal amendment has undoubtedly made the courts more liberal, not to say more lax, in their interpretation than they would otherwise have been."[74] Wilson's critique of the amending process presumably extended to the Article V convention mechanism, which, to my knowledge, he never advocated. Consistent with the above analysis, he did refer to the Supreme Court as "a kind of Constitutional Convention in continuous session,"[75] which, if taken literally, might obviate the need for an Article V gathering.[76]

Herman V. Ames Compiled Calls for Amendments

Professor Herman V. Ames of the University of Pennsylvania compiled the first, and one of the most comprehensive, of a number of monographs listing, and often analyzing, amendments that members of Congress had proposed to the Constitution. He devoted less than three pages to what he called "General Conventions." In this discussion he observed that states had issued calls for such conventions. He further observed that the convention that South Carolina called in the winter of 1832 and 1833 did not conform to the Article V model. He did not, however, directly address the issue of whether states or Congress had the authority to limit the agenda of Article V conventions.[77]

Walter Fairleigh Dodd Focused on State Conventions

In writing *The Revision and Amendment of State Constitutions*, which he published in 1910, Professor Walter Fairleigh Dodd (1880–1960) of Johns Hopkins University attempted to distance his own views both from those who thought that conventions were sovereign bodies and those who thought they were subordinate to the legislature. Counter to both arguments, he argued that a convention was "independent within its proper sphere."[78] He further explained what he understood to be the tasks of convention: "These are simply to propose a new constitution or to propose constitutional amendments to the people for approval; or, in states where the submission of constitutions is not required, to frame and adopt a constitution if they think proper."[79] He added, "In this sphere, and in the exercise of powers incidental to its proper functions, it would seem that constitutional conventions should not be subject to control by legislative acts."[80] Like a number of predecessors, however, Dodd was chiefly addressing *state* conventions.

Roger Sherman Hoar Portrayed Conventions
as a Fourth Branch of Government

In 1917, Roger Sherman Hoar (1887–1963) published his *Constitutional Conventions: Their Nature, Powers, and Limitations*, which chiefly upheld Dodd's view over that of Jameson. Hoar believed that, like each of the three branches of government, a convention is also "a regular organ of the state,"[81] or what he later calls "a fourth branch of the government,"[82] which shares powers independently of other branches. Hoar arguably muddied the waters, however, by focusing chiefly on state conventions and by indicating that legislative control over such conventions would thus vary from state to state. Moreover, he did not specifically examine the Article V convention mechanism.

J. Allen Smith Praised the Convention Mechanism as a Route to Revolutionary Change

The farther one gets from the Framers, the less likely one probably is to tap into their original intent, so far as scholars can reasonably ascertain it. Still, it is noteworthy that J. Allen Smith, a professor of political science at the University of Washington, who was among the greatest critics of the Founders, and what he believed to have been their betrayal of the more democratic goals of the Declaration of Independence, nevertheless took some hope in the amending process.

Writing in his classic, *The Spirit of American Government*, Allen observed that "The most important feature of the Constitution from the standpoint of democracy is the provision contained in article V, requiring Congress 'on the application of the legislatures of two-thirds of the several states' to 'call a convention for proposing amendments.'"[83] Focusing on the potential of conventions to rewrite the document, Allen observed that: "It in reality opens the door to the most revolutionary changes in our political arrangements. Congress can not refuse to call a general constitutional convention when two-thirds of the states demand it, and this convention might propose an entirely new constitution framed in accord with the most advanced ideas of democracy. It might also follow the precedent set by the framers of our present Constitution and prescribe an entirely new method of ratification, as our more conservative forefathers did when they disregarded the then existing provision governing the amendment of the Articles of Confederation."[84] In observing that states could call a general convention, Allen did not indicate whether they might also call for limited conventions. Consistent with contemporary attempts on the part of the states to force Congress to propose an amendment providing for direct election of U.S. senators, Allen further observed that:

> It is possible, if not indeed probable, that a serious and concerted attempt by the people to force changes in the Constitution by this method would sufficiently alarm the opponents of democracy and convince them of the wisdom and expediency of such amendments as would appease the popular clamor for reform without going too far in the direction of majority rule. To prevent the complete overthrow of the system, which might be the outcome if the states were compelled to assume the initiative in amending the Constitution, the minority may accept the inevitable, and, choosing what appears to them to be the lesser of two

evils, allow Congress to propose such amendments as the people are determined to bring about.[85]

Lester B. Orfield Did Not Think That
States Can Limit a Convention

In 1942, Lester Bernhardt Orfield, a professor of law at the University of Nebraska, wrote a book entitled *The Amending of the Federal Constitution* in which he addressed a limited constitutional convention more directly than had some of his predecessors. He identified the constitutional convention as "a method corresponding to the original organization which proposed the Constitution itself."[86] After first observing that only the states could initiate constitutional revision through a convention and that "All that Congress can do in bringing about a convention is of a purely advisory character, as by resolution inviting the state legislatures to apply for a convention," Orfield went on to deny "that Congress is a mere ministerial cog in the call of a convention."[87]

Writing at a time before the Supreme Court's acceptance of justiciability in congressional apportionment cases and specifically citing this inaction, Orfield acknowledged that Congress might successfully circumvent state calls for a convention, but he further opined that "A clear case is of course possible should two-thirds of the states all at one time request a convention for an identical purpose, and little discretion would seem to be left to Congress."[88] He further reiterated that Congress would have little leeway should the states request either a general convention or one for a specific purpose but concluded that even when two-thirds of the states contemporaneously requested convention applications for diverse purposes, this "would conclusively show a widespread desire for constitutional changes" that should prompt Congress to act.[89] He also observed that it seemed unlikely that state calls for the direct election of senators should be considered live after adoption of the Seventeenth Amendment.[90]

Orfield observed, "If the precedent of the Constitution were followed, the call would be addressed to the states, and would leave to them the method of selecting delegates; and the convention would vote by states."[91] Further arguing that "Where the states apply for a convention for general purposes, it would seem that the convention would be free to draft a new document," Orfield went on to say that "even though the application were for a limited purpose, it would seem that state legislatures would have no authority to limit an instrumentality set up under the Federal Constitution."[92] Orfield thought that the same was true of Congress: "Insomuch as Congress issues the call simply on the basis of the application of the state legislatures, there would seem to be no warrant for an attempt by Congress to limit the changes proposed."[93]

Citing the contrasting views that conventions were either sovereign or subaltern, Orfield ultimately sided with Dodd in believing that "a convention, though not sovereign, is a body independent of the legislature; it is bound by the existing constitution, but not by the acts of the legislature, as to the extent of its constituent power."[94] He thus concluded that "no restrictions can be placed on the scope of its constituent activity, but that its acts beyond this function would be void. Hence a convention would have no power to interfere with the President or Congress or the states, except of course, as the provisions of the proposed constitution might do."[95] Orfield further pointed out that states would ultimately have to decide whether to ratify anything that the convention proposed.

Cyril F. Brickfield Argued That States Can Limit a Convention

In 1957 Cyril F. Brickfield (1919–97), an attorney who would go on to lead the American Association of Retired Persons for twenty years, wrote a report for the House Judiciary Committee examining problems related to constitutional conventions. Relying chiefly on the distinction that Jameson had drawn between constitutional conventions and revolutionary conventions, Brickfield argued that a convention was bound by restrictions imposed by Congress.[96] He further thought that states could limit the agenda of such a convention.

He observed that:

> The States, of course, are given a major role under article V both in initiating a convention movement and in finally ratifying a convention's work. In addition . . . one of the major reasons for incorporating the convention method of amending the Constitution into our basic law was to create a remedy by which the States, in the event Congress was unwilling to act, could compel action. The convention method of amending the Constitution would be reduced to an unworkable absurdity both from the standpoint of the States having a voice in the convention process and from the magnitude of the operation and its ultimate effect on our Government, if only general conventions were permissible under article V.[97]

He therefore concluded that states could "ask for either a limited or general reformation of the Constitution."[98]

Analysis

My impression after surveying early sources is that they often discussed Article V conventions with a relative lack of precision that stemmed largely from the predominance of the method of congressional proposal and state ratification that can be traced back to Madison's decision to use the congressional method of proposing amendments as a way of preempting convention action. This decision in turn led many subsequent commentators to associate the congressional proposal method with a single amendment or amendments and the convention method with more systemic constitutional changes, like those inaugurated at the Philadelphia Convention of 1787. Although some writers continued to view the Article V convention mechanism as one of a number of tools within the Article V arsenal, few other than Jameson, who properly distinguished constitutional conventions from their revolutionary predecessors, specifically addressed whether state legislatures or Congress had the power to limit them, leaving the field relatively open for modern scholars to explore without many precedents to guide them.

CHAPTER 6

The Modern Debate over
Limiting Conventions

Scholars have expended far more ink on the question of limiting Article V conventions in the last fifty years than they did previously. There are so many arguments that it is often difficult to sort through them. In this chapter, I will assess the arguments by examining a report that a Special Constitutional Convention Study Committee of the American Bar Association issued arguing that states could limit the agenda of an Article V convention,[1] two scholarly responses arguing against a limited convention, and a further report by the U.S. Department of Justice that supported the ABA report's conclusions.

The American Bar Association Makes the Case
for Limited Article V Conventions

In the wake of the Supreme Court's reapportionment decisions and other innovations in constitutional interpretations during the Warren Court era, the 1960s were bedeviled by arguments as to whether states could call for a limited constitutional convention. In 1973 the American Bar Association (ABA) weighed in on the subject in a report formulated by a number of its members. Identifying the "central" issue surrounding an Article V convention as whether it "can be limited in its authority," the ABA cited two views: "There is the view, with which we disagree, that an Article V convention would be a sovereign assemblage and could not be restricted by either the state legislatures or the Congress in its authority or proposals. And there is the view, with which we agree, that Congress has the power to establish procedures which would limit a convention's authority to a specific subject matter where the legislatures of two-thirds of the states seek a convention limited to that subject."[2] In the preface to a fairly detailed review of debates at the Constitutional Convention, the ABA committee argued that these debates "make clear that the convention method of proposing amendments was intended to stand on an equal footing with the congressional method."[3] Thus, states should be able to issue a call for a convention to propose a single amendment or set of amendments just as Congress can propose such individual amendments.

Consistent with Judge Jameson's earlier analysis, the ABA report further distinguished the Convention of 1787 from an Article V convention: "While the Constitutional Convention of 1787 may have exceeded the purpose of its call in framing the Constitution, it does not follow that a convention convened under Article V and subject to the Constitution can lawfully assume such authority." The committee argued that "both pre-1787 convention practices and the general tenor of the amending provisions of the first state constitutions lend support to the conclusions that a convention could be convened for a specific purpose and that, once convened, it would have no authority to exceed this purpose." The ABA committee thus said that "the report of the Annapolis Convention of 1786 also reflected an awareness of the binding effect of limitations on a convention. That Convention assembled to consider general trade matters and, because of the limited number of state representatives present, decided not to proceed." The most notable evidence that the committee cited on this subject was a provision in Georgia's constitution that provided that when a majority of counties petitioned for a convention, the assembly would "order *a convention to be called for that purpose*, specifying the alterations to be made, according to the petitions referred to the assembly by a majority of the counties as aforesaid."[4]

Having reviewed this evidence, the ABA committee returned to the argument that the method whereby states proposed a convention was intended to be equal to that whereby Congress proposed amendments. An interpretation that allowed a convention to exceed its call "would relegate the alternative method to an 'unequal' method of initiating amendments. Even if the state legislatures overwhelmingly felt that there was a necessity for limited change in the Constitution, they would be discouraged from calling for a convention if that convention would automatically have the power to propose a complete revision of the Constitution." The ABA committee further cited experience at the state level, including judicial decisions, similar to those that Judge Jameson had cited, that "the electorate may choose to delegate only a portion of its authority to a state constitutional convention and so limit it substantially."[5]

The ABA committee summarized its case by observing:

A substantively-limited Article V convention is [1] consistent with the purpose of the alternative method since the states and the people would have a complete vehicle other than the Congress for remedying specific abuses of power by the national government; [2] consistent with the actual history of the amending article throughout which only amendments on single subjects have been proposed by Congress; [3] consistent with state practice under which limited conventions have been held under the constitutional provisions not expressly sanctioning a substantively-limited convention; and [4] consistent with democratic principles because convention delegates would be chosen by the people in an election in which the subject matter to be dealt with would be known and the issues identified, thereby enabling the electorate to exercise an informed judgment in the choice of delegates.[6]

The second of these four arguments further extended the first by equating single-issue amendments in conventions with the single-issue amendments that Congress has proposed, while the fourth argument raised an additional, and arguably powerful, consideration by suggesting that voters would want to choose delegates to a convention on the basis of which issues it would consider. It might be far more sensible to elect a medical doctor to a convention considering constitutional amendments relative to health care than to a convention to deal with legislative reapportionment or to rewrite the entire Constitution.

Charles L. Black Jr. Argues that Calls for Limited Conventions Are Nullities

One of the most vocal opponents of the ABA report was Professor Charles L. Black Jr. of Yale Law School, who summarized his arguments in an article published in 1979. Addressed as a letter to then Senator Edward Kennedy of Massachusetts, chair of the Senate Judiciary Committee, Black, who had written and published a previous letter on the subject to New York congressman Emanuel Celler seven years earlier,[7] took the view that Article V did not contemplate limited Article V conventions. Thus, any petitions for such conventions were therefore "nullities," and "thirty-four times zero is zero."[8]

Black based his first argument on what he called "'Plain Meaning' and Context." Imitating the practice of tracking a statute, Black asked how one would interpret a request, tracking the language of Article V, if a state legislature said "'Application is hereby made that Congress call a convention for proposing amendments,'" the exact language of Article V, and he concluded that the meaning of such a request for a general convention would be fairly incontrovertible. He then raised the question as to whether Article V "*in addition* to its incontestably plain conferral, on the legislatures of a very significant power, the power to force the call of a general constitutional convention," also permitted "a *different power*, not at all obviously meant by Article V." Whereas the ABA committee focused on the equality of Congress and the states to limit amendments to a similar subject, Black focused on what he believed to be the equality between Article V conventions and Congress: "The equality to be sought, as to national concerns, is an equality between the two national bodies to which the 'proposing' function is given." Moreover, seeking to deny "a 'greater includes the less' argument,"

Black argued that a general convention and a limited convention are "as different in kind as (1) the freedom to marry; and (2) the freedom to marry one of two or three people designated by somebody else."[9] Black further denied that it would be regrettable to discourage state legislatures from applying for limited conventions if Article V did not, indeed, intend for them to apply for them.

Black questioned why state legislatures would fear a convention that they would themselves have to ratify. Acknowledging that Congress could bypass state legislatures by requiring convention ratification, he still equated "fear of the headlong folly of such [state] conventions" as "a fear of the people who will elect them." He followed with two rhetorical questions: "Why, indeed, is one so afraid of the general national convention? Is it well to trust any part at all of the amendment process to people who, you think, would go wild if you turned them loose?"[10] Black further observed that the Framers distinguished between "'the people' and 'the legislatures,'" and gave the latter higher status, as they demonstrated by providing for constitutional ratification by state conventions rather than by state legislative approval.[11]

After quoting at length from the ABA committee report, he questioned both its use of convention debates and the conclusions that its members drew from it. He was skeptical of referring to the convention method as "the 'state' method," as he was of the committee's legislative history. As Black viewed the deliberations of 1787, they remained inconclusive. Black similarly denied that the ABA evidence from eighteenth-century constitutions had proven anything.[12]

Although Black had arguably done a better job in establishing that the Framers would have permitted general conventions than in showing that they required them, or prevented limited conventions, he did advance an additional argument to the effect that petitions for conventions in Congress during the first one hundred years of the nation's history all called for general conventions: "Think what this means. Through the controversies over the Alien and Sedition Laws, over the Embargo, over the 'internal improvements' bills, over the Bank of the United States, over the early fugitive-slave laws, *not one single state legislature* acted as though it thought it had the power to force Congress to call a convention limited to one of these topics."[13]

Having argued through most of his essay that the evidence was inconclusive, Black ended by questioning the maturity of those who proposed limited conventions by suggesting that "an application 'for the purpose of proposing' a minutely-described amendment is a mere travesty of grown-up constitutionalism, and indeed of the very word 'propose,' as applied to a solemnly assembled national constitutional convention."[14] This suggests that much of his argument may have stemmed less from his generic analysis of Article V than from concerns over some specific amendments that states had proposed and that he had labeled "A Threatened Disaster."[15]

Walter Dellinger Also Questions Limited Conventions

Walter Dellinger, a law professor at Duke University who would later serve as acting U.S. solicitor general in the Clinton administration, joined the debate over limited conventions with an article published in 1979. After surveying the debates at the federal convention, Dellinger identified two themes that emerged: "Congress should not have exclusive power to propose amendments; and state legislatures should not be able to propose and ratify amendments that enhance their power at the expense of the national government."[16] After distinguishing the processes of proposing amendments from that of ratifying them, Dellinger said that "the proceedings suggest that the framers did not want to permit enactment of amendments by a process of state proposal followed by state ratification without the substantive involvement of a national forum. Permitting the states to limit the subject matter of a constitutional convention would be inconsistent with the aim."[17]

Dellinger was especially skeptical of the right of the states to limit convention consideration to a single "draft amendment, the wording of which had been ordained in advance by the applying state legislatures." He observed that "if the [Framers'] aim had been to give the state legislatures the power to propose as well as to ratify amendments, it would have been unnecessary to provide for conventions."[18]

Dellinger thought that similar reasoning should apply to calls for conventions limited as to subject matter. Dellinger believed that "Congress could establish a precedent that applications are valid if and only if applying states understand that the convention will be free to set its own limits." From a practical perspective, he argued that "this determination would be significantly less intrusive than if Congress were to undertake with each set of applications to infer and enforce limits on the subject matter authority of the convention."[19]

Having thus argued against the ability of the states to call for a limited convention, Dellinger conceded: "There is, however, no basis in Article V for asserting that a convention is required to reappraise the whole Constitution, or that states would have to favor such revision before they could apply for a convention." Moreover, he suggested a mechanism by which such a convention could be limited: "If the prospect of a 'runaway convention' is frightening, then delegate candidates are likely to campaign for office on a pledge to limit the convention's agenda and that pledge is likely to have popular appeal." Further acknowledging that states might be less likely to call for unlimited conventions than for limited ones, and that a convention that was free to set its own agenda might "in spite of the recommendations of the applying states . . . consider subjects other than those recommended," he noted that "a majority of delegates would have to be persuaded to support those amendments on 'extraneous' subjects, and three-fourths of the states would still have to ratify them." Dellinger's bottom line, however, was that Congress should only call a convention if the requisite majority of states called for a general convention that left the convention to determine its own agenda.[20]

A Report to the Attorney General Argues for Limited Conventions

The U.S. Department of Justice issued a report to the attorney general in 1987, in which it reviewed the literature on the subject and advanced three major arguments for a limited convention. Its first argument was an argument based on "equality." This argument, which drew from debates at the Constitutional Convention of 1787, argued that states should have an equal right with Congress to propose amendments, and that since the latter could propose single amendments, the states should be able to do likewise.[21] A second argument focused on the need for contemporary consensus. By this reasoning, it seemed unwise to call an open-ended convention if states had only expressed a consensus for a convention on a single subject or set of subjects.[22] A third argument focused on the fact, explained in a section heading, that "Both the States and the Congress Have Interpreted Article V as Providing for Limited Conventions."[23] The report focused both on twentieth-century calls for limited conventions and on proposed legislation on the subject. The report argued that the states, Congress, and the judiciary might all serve to enforce limits on the scope of such conventions.

Paul J. Weber and Barbara A. Perry Point to Political Safeguards

Although most analysis of Article V conventions proceeds, much like this book, through a series of historical, legal, and constitutional arguments, political scientists Paul J. Weber and Barbara A. Perry chose an alternate approach in their book entitled *Unfounded Fears*. Arguing that "many scholars have done the nation a disservice by concocting hypothetical horribles" tied to the possibility of a runaway convention, Weber and Perry argued that there were numerous "political 'safety latches'" that would ensure that the convention mechanism was a "safe" mechanism.[24] Questioning whether "unsettled law is unsafe law," they sought to shift the focus. Whereas lawyers and theorists were asking the questions "What *could* a convention do?" or "What *should* a convention do?" which Weber and Perry believed were relatively inconclusive, Weber and Perry chose to ask, "What *would* a convention do?" which they thought that political experience could answer. They further thought that extensive experience at the state level would give guidance on a number of questions. They noted that only 6 out of 230 state conventions, the last of which occurred in 1908, exceeded their mandates.[25]

In looking at the national process, Weber and Perry began with protections that were built into Article V itself. These included the requirement for two-thirds of the states, all but one of which had bicameral legislatures, to propose amendments.[26] Weber and Perry further thought that it was likely that Congress and the Supreme Court would oversee the process of calling the convention, and noted that proposed legislation on the subject, which Congress has still to adopt, provided relatively clear rules. Under these rules, or something like them, Weber and Perry thought that the process of electing candidates to the convention would likely draw individuals with political experience who would take positions (opposing unlimited conventions if necessary) that would likely enhance their own prospects for electoral success.[27]

Weber and Perry further described a plethora of political factors that would likely constrain a convention. These included:

> The previously cited character of the delegates elected; the media attention that will be given to discrepancies between the campaign statements and promises and the delegates' actual words and actions; the number of delegates and divisions within the convention itself, which would make it extraordinarily difficult for one faction or a radical position to prevail; the delegates' awareness that the convention results must be presented to Congress, which might not forward any amendment that went beyond the convention mandate; the Supreme Court, which might well declare certain actions beyond the constitutional power of the convention; and most important of all, the need to get the proposed amendment ratified not only by the thirty-four states that called for the convention but by thirty-eight states.[28]

If Weber and Perry are correct, and Article V specifically mandates that three-fourths of the states must ratify any convention proposals before they become law, much of the controversy over what a convention *could conceivably do* are largely irrelevant because they fail to consider what a convention *would be likely to do*.

The argument might well be brought into further focus by closer analysis of the emotions convened by the term "runaway convention." Lawrence Lessig, who thinks that states have the right to call for a limited convention and who believes that Weber and Perry are correct, observes with reference to a "runaway convention," that

> it is not likely. At all. But if it happens, then it would happen only because that runaway convention had come up with the same sort of world-changing brilliance that our Framers did. And if it did, then why wouldn't we want the states to ratify it? Or put more strongly: If an "illegal proposal" were so strong as to overcome its own illegitimacy, and rally the support of thirty-eight states, it would have to be an incredible proposal. Not an incredible proposal for the Left or for the Right. To win the approval of thirty-eight states would require a proposal that cut across both Left and Right. What possible reason is there for us to fear a change that was supported by such a substantial majority?[29]

Further Weighing Costs and Benefits

At a time when there is such a diversity of opinion and such extensive commentary on the issue of constitutional interpretation, it is surprising that, apart from Weber and Perry's attention to political safeguards, there seems to be so much more discussion of, or speculation about, what the Framers *intended* the Article V convention mechanism to mean than there has of what it actually *should* mean. This is especially intriguing in light of the fact that many scholars who have devoted the greatest attention to the Framers' original intent with respect to this issue have openly acknowledged that their own conclusions are not definitive. In such circumstances, it certainly seems appropriate to consider which interpretation is likely to lead to the best outcomes. I believe that such considerations fall clearly on the side of those who think that limitations are appropriate.

The Arguments of John Harmon

The individual who has drawn the starkest contrast in the subject may be John M. Harmon, who authored a memorandum opinion for the U.S. attorney general in 1979. After surveying original sources, he concluded: "The basic constitutional choice is between a flexible application procedure and a rigid application procedure—between a procedure in which the legislatures are free to apply for what they want, and a procedure in which they may apply for a general convention only."[30]

Harmon continued in language reminiscent of the distinction that James Bryce drew in an earlier day between flexible and rigid constitutions:

> Under the flexible procedure the legislatures are free to do precisely what they are entitled to do under the rigid one, and Congress is empowered to do neither more nor less. Under the flexible procedure the legislatures are free to apply for

a general convention, if two-thirds of them are willing to solicit and entertain proposals on any subject; and Congress must respond whenever two-thirds of them have done so. The real difference between the two procedures lies, not in the way they allocate power between Congress and the legislatures, but in the way they allocate power between Congress and the convention itself. Under the rigid procedure the role of the convention is to follow wherever its delegates lead; and the convention is invariably empowered to do so, whatever the desires of the legislatures may be. Under the flexible procedure the convention is the servant of the legislatures. Its function is to respond to the extraordinary consensus that was the predicate for the call.[31]

Contrasts between the View that States Can Call for a Limited Convention and the View that They Cannot

Harmon's analysis is further clarified by examining other likely contrasts between a limited and an unlimited convention.

Safety

The most obvious advantage of interpreting Article V to allow states and/or Congress to call an Article V convention that is limited to a single amendment or set of amendments is that this would allow states to use a constitutional mechanism without fear of opening a Pandora's box or unleashing an evil genie that would be likely to bring about serious, unanticipated consequences. As chapter 3 indicated, Federalists chose the method of congressional proposal of individual amendments rather than convention proposal of amendments in hopes of averting a second convention that might undo their own work. It would seem no less urgent for modern elected officials to press for what they consider to be reasonable constitutional changes without opening the door to a parade of horribles no matter how unlikely they might seem to be.

Enforcement

Deciding that a convention can be limited does not, of course, establish how such limitations would be enforced. States could certainly send out a limited call; Congress could arguably refuse to send proposals other than such calls to the states for ratification; candidates could (and would) likely run on pledges to stay within the proposed agenda of such a convention. Even if states tried to ratify proposals that fell outside of a convention's proposed agenda, courts might decide that such ratifications were unconstitutional. By contrast, the view that favors interpreting Article V so that delegates to a convention could exercise unlimited power would leave state and national institutions relatively helpless in the event that radical delegates hijacked an Article V convention.

Stability

The issue of stability is largely redundant with that of safety, but though the two arguments are so often paired, they are distinct. If a convention can be limited to a specific issue or set of issues that do not appear to threaten human rights or call America's place in the world into question, then it is less likely to be politically, socially, or economically disruptive. Citizens and leaders will not have to lose sleep over what the convention is likely to do or what effects they might have on America's standing in the world. The people will not necessarily have to be quite as concerned about the timing of such conventions.

Likelihood of Use

As Weber and Perry's discussion of "fourth-quarter cautiousness reveals,"[32] it must, of course, be frankly acknowledged that whether the fear is real or imagined, the fear of an unlimited convention and the instability that it might cause is probably the central barrier to its use. If a relatively clear consensus emerged that Article V conventions could be limited and that they would be neither dangerous nor destabilizing, then states would be more likely to call them. Moreover, opponents of amendments would have to oppose them on the basis of their substance rather than on how they were being introduced—few individuals appear to have raised the specter of an unlimited convention who have actually favored the substance of amendments that they think states are most likely to propose.

Whether this would be good or bad would, of course, depend on the occasions for which states would call such conventions. Judging from convention debates, the Framers anticipated that states would use conventions chiefly in cases where Congress proved to be unresponsive to the people. As discussed earlier in this book, over the last century the three chief issues that have stimulated state convention requests have involved a liberal democratic reform (election rather than state legislative appointment of U.S. senators); a conservative reaction against court decisions relative to state legislative apportionment and the exercise of judicial power in general; and attempts to adopt balanced budget amendments, which while favored more by conservatives than liberals arguably cut across ideological lines.

This diversity (like a number of calls for conventions from the liberal/progressive side of the political spectrum) suggests that there is no inherently liberal or conservative bias among such proposals.[33] States could just as easily call a convention to approve gay marriage as to oppose it; to increase governmental powers as to narrow them; to expand rights (perhaps adding social and economic guarantees) as to restrict them; or to guarantee a national living minimum wage as to oppose it.

Although some scholars of the subject have joined Publius, Joseph Story, and other early commentators in defending the current amending mechanism,[34] such defenses were much more common during the first fifty years of the republic than thereafter. Chapter 3 of this book has documented the rising tide of criticism in the antebellum period, during the Progressive Era, and among modern scholars who want further to democratize the Constitution of the difficulty of the amending process. In such circumstances, an interpretation that opened up the process would be desirable.[35] Indeed, one might argue that the reason the current process has been so difficult stems chiefly from the fact that unfounded fears of a runaway convention have effectively stymied one of two relatively equal amending paths that the Framers originally anticipated. It is as though Article V has been attempting to fly with one rather than with two wings![36]

Biases in the Convention Mechanism

If states are convinced of the safety and stability of the Article V convention mechanism, they are, of course, more likely to introduce calls for amendments for convention consideration that Congress might otherwise oppose. States might favor more liberal or more conservative proposals than would Congress. There is likely to be more give and take between state and national authorities. Congress might seek, as did James Madison, to seize initiatives from the states in order to have greater control of the process.

Although this might lead to increased conflicts between Congress and the states, such tension might turn out to be healthy. Federalism might evolve in more positive directions, with Congress being more sensitive to state concerns, and states developing greater appreciation for congressional perspectives. Ultimately, as Weber and Perry point out, any measures that Article V conventions propose will require ratification of three-fourths of the state legislatures or of state ratifying conventions.

Much might well depend on the occasion or occasions for which the states called the first convention and on the reception that such proposals received in the convention itself and subsequently by states called to ratify any proposals that they offered. Should the process go relatively smoothly with an outcome that a majority of Americans favored, then they would be likely to use it again. Should the convention fail to propose any amendments, citizens might conclude either that the mechanism was ineffective or, depending on the reasons that the convention gave, might further think that the safety of the mechanism had been vindicated.

Those who believe that the Article V mechanism is an essential part of the Constitution certainly have an incentive to seek an initial convention that appears to confirm their own positive assessments. Even those who oppose any use of the mechanism would be likely to summon their patriotic interests in positively influencing such a body to help ensure that it results in a favorable outcome. The eyes of the nation and of the world would likely encourage delegates to be on their best behavior.

CHAPTER 7

Using Criteria and Ideal Types to
Think about the Big Picture

To date, the only successful national constitution that a legislative body has proposed for the United States as a whole emerged from the Second Continental Congress as the Articles of Confederation, and the only national constitution to emerge from a convention is the one that was formulated in Philadelphia in 1787. Although scholars most frequently identify the first constitution with its inadequacies, the Congress that proposed it was a far different body from that which currently meets in Washington, D.C. The inadequacies of the Articles did not so much reflect defects of the proposing body as they demonstrated the dearth of practical experience, state jealousies of their powers, and other factors, which a wooden amending process that states never effectively utilized perpetuated.

Commentators variously praise today's Constitution for its longevity and criticize it for some of the compromises—slavery, which has since been eliminated, and less-than-democratic mechanisms like the Electoral College and equal state representation in the U.S. Senate, which continue—that its Framers perceived to be necessary to secure state ratification. Twenty-seven amendments have expanded or modified the document, but the first ten were proposed and ratified together. The process whereby Congress proposes amendments is relatively well known, whereas the configuration and procedures of an Article V convention are less certain.

Criteria for Sound Amendments

In 1999 the Citizens for the Constitution developed eight "Guidelines for Constitutional Amendments."[1] They were as follows:

1. Does the proposed amendment address matters that are of more than immediate concern and that are likely to be recognized as of abiding importance by subsequent generations?
2. Does the proposed amendment make our system more politically responsive or protect individual rights?

3. Are there significant practical or legal obstacles to the achievement of the objectives of the proposed amendment by other means?

4. Is the proposed amendment consistent with related constitutional doctrine that the amendment leaves intact?

5. Does the proposed amendment embody enforceable, and not purely aspirational, standards?

6. Have proponents of the proposed amendment attempted to think through and articulate the consequences of the proposal, including the ways in which the amendment would interact with other constitutional provisions and principles?

7. Has there been full and fair debate on the merits of the proposed amendment?

8. Has Congress provided for a non-extendable deadline for ratification by the states so as to ensure that there is contemporaneous consensus by Congress and the states that the proposed amendment is desirable?[2]

To the extent that such guidelines are appropriate for amendments using the established process of congressional proposal and state ratification (and, in my judgment, they are quite sensible), then they would be equally applicable in considering proposals that an Article V convention proposed.

Additional Criteria for a Good Convention

Before describing how an Article V convention would or should operate, I further suggest that any decisions relative to constitutional conventions should promote at least six primary (albeit not necessarily exclusive) criteria, which I believe that the current method of congressional proposal and state ratification of amendments largely assures.[3] These are as follows:

- Attention to the public good;
- Democratic representativeness;
- Rational deliberation;
- Timeliness and efficiency;
- Promotion of governmental and societal stability; and
- Safety for the rights and liberties of the people.

Ultimately, of course, the aim should be to see that amendments that emerge from a convention are as sound as or better than continuing constitutional inaction, and these amendments should also be equal or superior to those that would emerge from the process of congressional proposal and state ratification. Moreover, under ideal circumstances Article V conventions would supplement the more-frequently used mechanism by offering needed amendments or constitutional reforms that Congress might fail to propose on its own or for which it may not be well equipped.

Attention to the Public Good

In his most notable essay, Federalist No. 10, Madison distinguished factional issues, or those connected to partial interests, from what he called "the permanent and aggregate interests of the community."[4] Acknowledging that "enlightened statesmen [like those who had drafted the Constitution] will not always be at the helm," and that liberty would multiply, rather than suppress factions,[5] Madison stressed that the Framers had designed both the system of representation that the Constitution articulated and the increased size of the nation, which would embrace significantly more diverse interests, to enhance the common good and to avoid problems of faction that he associated with ancient pure democracies.

Although many proposals for constitutional reform are hatched in the heat of partisan controversy, it is important that delegates to a convention, like members of Congress, understand that amendments should advance public rather than personal or merely partisan interests. Any proposals that either Congress or Article V conventions propose face the gauntlet of ratification in three-fourths of the states. Although this would likely weed out proposals with limited geographical or ideological support, it would be far preferable to design the convention itself so that it was attuned to national rather than partial interests.

Democratic Accountability

The Framers of the U.S. Constitution, who proclaimed that the new Constitution rested on the authority of "We the People," viewed constitutional conventions as a means of ascertaining and refining the public will. Unlike members of the three branches of government, who are there to make, enforce, and interpret the laws, convention delegates would examine and propose changes to constitutional structures and procedures, often with a view to whether the existing branches of government were effectively carrying out their representative responsibilities. One key standard would be that of democratic accountability.

Since 1787 Americans have extended the franchise to include African Americans, women, and individuals from eighteen to twenty-one. Similarly, the Seventeenth Amendment provided for the direct election of senators, and courts have applied the one-person-one-vote standard for legislative apportionment. A presidential election has not been decided by the U.S. House of Representatives since 1824, and the Twenty-Third Amendment has extended Electoral College votes to the District of Columbia. Under such circumstances, it is highly unlikely that the people would be inclined to accept the work of any convention unless they believed that the delegates were fairly chosen and apportioned and represented their interests. It would be unfortunate to see opposition to convention proposals develop not because of their inherent value or lack thereof but because of suspicions of the body that proposed them. State legislatures that desire real change need to recognize that asserting tight institutional control over such a body could thus prove to be highly counterproductive.

Rational Deliberation

Just as classical philosophers distinguished between individuals' temporary passions and their considered judgments, their wants, and their needs, so too it is important to distinguish between momentary blips in public opinion polls and more permanent shifts in societal and constitutional values. This requires considered judgment that debate, deliberation, and compromise can enhance, or what Amy Gutmann and Dennis Thompson have described as "deliberative democracy."[6] Like the rules the delegates to the Constitutional Convention of 1787 adopted at the beginning of their proceedings and the norms to which members of Congress adhere, regulations for Article V conventions should seek to foster mutual respect, full consideration of the issues, and reasonable compromises. Congress should work in conjunction with the states to see that delegates are so elected and rules are so formulated to these ends.

In his First Inaugural Address, Lincoln referred to the "*constitutional* right of amending" the Constitution or the "*revolutionary* right to dismember or overthrow it." He also argued for the kind of caution that would be wise for any convention to follow: "My countrymen, one and all think calmly and well, upon this whole subject. Nothing valuable can be lost by taking time. If there be an object to *hurry* any of you, in hot haste, to a step which you would never take *deliberately*, that object will be frustrated by taking time; but no good object can be frustrated by it."[7]

Timeliness and Efficiency

Ultimately, of course, any convention needs to decide what, if any, amendments to propose to the states for ratification. Just as too little deliberation could lead to highly partisan amendments that reflect passing fads and that are likely to generate suspicions and lead to unintended consequences, so too overly complicating convention procedures or overly prolonging convention proceedings (as by requiring a bicameral body, unrealistic supermajorities, or by facilitating minority filibusters), so that they obstruct what Justice Holmes called "the felt necessities of the time" would be similarly counterproductive and disappointing.[8] Similarly, a quick succession of fruitless conventions could likely lead to public disillusionment and undermine faith in national institutions.

Governmental and Societal Stability

Justice Joseph Story sagely argued that the amending process in general should be safe "for the stability of the government" and "for the rights and liberties of the people."[9] The idea of stability stems from the recognition that the constitutional amending process, however exercised, is an alternative to the violence and chaos of revolution. A convention should, as much as possible, approximate, if not replicate, the order that typically accompanies the method of congressional proposal and state ratification.

I hope to encourage practitioners and scholars to use conventions in the most appropriate occasions and make such conventions as predictable as possible. One practical argument for allowing the states to limit the scope of an Article V convention, which is certainly consistent with the original intent behind the amending process in general, is that this would create greater predictability and stability when this mechanism was being used.[10]

In its youth, when the United States was a relatively insignificant power, actions in America probably had greater ideological repercussions (many of which turned out to be fairly consequential) than economic ones. By contrast, conventions that states requested for the purpose of rewriting or instituting major changes in the Constitution, like those called to address matters of taxes or spending, might be particularly likely to influence national and international markets. With such potential influences, it would be especially important to replicate the kinds of checks that are in place in exercising the traditional method of congressional proposal and state ratification.

Protection for the Rights and Liberties of the People

Although Americans pride themselves on being democratic, they generally prefer this model of government because they believe that it is most likely to protect fundamental human rights and liberties, like those that the Declaration of Independence articulated and that the Bill of Rights and a number of subsequent amendments have sought to secure. Americans believe that citizens aspire to freedom and that if accurate information is available and proper deliberative mechanisms are in place, the people as a whole will never willingly sacrifice their basic liberties in a way that a single individual or group of individuals might do. Americans did not choose to entrench current understandings of such liberties against any future changes, but the Framers made the amending process arduous enough to block the people from adopting changes in basic constitutional structures or fundamental liberties on a whim. It is reasonable to hope that the convention mechanism would be at least as protective of such rights and liberties as the method of congressional proposal and state ratification, which has to date been extremely effective.[11]

Depending on the circumstances, a successful Article V convention might propose amendments or decide *not* to propose amendments, as, for example, in the case of an amendment that might attempt to strip citizenship from certain minorities. In each case, success would depend on whether the topic or topics under convention consideration were amenable to constitutional solution, and/ or whether the amendments that the convention proposed or rejected were considered to be wise or unwise. Although one would presumably not want to multiply such experiences unduly, publication of the result of the deliberations of a convention that considered and rejected a proposed amendment or amendments could arguably engender public faith that no such constitutional change was desirable.

Revisiting the Language of Article V

The U.S. Constitution divides power among three branches of the national government and between this government and that of the states. This gives multiple institutions the right to claim to represent the people in one or another capacity. Although the delegates to the Constitutional Convention undoubtedly worked on what they considered to be the people's behalf, their proposed Constitution did not become final until conventions in nine or more states approved. Amendments to this document require actions by both national and state institutions.

In Federalist No. 39, Madison observed that the new Constitution was "neither wholly federal nor wholly national."[12] Lester B. Orfield accordingly observed that "sovereignty in the United States, if it can be said to exist at all, is located in the amending body."[13] Similarly, Max Radin referred to the amending process as "the intermittent Sovereign."[14] Although it allows people to exercise their sovereignty when they adopt or amend constitutions, unlike the Preamble or the Ninth and Tenth Amendments to the Constitution, Article V does not refer directly to the people but to a number of their representative institutions (Congress, state legislatures, and conventions both to propose and ratify amendments).

In an attempt to highlight key issues in interpreting Article V and its respective allocations of power between state and national authorities, I have reprinted that provision below and italicized references to states, highlighted references to Congress in bold, and designated references to conventions in both boldface and italics:

> The **Congress**, whenever *two thirds of both Houses* shall deem it necessary, shall propose Amendments to this Constitution, or, on the Application of the *Leg-*

islatures of two thirds *of the several States*, shall call a ***Convention*** for proposing Amendments, which, in either Case, shall be valid to all Intents and Purposes, as Part of this Constitution, when ratified by the *Legislatures of three fourths of the several States*, or by **Conventions** *in three fourths thereof*, as the one or the other Mode of Ratification may be proposed by the Congress.

In the one entrenchment clause that remains in force, the article further provides "that no *State*, without *its* Consent, shall be deprived of *its* equal Suffrage in the Senate."

Four Ideal Types

Although it is easy to address each issue connected to Article V conventions on a piecemeal basis, it seems wiser to use a more systematic approach. The U.S. Constitution is based on the idea that "We the People" are the source and continuing support for all legitimate governments, but it also recognizes that no single entity can fully represent popular interests. In the process of surveying other studies on the subject, I have identified at least four ideal types with respect to the operation of Article V conventions, each of which draws from a different model of sovereignty. These are:

- The sovereign delegates convention model;
- The state-dominated convention model;
- The congressionally dominated convention model; and
- The mixed, or federal, convention model.

Each model takes a different approach as to who would control an Article V convention and how it would operate.

The Sovereign Delegates Convention Model

One view of the Article V convention, which grows from the origin of the convention as a means of expressing the public will, often in revolutionary circumstances, portrays the convention as a virtual sovereign, with power not only to propose new amendments but even to legislate. A delegate to the 1847 Illinois Convention stated this position when he said, "We are the sovereignty of the State. We are what the people of the State would be, if they were congregated here in one mass meeting. We are what Louis XIV said he was, 'We are the State.' We can trample the Constitution under our feet as waste paper, and no one can call us to account save the people."[15]

Because a convention is not a preexistent body (as a permanent board of censors would be), even proponents of this model generally acknowledge that another entity (generally understood to be either the states or the Congress) has to call for delegate selection and determine where delegates will meet. As to the actual powers of a convention once it has convened, I believe that John Jameson has sufficiently demonstrated that the people could call a truly constitutional convention for limited purposes, which could, however, include a complete re-writing of the document for subsequent state approval. It is accordingly appropriate for other governmental institutions to step in when a convention exceeds these powers, especially in cases where it seeks to exercise the power to adopt legislation.

More than any other, the model of convention sovereignty, especially prominent during the period preceding and immediately following the Civil War, has impeded use of the convention mechanism by feeding fears of a runaway convention. This model is inconsistent with the provision in Article V that specifically provides that three-fourths or more of the states would have to ratify proposals by an Article V convention before they became part of the Constitution. I accordingly think that this model has largely been found to be wanting.

The model might, however, have some validity with respect to convention rules. Whatever decision is made as to the convention's agenda, it seems reasonable that a convention should be able to formulate its own procedures. Ironically, in a recent book in which he argues that a convention is *sui juris*, or what he calls "a law unto itself," Thomas E. Brennan proceeds to mandate that any proposed amendments should "have the affirmative votes of three quarters of the states in the convention."[16]

The State-Dominated Convention Model

The second state-dominated model grows from precedents under the Articles of Confederation.[17] It further follows the Founders' arguments in *The Federalist* in recognizing the convention method of proposing amendments as the states' alternative to congressional proposal. It also fits with the seemingly obligatory language in Article V requiring that Congress "shall" call a convention at the request of two-thirds of the states. Professor Robert G. Natelson, who regards the Article V convention as a state mechanism from beginning to end,[18] is arguably the best representative of this model. Natelson believes that rules for conventions were well established at the time that the Constitution was written, that the "initial suffrage is one state/one vote with decisions made by a majority of states,"[19] that the "state legislature" should either choose commissioners or direct how they should be chosen, that states can "instruct" delegates and subject them to recall,[20] that states should pay the delegates,[21] and that states alone should set the agenda for the meeting. Natelson therefore seeks to import what he believes to be the original understandings of the eighteenth century into the term "conventions."[22]

Douglas J. Lising, a retired Army lieutenant colonel and founder of a computer services firm who favors calling a convention to restrict congressional powers under the commerce clause, observes that there is nothing in the Constitution "that specifies how the convention is to be organized or conducted." Consistent with his own concern for the rights of the states, he concludes, "Therefore, because powers not given by states to the Congress are reserved to the states, I believe the organization, conduct, and duration of the convention, once called, is at the discretion of the states."[23]

In a similar vein, Sidney Pulitzer, an entrepreneur who has been an adjunct professor at Tulane University, has recently suggested that two-thirds of the states should adopt identical resolutions to convene a constitutional convention, which he thinks they can govern. His plan proposes that each state would select in any manner that it wanted from three to seven delegates who would cast one vote, and each state would equally bear the costs of the convention. He further stipulated that "when 34 states have passed legislation ordering a Constitutional Convention, the Convention shall in every way be in compliance with the Constitution of the United States and all states in the nation are eligible to send a Delegation."[24] In such a scheme the congressional power in Article V to "call" a convention at the request of the states fades almost into nothingness. Indeed, Dustin Romney of Arizona, who favors calling an Article V convention chiefly to redress what he perceives to be the aggrandizement of federal powers, categorically states that "the State Legislatures control the process for calling a state-led convention, including the selection of delegates," although in proposing his own revision of Article V he spells this out with particularity.[25] The Compact for America, which advocates for a balanced budget amendment, similarly seeks to call and govern an Article V convention through an interstate compact agreement.[26]

Advocates of the state-dominated convention model typically refer to an Article V convention as a convention of states.[27] This is *not* the terminology of Article V, although it most certainly hearkens back to conventions that the states called prior to the Convention of 1787 and the adoption of the federal constitution. Ironically, those who defend the Article V convention mechanism by insisting that states would be represented equally may prove to be the greatest obstacle to calling such a gathering. How many large states will agree to call a convention in which they are equally represented, when they are currently represented according to population in the U.S. House of Representatives and (largely) in the Electoral College?

The Congressionally Dominated Convention Model

Consistent with the words of Article V providing that "the Congress . . . shall call a Convention for proposing amendments," a third ideal type would recognize the right of two-thirds of the state legislatures to apply for a convention but would vest chief authority for calling, organizing, overseeing, and judging the relevance of convention resolutions in Congress. This model arguably dates back to the English system of parliamentary sovereignty. It receives support from Supreme Court decisions, most notably *Coleman v. Miller* (1939),[28] in which the Court declared that key issues relative to the amending mechanisms were "political questions" for congressional resolution.

Under this model, Congress would decide which petitions for a convention to accept or reject (some advocates, among them Charles Black, urge Congress to reject *all* petitions for a limited convention), pay the delegates, determine where they would meet, set the time and length of their meeting, establish the convention's rules, including the majorities by which it would propose amendment, and exercise authority to choose whether resolutions were consistent with the convention's mission and whether they should therefore be sent forward to the states. Consistent with the configuration of Congress, members would be chosen from districts within individual states. Those who advocate this model might be particularly anxious to have Congress adopt legislation on the subject. The irony of this model is that, if carried to an extreme, it would arguably subvert the Founders' intention to bypass recalcitrant or out-of-touch Congresses.[29] Such an approach could, in short, leave the fox in charge of the henhouse.[30]

The Mixed, or Federal, Convention Model

Yet a fourth model, which I believe is most consistent with the U.S. Constitution and its recognition that no single entity can claim to be sovereign, further builds on Madison's description of the amending power in Federalist No. 39 as being "neither wholly federal nor wholly national."[31] This model focuses on the degree to which Article V divides responsibility between Congress and the states. Even while granting two-thirds of the state legislatures the power to apply to Congress for a convention, and three-fourths of either the state legislatures or of conventions within three-fourths of the states to ratify such amendments, Article V specifically requires Congress to call the convention (and this power would appear to include all powers "necessary and proper" toward that end) and to decide how such amendments will be ratified. This model recognizes that states do not collectively meet together *as states* outside of Congress, that states have different legislative calendars that would inhibit their collective action,[32] and that the representatives of states gathered together in Congress are more likely to be able to efficiently organize the event than are fifty individual state legislatures.

A mixed model would follow both the state-dominated convention model and the congressionally dominated model in choosing delegates from districts within existing state lines. It would, however, caution both Congress and the state legislatures against overly limiting the agenda of a convention and thus thwarting the advantages that delegates from throughout the nation could bring to such a discussion. It would also warn against being overly prescriptive with respect to a convention's operations, including the choice of a leader and the composition of committees. If the states and Congress cooperate in providing methods for selecting good members openly and fairly, the delegates themselves should be able to resolve many of the day-to-day issues of how such a body should operate.

A Presidential Convention Model

Jack A. Wilson, a retired attorney and professor who advocates a modern convention as an antidote to judicial attempts to change the Constitution, has argued for yet another option. He suggests that the U.S. president can call a convention under the authority in Article II, Section 3 to "give Congress information on the state of the Union, and recommend to their consideration such measures as he shall judge necessary and expedient."[33]

As long as a president retains the same right of freedom of speech as other citizens, it is difficult to quarrel with the idea that he could give speeches imploring states to petition for an Article V convention. A president might even give a speech to a joint session of Congress advocating that it propose an amendment that would authorize presidents to call such a convention. The thought that a president could convert the power to make recommendations into a power to convene a convention apart from Article V processes, however, pushes presidential powers beyond the breaking point. If it became a precedent, a president could just as easily propose passing legislation by 40 percent majorities or allowing the House of Representatives, rather than the Senate, to confirm Supreme Court appointments.

It is almost inconceivable that such a convention could meet in the absence of congressional appropriations. When it made recommendations, would they go into effect simply when ratified by three-fourths of the states, or would another step be required? If a president believes a convention is necessary, then the president can certainly advocate it, but under the Constitution, a president could do no more than recommend such a gathering.

Drawing from Akhil Reed Amar's idea that the nation should consider "a different species of rules that should properly go into effect—that should 'sunrise'—only after a substantial time delay"[34]—Professor Edward B. Foley has recently proposed creating what he calls a Posterity College. As he envisions it, this body, which he believes should consist of 538 members and 2 cochairs appointed by Congress, would consult over a period of a year and formulate amendments for congressional consideration that would, if adopted, go into effect fifty years later, when they would be unlikely to affect existing political dynamics. Unlike

Wilson, however, Foley anticipates that the Posterity College would be merely "an advisory body to Congress, which would retain the power under Article V to turn the Posterity College's recommendations into official constitutional amendments to be sent to the States for ratification."[35]

Advantages of a Convention

Having already canvassed various dangers like uncertainty, instability, and the possibility that a convention might undermine cherished civil rights and liberties, it is important to stress that a convention might have certain advantages. First, it could serve to show that the Constitution is more responsive to change than its advocates have believed, especially if the amendments it proposes prove to be both wise and successful. Second, it could redirect attention to core constitutional values that sometimes get lost in the debates over particular issues of public policy and in elections that focus on the qualifications of particular individuals. Third, it could serve as a forum for reasoned deliberation and debate about fundamental issues chiefly among individuals who are not dependent for their livelihoods on public support. Fourth, it could serve an important educative function. Professor John Davenport thus anticipates that "the whole process of holding a convention and debating these issues would educate a large majority of the American public about constitutional issues to a level of understanding not previously seen. The massive public discussion and debate that would follow the call for a convention by the states would be very productive and make good amendments much more likely in the outcome."[36]

A Look Ahead

It is wise to establish criteria by which Article V conventions and their proposals can be judged. It is also useful to consider models that might provide for their most effective governance. I believe that a federal model that mixes state and congressional authority with due deference to the convention itself is most likely to provide such success.

Just as the ultimate proof of any pudding is in the eating, so too the people are more likely to judge the success of Article V conventions by the wisdom of the amendments that they decide to propose or refrain from proposing than by the theories by which they were established. Although such outcomes cannot be known in advance, scholars and legislators can begin thinking about how Article V conventions would operate. The next two chapters will examine such issues with a view toward formulating solutions that are best designed to facilitate needed changes.

CHAPTER 8

The Selection and Likely
Characteristics of Delegates

When U.S. citizens think about representation, they are probably most likely to think about members of their state legislatures, the configurations of which vary somewhat from state to state, or members of the U.S. Congress. The U.S. Constitution delineates the fundamental makeup of the Congress in Article I, and its operations are well publicized and closely scrutinized.[1] Members of the House of Representatives, each of whom must have been a U.S. citizen for seven years, state inhabitants at the time of their election, and at least twenty-five years of age, are apportioned among the states according to population, elected from districts, and serve two-year terms. Article I, Section 2 further specifies that voters "shall have the Qualifications requisite for Electors of the most numerous Branch of the State Legislature," and the Seventeenth Amendment makes a similar provision for senators. The Constitution requires that senators must be U.S. citizens for nine years, state residents, and at least thirty years of age. Consistent with the Great Compromise, the Constitution apportions senators equally among the states whose voters now select them on a statewide basis for six-year terms.

Congressional Lawmaking

Legislative action requires the consent of both houses, each of which accentuates legislative specialization. This is enhanced through members' service on committees and subcommittees, which are often, in turn, tied to interests within members' own states and districts. Almost all members identify with two major political parties; these members select respective majority and minority leaders for each house, and they have, in recent years, become increasingly partisan. The Senate is especially known for tying up legislation through long debates known as filibusters, which currently require the consent of sixty or more members to terminate. Legislation is subject to presidential veto, which two-thirds of both houses can override, and to judicial oversight and review if appropriately challenged in concrete cases by parties with legal standing.

Because the system is so complex, legislation is difficult to enact and arguably even more difficult to repeal.[2] For many members, serving in Congress is a career. Perhaps in part because members of Congress and their staffs spend so much of their time on constituency services, a high percentage of voters generally like their own representatives, most of whom they regularly return to office. Ironically, members of the public also report highly negative views of the manner in which Congress acts collectively.[3]

Records describe the proceedings at the Convention of 1787 in detail. However, because it operated largely outside the existing constitutional framework, because the nation and its mores have changed significantly since then, and because another convention might have a more limited agenda, the Convention of 1787 does not necessarily indicate how a contemporary Article V convention would work. As Weber and Perry have suggested, however, there is enough history of conventions at the state level and sufficient scholarly writing on the subject at the national level to anticipate with a fair degree of certainty how an Article V convention would be likely to operate, to suggest how such a convention should operate, and to compare and contrast its probable operations with those of the existing Congress. Writing about amendments in general, the Citizens for the Constitution argued that "advocates of amendments of any kind should focus not only on the desirability of the proposed change, but also on the costs imposed by attempts to achieve that change through the amendment process as contrasted with other alternatives."[4] This chapter tries, in a similar way, to examine the costs and benefits of pursuing the convention option versus the option of congressional approval and state ratification.

Lawmaking Responsibilities
versus a Sole Focus

Thus, one of the most obvious differences between an Article V convention and the current Congress and state legislatures is that the latter bodies perform a variety of lawmaking and other functions. One of the responsibilities of Congress is, of course, that of proposing amendments by two-thirds majorities in both houses. Many state legislatures also play a role in introducing state amendments, which are typically ratified in referendums. Rarely, however, is this duty of proposing amendments likely to dominate legislators' time. In addition to adopting a budget, drafting laws, and conducting oversight, Congress is responsible for declaring war. The House decides whether to impeach officials who commit bribery, treason, or other high crimes or misdemeanors. The Senate has additional responsibilities in ratifying treaties; confirming ambassadors, judges, and justices; and conducting impeachment trials.

Members of both houses, all of whom are eligible for reelection, are engaged in almost constant fund-raising efforts and campaigning (this is especially true of members of the House of Representatives, who serve for two-year terms), and typically serve on multiple committees and subcommittees. Members of Congress and state legislators and their staffs fulfill a variety of constituency services and often return to their districts to ascertain sentiments and mend fences.

In addition to the pressures of time that multiple tasks impose, constituents probably rarely if ever elect members of Congress or of state legislatures with a view toward their stance on proposing individual amendments; James Madison's success in winning a seat in the first House of Representatives over James Monroe seems largely to have stemmed from his promise to support a bill of rights and was the exception that proves this rule.[5] Unless individuals have campaigned specifically on a platform favoring or disfavoring constitutional changes, it is unlikely that members of the public are paying much attention to the issue, if they are even aware of it. This relative inattention to constitutional issues and the desire to emphasize the sovereignty of the people over that of the lawmakers were key reasons the nation moved relatively early in its history from a system in which legislatures proposed and sometimes ratified constitutions to one where specially called conventions proposed constitutions that the people then ratified.

Vikram Amar accordingly notes:

> Even if an overwhelming majority of voters in a state embraced federal term limits and did not like the fact that their state legislatures refused to apply for a constitutional convention, voters in each state legislative district would have to weigh that discontent along with a number of other preferences in deciding whether to punish their state representative. Worse still, because punishing an incumbent could cause voters in a state district perhaps to lose legislative seniority unless voters in other districts all across the state were engaged in similar punishment, a "prisoners' dilemma" would make regular elections even less useful.[6]

By contrast, Jack Wilson points out that "a convention would not have to concern itself with the routine legislative business that in Congress distracts attention away from and overshadows debates on constitutional amendment matters. In a constitutional convention, then, the total energy of the delegates may be devoted to formulating proposed amendments that will represent cohesive compromises relating to the fundamental law of the land."[7]

Comparing the Likely Members of an Article V Convention to Typical Legislators

With a view toward the Convention of 1787, whose members Jefferson once described as "an assembly of demi-gods,"[8] it is easy to idealize individuals who attend conventions over those who are typically elected to legislatures. In actuality, perspectives have varied widely on how convention delegates would be likely to compare to legislators. Political scientist Frank J. Sorauf hazarded that if delegates were selected, as he thought they almost surely would be, on a nonpartisan basis, then "it seems safe to assume that a mixture of public figures, political neophytes, and state and local politicians and office-holders would be chosen." He explained that "the delegates would in other words be largely 'blue ribbon'—middle class, civic-minded, and somewhat inexperienced in government and politics."[9]

Convention Delegates Would Be Superior to Legislators

Historians generally consider the work of writing and "founding" (albeit not necessarily amending) a constitution to be a more noble and enduring enterprise than the process of writing more ordinary laws.[10] A number of commentators have accordingly argued that a convention would draw more serious and prominent individuals who would give greater attention to the magnified task. Citizens might also give more thoughtful consideration to choosing delegates for conventions than for legislatures. The narrower or more trivial the subjects of a convention would be, however, the less likelihood there would be that it would fit this model.

Focusing on the state level in the nineteenth century when only men were eligible for legislative offices when the office was rarely considered to be a full-time job, Judge John Jameson anticipated that a group of convention delegates might be more likely to comprise superior delegates who were less tied to party interests. He explained:

> The legislature is a body chosen for temporary purposes. It is a mirror of po-
> litical passions and interests, and, with the best intentions, cannot be expected
> to be free from bias, even in questions of the highest moment. It is composed,
> moreover, in general, of politicians rather than of statesmen. Indeed, if a man
> shows himself, by culture and the breadth of his views, to be fitted for the high-
> est trusts, it is nearly certain that he will not be found in the legislature, but be
> left in obscurity at home. But, when a Convention is called, it is sometimes pos-
> sible to secure the return of such men. It is not necessarily because such a body
> is recognized to be, as it is, the most important ever assembled in a State, but
> because the measures it is expected to mature bear less directly on the interests
> of parties or of individuals. Party management, therefore, is not usually so much
> directed to the seeking of control of a Convention as of a legislature.[11]

James Bryce echoed this sentiment in commenting specifically on the experience of the states: "Experience has, moreover, shown in the United States . . . that a set of men can be found for the work of a Convention better than those who form the ordinary legislature of the State, and that their proceedings when

assembled excite more attention and evoke more discussion than do those of a
State Legislature, a body which now receives little respect, though perhaps as
much as it deserves."[12] Walter Fairleigh Dodd also expected convention delegates
to be superior to legislators:

> Both the legislature and the convention are chosen by the people, and when it
> is remembered that abler men are usually chosen to conventions than to legisla-
> tures, it is perhaps clear that conventions are apt to be equally as competent to
> exercise the limited powers committed to them as are legislatures to instruct the
> conventions as to what they shall or shall not do. The convention is less apt to
> abuse its power in the drafting of a constitution, than is the legislature in placing
> limitations upon the convention, if the legislature were assumed to have such
> power. This practical consideration is particularly strong with reference to those
> states whose constitutions require that the work of a convention be submitted
> to the people.[13]

Similarly, John Burgess proposed in the 1920s that constitutional conventions
should be the exclusive mechanism used for proposing constitutional amendments. He focused both on what he expected to be the quality of the delegates
and on their attention to a single task: "Constitutional Amendments are matters of such fundamental and vital importance that they should be drafted and
voted on only by men of the highest quality as jurists, publicists and statesmen,
men chosen by the original holders of the suffrage and chosen for that purpose
primarily and alone. No mixing of the subjects of Amendment with any other
subjects, making compromises instead of principles out of them, should be toler-
ated."[14]

A modern advocate of using the Article V convention mechanism expects
convention delegates to be superior to legislators because he believes that they
will be drawn from a much wider pool. Jack A. Wilson thus explains:

> Persons of such capability who may be precluded from serving in Congress for
> one reason or another, may choose to be delegates to a constitutional conven-
> tion. The requirement to go to Washington for a 2 year or a 6 year term, with the
> related high expenses and cost of living, not to mention the dislocation of one's
> family and other such considerations, or for one of a hundred other reasons,
> is enough to dissuade many from seeking a Congressional office. The arduous
> requirements for running for Congress is enough to dissuade many. However,
> many qualified and devoted citizens could and would be delegates to a constitu-
> tional convention which would be assembled for only a relatively short period
> of time.[15]

Wilson also believes that governmental employees who are precluded from seeking other offices would also be eligible to attend.[16]

Legislators Would be Superior to Convention Delegates

By contrast, readers may remember that in Federalist No. 49 James Madison opposed Jefferson's idea allowing two of three branches to call a convention because
he feared that "it would inevitably be connected with the spirit of pre-existing
parties, or of parties springing out of the question itself."[17] Moreover, the relative
lack of experience with the convention mechanism at the national level can lead
to concerns.

Thus, Sidney George Fisher, who admired the British model of parliamentary
sovereignty, believed that members of Congress were far less likely to be subject
to party passions than those specifically chosen for conventions. In more recent
times, attorney Ralph M. Carson has argued, "By contrast with the situation in
1787, delegates to a national constitutional convention of the present day would
be subjected to impossible conflicts and pressures destructive of any possibility
of calm deliberation."[18] The reluctance to call an Article V convention might further stem from doubts about the kinds of individuals who might serve in such a
body.

Convention Delegates and Legislators Would Be Similar

Assuming that they would be chosen by similar voters from similar districts, the
most realistic comparison of legislators and convention delegates might conclude that although the tasks of the latter might be both nobler and more limited, they would typically be similar.[19] Noah Webster, the great lexicographer
who had published his own plans for governmental reform during the Articles
of Confederation,[20] thus observed in 1788 that a convention consisted of "a body
of men chosen by the people in the manner they choose the members of the
Legislature, and commonly composed of the same men; but at any rate they are
neither wiser nor better."[21]

Elmer E. Cornwell Jr. summarizes three major types of delegates that he and
colleagues discovered in examining state constitutional conventions. They were
what he called "reformers, standpatters, and aspirants."[22] Reformers were eager to
implement innovations in political thinking, standpatters preferred to adhere to
the status quo, and aspirants were primarily motivated by personal goals, which
they hoped to advance by their participation.[23] These divisions seem similar to
what one might find in examining state legislators.

It is arguably far more difficult to resolve such issues in the abstract than
by considering how an Article V convention would be likely to operate. This
chapter addresses this question by examining three key questions. These involve
congressional authority with respect to a convention, the methods for choosing
delegates, and other matters relative to the delegates.

Congressional Authority with Respect to an Article V Convention

As chapter 7 indicated, Article V mixes state and congressional responsibilities with respect to conventions to propose amendments. To date Congress has taken the lead in proposing all twenty-seven amendments that states have ratified, but the convention mechanism allows two-thirds of the states to take similar initiatives, with the understanding that states petition but that Congress actually calls the convention. As indicated in the last chapter, I am among those who believe that while Congress thus has a role, it should exercise this role in a way prudentially consistent with the manner in which Article V divides power between it and the states. I would especially caution against a proposal, advanced in a novel designed to restore "God's original plan for America," that would allocate fifty at-large delegates to be chosen by members of the U.S. House of Representatives or that would allow the Senate to choose twenty constitutional law scholars to advise an Article V convention.[24] Such interference would be especially troubling in the case of a convention called particularly to circumvent what citizens perceived to be congressional abuses or defects.

Scholars of the subject almost universally acknowledge that Congress has to exercise some judgment as to whether two-thirds of the states have contemporaneously requested a convention either for a general convention or to examine a particular subject area. Similarly, there is general consensus that the seven-year period that a number of amendments (the Eighteenth and the Twentieth through Twenty-Second) have included for their own ratification is a reasonable period within which to consider applications to be contemporaneous.[25] Opinions and precedents with respect to whether states can withdraw ratifications of pending amendments are closely divided,[26] but on a related subject, to date at least, Congress has not been counting petitions for conventions by states that have subsequently rescinded them. Because the convention method is an alternative to the method of congressional proposal, it is legitimate to ask whether Congress could go beyond its obvious authority to make such judgments in an attempt simply to stymie any Article V convention.

Could Congress Ignore State Calls for an Article V Convention?

There are both legal and political reasons to suggest that Congress would heed calls for contemporaneous calls for a convention by two-thirds of the states. First, the language of Article V, which uses the word "shall" rather than "may," appears obligatory, and Alexander Hamilton described and defended it as such in previously cited arguments in Federalist No. 85.[27] In addition to any moral obligation that such language would carry with it (and ammunition that it would give challengers at election time), the wording of Article V might also provide a basis for state legislatures that had issued calls for such a convention to establish standing to seek judicial review if Congress ignored their requests. Second, Congress, whose members are drawn from districts within the states that called for the convention and face reelection there, would likely find itself subject to extreme pressure to call a convention if, after more than two hundred years, states finally rallied the supermajority required to request it.

On at least one occasion (the Seventeenth Amendment) calls for an Article V convention likely stimulated congressional action toward proposing it. If Congress is genuinely afraid of the convention option and would prefer to take its own initiative, it could act in a similar fashion in the future. Depending on how broad or narrow the call for a convention turned out to be, Congress might seek to bypass a convention by proposing an amendment on its own. If Congress so acted in response to calls from two-thirds of the states requesting a convention to consider the text of a particular amendment or amendments with identical language, states may not care whether Congress actually called a convention or not, although it would surely be preferable for Congress to propose such an amendment before receiving the petition from the thirty-fourth state rather than after it.[28]

If Congress sought to substitute a narrow amendment for a broad call, courts might or might not choose to intervene, depending in part on whether they received an appeal from a person with appropriate standing. If congressional actions enraged states, they could, of course, engage in a second round of convention requests, which gives Congress a fairly good incentive to act prudently. Similarly, voters could punish members of Congress that they thought were obstructing the convention process.

Robert Berry, who has written two e-books in favor of an Article V convention and who believes that states can hold a limited Article V convention, nevertheless argues that they should not call for a limited convention. He reasons that "a limited application leaves it to Congress' discretion whether to aggregate it with other states issuing similar, though not identical, applications."[29]

It is not altogether clear, however, what would happen if thirty-three states applied for an Article V convention on a particular topic, Congress then voted by two-thirds majorities of both houses for an amendment that appeared to address this concern, and yet another state petitioned for a convention. The issue would most likely be resolved politically rather than legally. States might generally agree that there would be no need for a convention if Congress acted expeditiously, but those who secretly hoped that a single-subject convention might morph into a general convention (who would not arguably be entitled to much consideration) or those who believed that this is what the states had called for (who would be on much stronger ground) might still be unhappy.

Because Article V outlines a multilevel process, proponents of amendments have a general interest in encouraging forces at both state and national levels to work together cooperatively. Ultimately, proponents of a single amendment or set of amendments are unlikely to care whether two-thirds of the states or two-thirds majorities of both houses of Congress propose amendments that they favor. Proponents of change would likely be disappointed if they thought that Congress were using its own power to propose a weaker amendment or set of amendments simply to preclude a convention from proposing more far-reaching changes, although this was arguably part of James Madison's strategy in proposing the Bill of Rights.

Advocates of change who thought that Congress had responded inadequately would have a number of options. They could seek judicial review, work to defeat the congressional proposal or proposals and renew the call for a convention, or encourage members of Congress to propose stronger amendments more to their liking.

What Ancillary Powers Accompany the Congressional Power to Call an Article V Convention?

Although Article V vests two-thirds of the *states* with authority to apply for an Article V convention, it grants the responsibility to "call a Convention for proposing Amendments" to *Congress*. After listing numerous powers of Congress, the last provision of Article I, Section 8 further vests it with the power "to make all Laws which shall be necessary and proper for carrying into Execution the foregoing Powers, and all other Powers vested by this Constitution in the Government of the United States, or in any Department or Officer thereof." Even before the Supreme Court's historic decision in *McCulloch v. Maryland* (1819) legitimizing the congressional establishment of a national bank that the Constitution did not specifically enumerate,[30] this provision served as the basis for the exercise of implied powers.

Robert G. Natelson argues that "the Necessary and Proper Clause of the Constitution does not apply in this setting, as some writers have claimed. That Clause applies only to Congress in its capacity as a legislature and pertains to other 'officers' and 'departments' of the government of the United States. No Article V assemblies fit within that category."[31] This argument seems to ignore the clause's plain statement that it applies to "all other Powers vested by this Constitution in the Government of the United States" which would most certainly include the congressional power to "call a convention for proposing amendments" at the request of two-thirds of the states and thus assumes, rather than proves, that Congress has no authority to adopt laws on the subject of Article V conventions.

Because state legislatures that issue calls for Article V conventions have no official capacity to act collectively other than through Congress, it is appropriate for Congress to set the time and place of the convention, decide how many delegates there would be and how they would be allocated (aside from the desire to keep overall numbers consistent with those of other deliberative bodies, this would largely be irrelevant if Congress decided that states should all have an equal vote), and establish procedures sufficient for the delegates to convene.[32] In general, Congress's job under Article V is that of facilitating a convention for which states have petitioned consistent with the goals that the previous chapter has identified. In practical terms, Congress would be particularly wise not to appear to be obstructing a convention that states have called specifically in response to perceived abuses of congressional powers.

Once delegates began meeting collectively, they should be able to specify their own procedures, subject, of course, to constitutional understandings of due process and the constitutional provision that any amendments the delegates propose would require consent by three-fourths of the state legislatures or of state ratifying conventions. Grover Rees III has thus observed that "once the delegates have been selected, the most persuasive argument for congressional regulation of the convention process—that certain decisions simply must be made and that nobody but Congress is in a position to make them—no longer exists."[33]

What about State Compacts?

One group that would challenge my dismissive approach to states planning for an Article V convention is the previously mentioned Compact for America, whose leaders have plans for the states to enter into a compact for a balanced budget amendment of considerable complexity,[34] which they had hoped to ratify by July 4, 2015.[35] This group believes that states have the power to call and control a convention to which each state would send its governor and which would be limited to consideration of the single amendment that they proposed.[36]

I have serious reservations about this approach, in part because I question the value of such nondeliberative conventions (a topic I will address in chapter 10), but chiefly because it appears to conflict with the provision in Article I, Section 10 that prevents states "without the Consent of Congress," from entering "into any Agreement or Compact with another State."[37] In *Virginia v. Tennessee*,[38] the Supreme Court did decide that Congress did not formally have to approve all agreements, but *U.S. Steel v. Multistate Tax Commission* decided that it did apply to those that "enhance state power quoad [with respect to] the National Government."[39]

The Compact for America would appear to be a quintessential example of a case where states are seeking to displace the power that Article V vests in Congress to call an Article V convention at the request of the states. Moreover, in striking down provisions within state constitutions limiting ratification of federal amendments, the Supreme Court ruled in *Leser v. Garnett* (1922) that "the function of a state legislature in ratifying a proposed amendment to the Federal Constitution, like the function of Congress in proposing the amendment, is a federal function derived from the Federal Constitution; and it transcends any limitations sought to be imposed by the people of a State."[40] In any event, the compacts clause would appear to give Congress the clear right to displace such state plans, undermining any confidence that it could succeed.

How Large Should an Article V Convention Be, and How Would Delegates Be Apportioned?

Although discussion of the size of an Article V convention might just as easily fall within the operational and logistical issues covered in the next chapter, it also has an important bearing on how delegates would be selected. The three most obvious starting points for considering this question are the Constitutional Convention of 1787, the makeup of the current Congress, and the Electoral College.

The Precedent of 1787

Twelve state legislatures selected seventy-four men, fifty-five of whom attended the Constitutional Convention of 1787, which drafted the current Constitution. States sent from two to eight delegates, some of whom arrived late and others of whom attended rather sporadically. As under the Congress of the Articles of Confederation, each state cast a single vote.

Some individuals, especially those who view the Article V convention chiefly as a *state* instrument, believe that an Article V convention should operate in a similar fashion, albeit with a larger number of delegates to reflect fifty states rather than twelve.[41] A recent proposal for a convention to propose ten amendments would allow each state to send up to three delegates, chosen however the state legislature decided.[42] Although this would arguably aid deliberation by keeping the size of the convention small, it would conflict with current egalitarian ideas of representation as established by representation in the U.S. House of Representatives according to population, the inclusion of these numbers in the Electoral College, the direct election of senators in the Seventeenth Amendment, and amendments reducing restrictions on suffrage. Moreover, states already have an opportunity to vote on an equal basis when they decide whether or not to ratify convention deliberations.

The Congressional Precedent

The Constitution created a bicameral Congress that represented states in the House of Representatives according to population and in the U.S. Senate equally. Consistent with the stipulation that there be no more than one representative for every thirty thousand inhabitants, Article I, Section 2 allocated sixty-five representatives to the first thirteen states. This number continued to grow with the increased number of states and their growing populations.

Writing at a time when the nation was much smaller, James Madison indicated in Federalist No. 55 that the House of Representatives would need a minimum number of members in order "to secure the benefits of free consultation and discussion, and to guard against too easy a combination for improper purposes." He immediately qualified this statement by noting that "the number ought at most to be kept within a certain limit, in order to avoid the confusion and intemperance of a multitude." In one of his more quotable observations, he ruminated: "In all very numerous assemblies, of whatever characters composed, passion never fails to wrest the scepter from reason. Had every Athenian citizen been a Socrates, every Athenian assembly would still have been a mob."[43] Alice Slu, the associate director of the Center for Deliberative Democracy, reports that the number of participants in deliberative polling projects ranges from two to six hundred members.[44]

Although some critics believe that the current size of the U.S. House, which resulted after the 2010 census in a typical House district of approximately 710,767 constituents,[45] is inadequate,[46] Congress capped the size of the House at 435 in 1911,[47] and the number of senators (currently 100) is always twice the number of the states that are represented there. The size of the House is considerably larger than that of the Senate, but both bodies are large enough that they conduct most of the work of investigating, drafting, and debating bills in committees and subcommittees rather than on the House floor. Largely because it is a smaller body, the rules of the Senate, including widely criticized provisions for filibusters, are considerably more flexible and informal than those of the House.

The Electoral College Precedent

Reflecting the Great Compromise, the Founders provided that states would be awarded electoral votes according to their joint representation in the U.S. House and Senate. The Twenty-Third Amendment has further provided for three votes for the District of Columbia. This means that the 538 electors are currently selected to choose a president. These delegates, however, meet in their collective states and serve to record votes of their constituents rather than engaging in deliberation, so the model does not indicate desirable numbers for deliberative purposes, although it might serve as a compromise between those who favor equal state representation and those who want states to be represented according to population.

Choices of Convention Sizes

A convention would therefore likely be one of five sizes. First, if states sent from two to eight delegates, it could have from one to four hundred members. Second, it might have 435 members, the same number as the current House of Representatives. In such a case, voters in each congressional district would likely select one delegate. A third possibility is that the convention would have 535 delegates based on the combined numbers of the House and the Senate; a compromise might cut the number by fifty by granting each state only one vote for its two Senate seats. In this case, it seems likely that each district would select one delegate per district and states would choose one or two on a statewide basis. A fourth possibility, a variant of the third and patterned on the current configuration of the Electoral College, would set the number of convention delegates at 538 and allow the District of Columbia to select three delegates. Congress might further increase this number by assigning additional representation to citizens in U.S. territories, although neither they nor members of the District of Columbia would have any role in ratifying the proposals.

Yet a fifth option, which would dismiss most of the considerations I have provided for limiting the size of the convention, would call for a very large convention of delegates, many of whom would "attend" only through cyberspace. Thomas E. Brennan has thus advocated a convention of 6,166 delegates, of which "only a very small percentage" would actually assemble.[48] The larger number was derived from the idea, attributed to James Madison, of one representative for each fifty thousand inhabitants, a proposal that a group known as Thirty-Thousand.org (TTO) has advocated.[49] Although he does not specify the number of delegates, Robert Schumaker is among those who think that "we must use the technology that exists today to facilitate the remote access and participation of convention delegates in the process." He further argues that such a "virtual convention of the states would eliminate the need for delegates to travel or be housed in order to participate," and that "this would diminish the influence of interest groups and ensure significantly better transparency."[50]

I favor a sixth option, a variant of the first and third, that would assign each district, including residents of the District of Columbia, 1 vote, for a total of 436 delegates. This would thus enfranchise U.S. citizens living in the nation's capital. This would also be a more manageable number and would allow some representation for each state without overly advantaging the smallest states, which already have an equal role in the ratification process.

If Congress concluded that a smaller convention would be more likely to minimize such passions and successfully formulate and debate issues, it could allow fewer delegates to cast weighted votes that reflected their states' populations, although this might stir resentments among delegates within the convention itself. Alternatively, Congress might divide the number 435 or 538 by three (resulting in conventions of 145 or 179 delegates), giving each state at least 1 delegate and (in the case of California, which has 55 electoral votes), up to 18.[51] When states called conventions to ratify the Twenty-First Amendment, representation ranged from a low of 3 delegates in New Mexico to 329 in Indiana, but only six conventions had more than 100 delegates.[52] If ratification conventions are chiefly designed to register and/or build strong consensus rather than to engage in much deliberation, they might arguably be larger than conventions designed to formulate amendments.

Will Delegates Vote Individually or by State?

Consistent with voting procedures under the Articles of Confederation, delegates to the Constitutional Convention of 1787 voted as delegations, with each state casting a single vote. In accord with the current practices of both houses of Congress, however, most scholars believe that convention delegates would cast their votes individually.[53] This would be similar to procedures in national nominating conventions where states typically split their votes among candidates rather than using the unit rule.

The state delegations to the Constitutional Convention of 1787 were represented equally largely because this is how they had been represented in Congress under the existing Articles of Confederation, where states exercised primary sovereignty. Given current representation in Congress, it seems unlikely that more-populous states would be willing to call a convention in which states, which already have equal weight in the ratification process, would propose amending measures on an equal basis. It would be ironic if the issue of state representation, which played such a decisive role in 1787, would serve as a similar bone of contention in the twenty-first century. One solution would be for a convention to require a majority (or whatever vote it deemed appropriate) of delegates *and* a majority of states to pass all proposals, subject, of course, to eventual ratification by three-fourths of the states.

Methods for Choosing Delegates

The method of selecting delegates would likely affect both the degree to which they would focus on the public good and on the public's perception of whether the delegates represented their interests. Although I have largely assumed in the section above that voters would choose convention delegates, there are actually three primary ways that convention supporters have suggested selecting such delegates. They are as follows:

- Appointment by state legislatures or other state officials;
- Random selection from among citizens; or
- Election.

These methods could, of course, be combined, as in national nominating conventions, which mix methods of delegate selection, by providing that some delegates would be appointed and others elected.

Appointment by State Legislatures or Other State Officials

Members of Congress might seek to exercise their power to call a convention by trying to select some or all of the delegates, but this seems inconsistent with the Founders' decision, incorporated into Article V, to allow states an alternative to the congressional method of calling conventions, and would likely stir great controversy. Some commentators, especially those who emphasize what chapter 7 described as the state-dominated model, believe that state legislatures could appoint delegates, perhaps with the approval of state governors, much as they appointed members of the U.S. Constitutional Convention of 1787 or U.S. senators prior to the adoption of the Seventeenth Amendment.[54]

Robert G. Natelson has supported this approach by observing that the convention models with which the Framers were most familiar provided the following:

(1) Election by one house of the state legislature, subject to concurrence by the other, with a joint committee negotiating any differences;
(2) Election by joint session of both houses of the state legislature;
(3) Designation by the executive;
(4) Selection by a designated committee.[55]

Although this would conflict with the increasing democratization of the United States, if citizens perceived that such officials acted with a clear view of the public good and if they had respect for the delegates who were selected in this manner, they might acquiesce in such selection. State legislators would have to decide whether it would be appropriate to appoint themselves as delegates to such a convention, and whether citizens would tolerate such a practice.

Especially if states were calling for a convention to deal with an especially complex or technical issue—for example, reorganization of the Federal Reserve System—they might justify such appointments on the same ground that the Constitution currently provides for presidential appointment and senatorial confirmation of federal judges and justices who must be familiar with the U.S. legal system. Blue ribbon panels might serve as yet another appropriate model. Even if states decided that such selection should be open to voters, they might limit the selection to members of a set of designated experts. Keith W. Miller, an advocate of a convention, has suggested that half the delegates "should be drawn from university scholars in political science, government, and law."[56]

Random Selection of Some or All of Delegates

Another alternative is that of selecting convention delegates, or at least a portion of them (Miller suggests 50 percent), by lot,[57] perhaps from among citizens or registered voters who were eighteen (or twenty-five) years or older. Such a convention, patterned after juries, might be more representative of general opinion and less inclined to represent special interests. Such conventions have special appeal to those who believe in the wisdom of the people. In describing such a convention, Harvard's Lawrence Lessig thus observes that a convention "should not be a convention of experts. Or politicians. Or activists. Or anyone else specific. It should be a convention of randomly selected voters, called to a process of informed deliberation, who then concur on proposals that would be carried to the states."[58] Iceland recently drew 950 individuals at random to form a national assembly, which subsequently approved of a convention that consisted of 25 individuals that Professor Thorvaldur Gylfason described as being from "a roster of 522 candidates from all walks of life, most of them with no particular political or special interest affiliations."[59]

One difficulty with such a gathering composed partly of amateurs is that delegates who have not studied government or served in previous offices might either feel overwhelmed with the responsibility or largely defer to those who had. In contrast to individuals with such educations and experience, ordinary citizens would be at a clear disadvantage when it came to giving speeches or analyzing proposed constitutional changes. In describing citizens forums, Bruce E. Cain thus observes that "citizens do not start from an equal position. Some of them will have more knowledge and stronger opinions to begin with, which can affect group dynamics and outcomes."[60] Moreover, apart from juries, which have a different function and which are guided by skilled attorneys and judges, it is difficult to identify another American precedent for such a gathering. Immediately after advancing the idea of randomly selecting delegates, Lessig observed, "I recognize that of all the insanity strewn throughout this book, this will strike readers as the most extreme."[61] Even representatives to national nominating conventions who may not have held elective office have usually been active in party politics. I believe that it would be far better to concentrate on democratic *selection* of the delegates and democratic *ratification* of proposed changes in the Constitution through constitutionally specified processes than on their democratic *formulation.*

Election of Delegates

Voters select members of Congress, who make ordinary laws, and the president (through the Electoral College), who is responsible for enforcing them. Voters also select state legislators and governors, and some states also provide for the election of their judges. Primary elections account for the selection of most members of national nominating conventions.

Conventions were initially invented to represent the power of the people, and they were the means by which the U.S. Constitution was ratified. Since then, the nation has increasingly emphasized equality, which is incorporated into the Fourteenth Amendment. Similarly, the adoption of the Seventeenth Amendment, which provided for the direct election of senators, and the Fifteenth, Nineteenth, Twenty-Third, and Twenty-Sixth Amendments have widened suffrage. These developments make it much more likely that voters would select delegates in popular elections from existing congressional districts and that they would be most likely to garner public confidence.

What Would Be the Appropriate Geographical Basis for Electoral Districts?

If Congress apportioned delegates on the basis of the total number of representatives and senators and did not choose to specify how they would be elected, most states would probably elect one delegate from each district and two delegates on a statewide basis. When states ratified the Twenty-First Amendment, with no congressional guidance on the issue, twenty-five voted on a statewide basis for delegates, fourteen used districts, and four used a combination of the two.[62] Although representation based purely on the total number of representatives would more closely approximate equal protection (it would not completely do so because each state would have at least one delegate regardless of population), either system would probably pass muster under the Equal Protection Clause, especially if the Supreme Court followed precedents relative to other amending issues and largely deferred to congressional judgments on the subject.

A statewide election might draw candidates with wider reputations than those known simply within a district, but it might also draw individuals simply for their celebrity status.[63] One advantage of electing most delegates from single-member districts is that this system would be less likely to freeze out delegates from one or the other major party as might happen if a political party advanced an entire slate of candidates who won a narrow majority in statewide balloting. Paul Weber said that he thought that "there is about as much chance of having a proportional kind of election as the proverbial snowball, simply because the American people are not used to it, they don't know how to do it, and in these kinds of procedural matters we tend to be extraordinarily conservative."[64] Although systems of proportional representation are more common in Europe than in the United States, if candidates ran under partisan labels, such statewide systems of proportional representation might accomplish the same goal of seeing that both parties received representation.

State representation would provide a diversity of geographical and regional representation. If a convention should "look" like the American people that it represents, those deciding how delegates should be chosen might want to consider what kind of elections might result in a convention that reflects national demographic characteristics, especially with respect to sex and ethnicity. After the last congressional elections, the current single-member-district system of electing members of the House of Representatives resulted in the election of eighty-one women, forty-two African Americans, two Native American Indians, eleven Asian Americans, and thirty-five Hispanic delegates, or about 32 percent (some categories overlap) women and minorities.[65]

If Delegates Were Elected, Who Would Select Them?

I cannot identify sound reasons that any voters who are otherwise eligible to vote in state or congressional elections should be excluded from voting for Article V convention delegates, although if delegates were nominated by political parties, nonparty members might be excluded from primary elections. Given the Supreme Court's solicitude for the importance of voting rights,[66] as well as amendments that explicitly deny linking the vote to race, sex, or age eighteen or above, it seems highly unlikely that states would attempt to restrict voter eligibility for choosing convention delegates or that courts would approve such restrictions if states attempted to impose them.

Issues Relative to the Delegates

In addition to deciding how to select delegates, a number of other issues relative to delegates would require resolution. These would include who would be eligible to serve as delegates; what kind of delegates a convention would be likely to attract; whether delegates would run under party labels; whether delegates would run on platforms; and how long delegates would serve.

Who Would Be Eligible to Serve as Delegates?

Congress might attempt to specify conditions of eligibility for delegates, or it could defer this issue to state consideration and determination. Although I do not expect significant variation from one state to another, I favor the latter course, with due deference to principles of equal protection prohibiting restrictions based on race or sex. Although it would lack uniformity, a mix of qualifications might actually add some diversity to the delegation.

One could argue that the task of drafting amendments has more lasting consequences and is therefore more durable than that of formulating laws and that standards should therefore be more stringent, but I think that it would be reasonable (and most simple) for states to use the current standards that they use to select members of their legislatures or for members of the U.S. House of Representatives.[67] Qualifications for the House require individuals to be twenty-five years of age, be U.S. citizens, have seven years of national residency, and be inhabitants of their states. States might also use Senate qualifications (thirty years of age, U.S. citizenship, nine years of national citizenship, and state residency) for the second branch should the convention divide into two houses.[68] If the convention followed the congressional model, members of the convention would have to seat all delegates who met the minimal requirements although delegates might, like members of Congress, have the power to expel obstreperous members or those caught up in scandals that might demean the reputation of the body by a two-thirds vote.[69]

Would Members of Congress Be Eligible to Serve?

A key question is whether sitting members of Congress would be able to serve as Article V convention delegates, as some, including James Madison, did in the Convention of 1787. This question has both a constitutional and a practical dimension.

CONSTITUTIONAL CONSIDERATIONS

The legal issue arises from the provision in the Constitution (the incompatibility clause), which was not contained in the Articles of Confederation under which delegates were selected in 1787. This clause specifies: "No Senator or Representative shall, during the Time for which he was elected, be appointed to any civil Office under the Authority of the United States, which shall have been created, or the Emoluments whereof shall have been increased during such time; and no Person holding any Office under the United States, shall be a Member of either House during his Continuance in Office."[70] If being a delegate to a convention were considered to be such a "civil Office under the Authority of the United

States," members of Congress who were selected to attend a convention would have to decide whether to refuse the appointment or resign much like members of Congress currently do when they are selected as part of the president's cabinet.

The Constitutional Convention Study Committee of the American Bar Association did not believe that the incompatibility clause barred congressional service: "The available precedents suggest that an 'office of the United States' must be created under the appointive provisions of Article II or involve duties and functions in one of the three branches of government which, if accepted by a member of Congress, would constitute an encroachment on the principle of separation of powers underlying our governmental system."[71] Weber and Perry further observed: "There is certainly adequate precedent for multiple membership. Twenty-one of the original fifty-five members elected to the Constitutional Convention of 1787 were past or active members of the Continental Congress. Nine members, including James Madison, were active members of both bodies. Edmund Randolph was both governor of Virginia and a convention delegate. Madison had the further distinction, as did several other delegates, of also being members of a state ratifying convention!"[72] It is important to reiterate, however, that the Constitutional Convention of 1787 was not called under the authority of Article V and was not subject to the constraints of the current Constitution. Moreover, there would be far less danger of conflicts of interest between those who previously served and those who were currently serving in governmental offices.[73]

Although neither the study committee nor Weber and Perry specifically say so, James Madison had argued during the 1797 impeachment of Senator William Blount of Tennessee that members of Congress were not officers of the United States. Unfortunately, the precedent is inconclusive because the Senate did not give reasons for dismissing the impeachment case, and some thought that it did so because it had already expelled him.[74]

PRACTICAL ISSUES

Even if the constitutional issue were resolved in favor of allowing sitting members of Congress to participate, Congress might decide to prohibit their members from serving.[75] Even if it did not, practical considerations might prove to be important as to whom voters decided to elect. Members of the current government could certainly bring expertise to bear on the subject. Contrariwise, allowing members of Congress to attend a convention might divide their loyalties and interfere significantly with their attendance. This would be especially true if the convention were held outside the District of Columbia and if it were a convention called to examine the Constitution as a whole rather than a more limited assembly called to affirm or propose a single amendment. Allowing members of Congress to participate in a convention would give them a second bite at the apple since, as members of Congress, they already have the right to introduce proposed amendments in that body. It is possible that members of Congress might also bring a more partisan perspective than other delegates or that they might be more likely to tailor what they said and how they voted to short-term political considerations.

One disadvantage of downplaying partisanship at an Article V convention (or of allowing states to set too strict an agenda for such a convention) is that because they are elected under party labels and constantly see partisanship played out in national counsels, members of Congress may well have a better understanding of what amendments are politically feasible (those that three-fourths or more of the states are likely to ratify) than would members of states where single parties are more likely to dominate. To date three-fourths or more of the states have ratified twenty-seven of thirty-three amendments that Congress has proposed to them. Politically inexperienced members of conventions may not be as cognizant of such realities.

It would be particularly ironic to elect members of Congress, especially those within the majority, to a convention that states specifically called to bypass what they considered to be congressional intransigence. However, if state voters select such individuals, this could send a powerful signal that they did not share the same lack of faith in their members of Congress as their state representatives who voted to call the convention.

Would State Legislators Be Eligible to Serve?

Although most discussion to date has centered on the eligibility of members of Congress, it might be more relevant to consider whether state legislators should be able to serve. Those who see an Article V convention as a mechanism to empower the states might logically conclude that the best way to do this is to give state legislators some say, perhaps the dominant say, in the proceedings.

I know of no *constitutional* barrier that would prevent state legislators from running as delegates, unless it would be provisions within individual constitutions themselves. As in the case of members of Congress, however, voters might be wary of sending individuals commissioned to represent them in one forum to another forum that was meeting elsewhere at the same time. Similarly, voters might fear that such legislators, especially those who had voted on the call for a convention, would bring their partisan perspectives with them.

One advantage of electing at least some state legislators would be that if they came from states whose legislature petitioned for a convention, they would be more likely to understand the impetus behind such a petition. If Congress subsequently sent convention proposals to state legislatures for approval (and

Congress could choose instead to send them to state conventions), legislators attending the convention to propose amendments might have a clearer sense of whether their fellow representatives would be likely to approve them and might serve as effective spokespersons for the proposals that had been forwarded.

Alternately, there might be something unseemly about a process that began with petitions from state legislatures, continued with a convention largely consisting of state legislatures to formulate proposals, and then ended up with state legislative ratification of the amendments! This could arguably be a poor substitute for the more regularized Article V process whereby members of Congress propose amendments, and state legislatures (or special conventions called within the states) ratify them. This does not necessarily mean that state legislators should be prohibited from serving, but it would caution against peremptorily granting such legislators such a privilege.

What Kind of Delegates Would a Convention Be Likely to Attract?

Professions like law and business provide a large majority of the members of most legislative bodies and would likely also be well represented in an Article V convention. Weber and Perry anticipated that delegates were most likely to include "those who have an active interest in the purpose of the convention and who are willing to take a position for or against amendments; who like the public spotlight and whose personal affairs can withstand public scrutiny; who have name recognition (and therefore a chance of winning in a relatively short campaign period); who have financial and organizational support; and who have some experience in waging campaigns and can devote time to campaigning."[76]

Individuals with certain types of expertise might also be drawn to conventions on particular subjects. Should states, for example, call for an amendment related to health care, medical doctors might be more inclined to run and be elected; economists might seek election to a convention designed to propose balanced budget amendments; clerics and First Amendment experts might be particularly interested in a convention that was considering introducing prayer and Bible reading in public schools. Apart from legislators, it seems unlikely that legislation would exclude members of any profession.

Many working-age individuals would find it difficult to take time off from their regular jobs without reimbursement, and even those receiving pay might find it difficult to absent themselves from their regular jobs. Partly because of this, I would not be surprised to see numerous retirees, particularly former state or national legislators, vying for delegate positions. Although political parties do not reimburse the expenses of delegates to national nominating conventions, which last less than a week, members of state legislatures and members of Congress receive salaries, and denying such compensation to convention delegates would be far more likely to make them less demographically representative of the population.

Because one could not know in advance how long a convention would last, the government might choose to reimburse delegates for transportation to and from the convention and then pay them on a per diem basis. Congress should set the rate of pay both to be adequate for those without other income and to avoid providing perverse incentives for delegates either to leave without adequate deliberation and debate or to string out proceedings simply to increase their reimbursement.

Would Delegates Be Selected under Party Labels?

Currently, only two members of Congress (Angus King of Maine and Bernie Sanders of Vermont, both of whom caucus with the Democrats) consider themselves to be independent of the two major political parties. Such labels are, indeed, the only cue that ballots typically provide to the views of individuals who are running for such offices. Although partisan elections help voters to choose between rival sets of policies, observers increasingly blame partisanship both for governmental gridlock and for rewarding, rather than controlling, special interests.

The nation's primary experience with nonpartisan elections has been with those for state judiciaries or for local offices like school boards. Many individuals who have held elective offices are so readily identified with political parties that it would be difficult for voters to ignore this identity even in elections where the ballots did not contain this information.

Except in times of genuine party dominance, a deliberative convention would appear to be almost doomed from the outset if its members expressed their intention to cast straight party-line votes. Writing in 2014, Lawrence Lessig observed, "There are 18 state legislatures controlled by the Democratic Party, and 27 state legislatures controlled by the Republicans. There is no serious chance that a partisan amendment would not find 13 states to veto it. It just can't happen."[77] I suggest that delegates should seek to avoid even the appearance of partisanship.[78] Political parties could help if they agreed beforehand either to encourage delegates to stick to a specified agenda, or, in the case of a more general convention, set certain contentious issues about which there is intense public division on a shelf rather than engage in debates about them.

Professor Larry Sabato, who favors an Article V convention, thus observed that "besides avoiding pitfalls such as parliamentary government or a national initiative process, the new Constitutional Convention would have to steer the

ship of state around the shoals of hot-button social and cultural issues." Singling
out the issues of "abortion, gay rights, the death penalty, gun control, and the
like," Sabato argued that "opinion is intensely divided on all of them, and they
are best fought out on the political landscape, in the legislatures and election
campaigns, until such time (if ever) that there is a national near-consensus on
them."[79] Similarly, in arguing for a convention to address a set of reforms to the
two-party and current electoral systems, Professor Jonathan Turley argued that
"to be successful, a convention would have to be limited to addressing political
reforms and not get sidetracked by divisive issues such as same sex marriage or
abortion."[80] Despite all the important changes they made in the existing government, the delegates to the Convention of 1787 did not settle the issues of slavery or women's rights or numerous other issues that the nation has subsequently
resolved, sometimes through constitutional amendments. Ultimately, delegates
might have to decide whether their primary goal was to make a statement or to
propose changes that had a reasonable chance of state confirmation.

Would Delegates Run on Platforms?

There is considerable debate over whether individuals running for public office
should sign pledges indicating that they will not raise taxes, increase spending,
or the like. Although this sends clear signals to voters about where they stand,
it gives candidates little flexibility once they enter office. A critical issue to consider with respect to Article V conventions is the extent to which voters would
select delegates on the basis of their precommitment to a particular proposal or
agenda.[81] The dilemma is that the First Amendment would make it difficult, if
not impossible, to prevent individuals from announcing their stances prior to
election, even though narrow commitments to one or another solution could
effectively torpedo effective deliberation. States that provide voter referendums
often find that interest groups spend vast amounts of money to promote their
views.

States might call for a proposal (much like those that face ratifying conventions) that would lend itself to a fairly easy division into two sides—an amendment, for example, to permit prayer in public schools or to impose congressional
term limits. A convention called to address issues of federal spending and deficits
might permit considerably more leeway. It is not altogether clear that delegates
to a convention would differ significantly in this respect from members of Congress or state legislators except to the extent that legislators will typically con-
front a far greater array of issues, and thus be elected on their stances on them.

Weber and Perry have argued that the election process is one of the strongest
guarantees that delegates will, in fact, address the concerns that motivated the
calling of the convention. As Weber and Perry explain:

Since candidates will be asked and forced to answer the "confrontational" and "runaway" questions before they are elected, a logical assumption is that they will take positions that are in accordance with their personal beliefs on the substantive issues and that are most likely to enhance their chances of being elected on the procedural issues. Except for instances of the collapse of societal infrastructures (e.g., in times of war or famine) those who are elected are those who take safe, or centrist, positions on procedural questions. At the very least, voters will know how candidates stand on the critical questions and cast their votes accordingly.[82]

Such public scrutiny would be much further removed if state legislators sought to appoint convention delegates.

How Long Would Delegates Serve?

Madison's opposition to periodic constitutional change as expressed in *The Federalist* and the convention's failure to follow some state precedents in creating Councils of Revision clearly indicated that an Article V convention is not meant to be a permanent body.[83] The Framers certainly did not intend for it to be an alternate lawmaking institution. This suggests that members should have a fixed term. Too short a term (a month or two) would likely prevent the convention from organizing itself, whereas terms of too great a length (longer than a year) might discourage members either from running for office or from acting expeditiously. In describing how a Posterity College (designed to offer suggestions to Congress for amendments that would not go into effect until fifty years after they were ratified) might operate, Edward B. Foley anticipated that they might "meet for one weekend per month for a year, with the expectation that members would do their 'homework' between meetings, and then, when the body is ready to debate and vote on specific proposals, it could meet full-time for two weeks."[84]

Since most delegates would need to know the extent of their obligations before accepting office, Congress (the only body that could ensure uniformity since the convention could not meet until delegates were first selected) should establish term lengths with due sensitivity to the need not to use such terms to undermine the convention's work. Terms would not necessarily be the same for one kind of convention as for another. It might be wise to adjust terms according to the proposed agenda of the convention. Should two-thirds of the states petition for an Article V convention to rewrite the entire document, they would likely need more time (the Constitutional Convention of 1787 met from May through September) than were they to convene to decide on whether to take an up-or-down vote or formulate language for an amendment providing for a balanced federal budget or for congressional term limits.[85] This time might be decreased if the convention were largely considering a proposal advanced by an outside body of experts.

Analysis

Absent the reincarnation of George Washington, James Madison, and Gouverneur Morris, the nation should probably not expect to see a pantheon of refounders, but there is good reason to suggest that it should be able to anticipate basic competence and patriotism. Voters would most likely select the majority, if not all, of delegates from existing congressional districts. It seems likely that such elections would weed out those who sought substantially different objectives than what the people favored. Their orientation might further be affected by whether they ran on partisan or nonpartisan ballots and by whether sitting members of the government were eligible. If the nation were seriously considering fundamental reforms rather than contemplating proposing a single amendment or set of amendments, some officeholders might be willing to resign in order to take part in what they considered to be a more important endeavor. Likewise, terms would likely vary depending on whether the convention were addressing a single issue or small number of issues, or seeking to rewrite the entire document.

CHAPTER 9

Organizational and Logistical Issues
Related to Article V Conventions

Having examined issues relative to the size of the convention and the selection and likely profiles of its delegates, it is appropriate to consider other operational and logistical issues, again with a view toward the resolution of such matters with respect to the current Congress. It is a truism that the devil is often in the details. Although the Constitution specifies some of the central organizational aspects of Congress (the fact that it is bicameral, the terms of its members, the basic leadership structure, the requirements to adopt legislation, and the like), it does not provide similar details for organizing Article V conventions.[1]

This chapter will accordingly address key organizational issues, including what preliminary steps might facilitate such a convention; who would fund the convention; how large an Article V convention should be; whether a convention should be unicameral or bicameral; what role committees should play; to what degree convention proceedings should be public; what majorities should be required to send amendments to the states; whether all states would be likely to participate; where the convention should meet; what would be the likely staff needs of the convention; what ceremonial trappings would be appropriate; and who would lead the convention.

What Preliminary Steps Might States Take
to Facilitate Such a Convention?

Although Article V requires Congress to call a convention at the request of two-thirds or more of the states, there is nothing to prevent states from attempting to facilitate the success of its petitions by attempting to organize in advance. In a recent e-book entitled *Amendments without Congress*, Robert Berry, who is particularly concerned about the growth of the federal government and deficit spending, has proposed that each state should send five delegates to a conference in Denver, Colorado, which he designates as a "Conference for Proposing Amendments (COPA)." Likening the conference to "a dry run for a Convention for Proposing Amendments, in much the same way the First Continental Congress was for the Second," he thinks that delegates to such a conference could "coordinate the language that will be used for the actual Article 5 application to Congress demanding the official Convention for Proposing Amendments." He believes that delegates might do a good bit of their work through electronic media in advance of such a meeting. He further suggests that a COPA might transmit "specific amendments . . . directly to Congress with a diplomatic message saying in essence, 'Ignore these at your peril.'" If the plan works, "the states know they will get their chance to decide the fate of the individual amendments either during the ratification phase, if Congress capitulates and proposes them, or in an actual amendments convention."[2] Berry, who has written a follow-up book advocating specific amendments,[3] notes that Republican Mike Leavitt of Utah advocated a similar Conference of the States in 1994, but that fears of an unlimited convention led only fifteen states to pass Resolutions of Participation.

In proposing another constitutional convention in 2000, Professor Richard Labunski suggested that the movement for a convention might model itself on the antebellum Peace Convention or on the National Issues Convention that was held in Austin, Texas, in 1996.[4] He further suggested that the impetus for such a convention might begin at the county or congressional level where individuals could elect representatives to state conventions of fifty-two people or fewer. Each state could in turn select two delegates to a national "preconvention" in Washington, D.C., that would identify "the *problems* that will be addressed by constitutional amendment"; "the specific *sections* of the Constitution that will be considered for revisions"; and "in *general terms* language that may be appropriate for the new amendments."[5] He believed that the people might use the Internet to pressure their representatives in Congress to call for an Article V convention.

Similarly, Michael B. Rappaport, who believes the Article V convention mechanism has been moribund largely because of problems involving state coordination, has proposed that states should hold preconventions where delegates would agree on the text of a single amendment. He further favors amending Article V so that the Constitution would "authorize conventions that are both voluntary and advisory."[6]

One might hypothesize that such conferences or preconventions would aid the cause if they appeared to be orderly and if their proposals appeared reasonable. Contrariwise, troubles there might doom the larger enterprise or give opponents greater time to muster opposition. No such meetings would, of course, have the constitutional authority to propose amendments directly to the states, although they could certainly forward proposals that they thought were worthy of congressional or convention consideration.

Who Would Fund the Convention?

Those who chiefly see Article V conventions as an instrument of individual states tend to favor state funding of delegates, while those who desire such conventions to have a nationalistic perspective generally want Congress to fund them. At the Constitutional Convention of 1787, the national government provided general expenses, but states paid the salaries of individual delegates. The convention decided that members of the new government that it proposed would be paid from the national treasury.

Congress exercises the power of the purse and is accustomed to appropriating and spending money in a way that states do not collectively do. A system of state payments would likely lead to discrepancies in reimbursements among individuals from different states. I would therefore recommend that Congress fund the body, perhaps paying delegates per diems. An alternative would be for a private foundation or group known for nonpartisanship (perhaps the League of Women Voters) to foot the bill.

Given the desire to focus on the public interest, it would be wise to prevent delegates from receiving any outside gratuities, including speaking fees, during or in the months immediately following their service to the convention. Congress should similarly consider whether it would limit interactions between delegates and representatives of interest groups during its deliberations, and, if so, how? At the very least, Congress should subject convention delegates to the same laws against bribery as other governmental officials face.

Should a Convention Be Unicameral or Bicameral?

Most conventions in American history, including the one that wrote the current Constitution, have been unicameral bodies. One could argue that Article V conventions should be bicameral so that they reflect the method of congressional proposal of amendments, which includes majorities of both houses. By contrast, I believe that an Article V convention with one house would be adequate because two-thirds of the states, all but one of which are bicameral, would first have to apply for a convention, which would then meet and deliberate separately. Apportioning state votes according to the total number of representatives and senators might increase pressure for a bicameral body, especially if two delegates from each state were elected from the state as a whole, but the electors who meet in state capitals to cast votes in the Electoral College are not so distinguished from one another.

What Role Should Committees Play?

The Constitutional Convention of 1787 frequently resorted to committees, particularly when it encountered issues that required compromises.[7] A body of from 435 to 538 members would almost surely require that the convention, like the current Congress, do even more of its work in committees, especially if it were addressing multiple subjects or attempting to rewrite the Constitution.[8] These would undoubtedly include a Rules Committee, committees to examine various amending proposals, and a Committee of Detail and a Committee of Style (especially if the convention were redrafting the entire Constitution). Unlike congressional committees, whose chief work is oversight and drafting legislation, convention committees would only be responsible for formulating or refining constitutional amendments.

Political scientists sometimes use the term "iron triangles" to describe the cozy relationships that can develop among members of congressional committees, the groups that they are supposed to be overseeing, and associated interest groups. Because the committees at an Article V convention would be new and members would be unlikely to seek reelection or reappointment, they might avoid such problems. From a more negative standpoint, convention delegates would not necessarily have the same expertise and experience as members of established congressional committees who have served in such capacities for many years. A convention could likely select members of such committees on the basis of their educations and life experiences.

To What Degree Should Convention Proceedings Be Public?

The delegates to the Convention of 1787 held their proceedings behind closed doors, and some proponents of an Article V convention think that it should do the same.[9] Although such secrecy could enhance deliberation, it is unlikely that an Article V convention could or would attempt to exclude news coverage. Not only have communications significantly improved since 1787, but norms with regard to such publicity have changed. The larger the convention, the more difficult it would be to avoid leaks and to keep secrets. A convention would almost surely keep a journal or record of its proceedings, especially if it were proposing a new constitution. James Madison's *Notes of the Federal Convention of 1787* were not published until after all the participants had died. If notes of an Article V convention were published, judges would have to decide how, if at all, to use them in interpreting any changes in the Constitution that they initiated.

Congress, of course, is also an open body, and members have to submit amending proposals under their names. It seems likely, however, that a convention would receive greater public scrutiny than Congress generally does, both because a convention would be focusing only on constitutional change (and not legislation, confirmation, and other congressional tasks), and because it would be so unique. Congress and/or the convention would have to decide whether to allow video recordings of the proceedings (Congress currently allows this, but the Supreme Court does not). Televising the proceedings, perhaps on C-SPAN, would certainly increase public awareness and interest and could serve an important educative function, but it might also encourage political grandstanding among delegates, and possibly demonstrations in the city that was hosting the convention.

Although it seems somewhat counterintuitive (since the stakes are higher), a convention charged with completely rewriting the Constitution might be able to make a stronger case for secrecy than one charged simply with proposing one or more individual amendments, especially if the people were to be presented with a yes-or-no decision on a finished document. In such a case, compromises might have to be included to enhance the feasibility of the document as a whole (much like the compromises in 1787 involving state representation and slavery) that would be impossible to negotiate in the harsh light of publicity. This would not necessarily make such secrecy more feasible, but it would provide a greater incentive for it.

Should Delegates Be Sequestered?

Charles R. Hooper, a social worker who advocates an Article V convention, has not only suggested that delegates should take "an oath of secrecy" but has also proposed that they should be "sequestered like a jury," so that they would be insulated "from any outside influence until the convention has adjourned."[10] Professor John Davenport has made a similar suggestion.[11] This would go far beyond the secrecy rules adopted by the Constitutional Convention of 1787.

I believe that this would be unwise largely for the same reasons that total secrecy would be unwise. Even the judiciary, which conducts its deliberations almost completely behind closed doors, does not require its members to stop reading newspapers or watching television. Jurors are sequestered because the evidence that they can consider is strictly governed by rules of evidence that are designed to protect the innocent and ensure fair trials. Moreover, sequestration is more practical for a body of 12 people than for one of 435 or more. By contrast, delegates considering constitutional changes should have access to information of all kinds. Completely cutting off delegates from all correspondence would likely do less to ensure their impartiality than it would to isolate them from public opinion and breed suspicion of their activities.

What Majorities Should Be Required to
Send Amendments to the States?

The Constitution clearly requires two-thirds of the states to petition Congress to call an Article V convention, and it just as clearly requires two-thirds majorities of both houses of Congress to propose amendments to the Constitution and three-fourths of the states to ratify them. It does not specify the majorities by which a convention would propose amendments for possible state ratification.[12] The Constitutional Convention of 1787 followed the example of the Congress under the Articles of Confederation and voted by a simple majority of states (although this required additional majorities within each delegation), but it allowed for revotes on issues as consensus shifted, and, as explained above, it seems likely that delegates to an Article V convention would cast individual votes.[13]

Congress could choose to specify (and a convention may or may not accept this instruction) that the convention muster either a majority vote or two-thirds vote to propose amendments, or it could leave such matters for the convention to decide on its own.[14] The latter would most likely provide the better incentive to make a decision that would lead to its own success. A general convention proposing a new constitution might think it more necessary to vote by supermajorities than would a more limited convention focusing on a single amendment or set of amendments. Lincoln Oliphant observed that the U.S. Senate adopted an amendment in 1971 that would have required an Article V convention to propose amendments by a two-thirds vote, but that since two-thirds of the states would have already issued a call for a convention, such a majority seemed unnecessary.[15] A convention could provide information to the public with regard to the majorities by which delegates had proposed each measure.

A possible compromise, which would require the parliamentarian to engage in a bit of math, might call for votes by both a majority of delegates and a majority of states. If there were particular public concerns about the possibility that a general convention might undermine existing civil rights and liberties, delegates might provide reassurance by requiring greater pluralities for any changes to provisions within the Bill of Rights or the Fourteenth Amendment.

Allowing for a mere majority vote to propose amendments at a convention might ultimately prove to be more symbolic than real in that the primary obstacle to adoption of amendments would more likely be the requirement for three-fourths of the states to ratify than the majority, or supermajority, required to propose. A simple majority vote at the convention to propose an amendment or series of amendments that had little chance of victory would be a pyrrhic victory. A two-thirds majority, like that which the Constitution requires of Congress to propose amendments, could caution delegates against proposing amendments that had little chance of confirmation.

As the review of U.S. amending history has demonstrated, amendments often take considerable time to germinate. There would be nothing to prevent members of Congress from reintroducing an amendment in that body that failed at an Article V convention. A convention would presumably have the same powers that Congress has exercised to include a time limit for ratification within its proposal or could choose to omit one.

Could a Convention Alter the Requirement for Three-Fourths of the States to Ratify Amendments?

One fear that is closely tied to the idea of a runaway convention is that a convention might seek to reduce the Article V requirement that three-fourths of the states must approve proposals before they become amendments. This concern likely stems from the fact that the Constitutional Convention of 1787—which, to reiterate, was not an Article V convention—did something similar with respect to the unanimity requirement under the Articles of Confederation. The situation is itself more ambiguous than it might at first appear since the 1787 convention also specified that the new document would only go into effect among ratifying states, but nevertheless the issue is important.

There is no reason to believe that the current Congress, existing state legislatures, or the U.S. Supreme Court would acknowledge the constitutionality of a procedure that departed from Article V guidelines any more than it would do so if members of Congress sought to propose amendments with less than a two-thirds vote or inform states that they could ratify them with less than a three-fourths majority of the states. From a practical standpoint, numerous individuals who might otherwise support the substance of Article V convention proposals might oppose such unconstitutional procedures. A convention could, of course, propose an amendment, subject to approval by three-fourths of the states, to lower majorities required by current amending procedures, but so could Congress.

Would All States Be Likely to Participate?

Only twelve of thirteen existing states sent delegates to the Constitutional Convention, and, like Congress, a convention would probably require a majority quorum to operate. Congressional vacancies rarely last very long. One of the purposes of the Seventeenth Amendment was to remedy the situation created when state legislatures, which met fairly sporadically, failed to agree in a timely manner on whom they wanted to send to the U.S. Senate, leaving them with only partial representation in that body. Similarly, states might want to elect alternate delegates or vest an official (perhaps their governors) with the right to appoint replacements for delegates who could not attend.

It takes two-thirds of the states to petition Congress for an Article V convention. Given the potential stakes, it is doubtful that any states would refuse to send delegates, although one might imagine a scenario in which states hit a snag in conducting elections or in which a walkout, or threatened walkout, by disillusioned delegates could jeopardize the work of an Article V convention. Working against the latter possibility is the fact that states could just as easily express opposition, and likely more effectively, by staying and opposing measures with which they disagreed. A convention might be expected to reflect national opinion on an amending issue or set of issues better than would a congressional committee.

Where Should the Convention Meet?

The Constitution does not specify where an Article V convention would meet. There would be advantages to meeting in Washington, D.C., with its access to world-class libraries, governmental offices, and sitting officials, especially if some of them were simultaneously serving as convention delegates. The capital is served by airports and hotels and is a media hub, and its police forces are accustomed to providing security for keynote meetings.

Because it is the seat of government, however, it is subject to frequent criticism. Political commentators, who may themselves be part of a media elite, rarely use the term "inside the beltway" as an accolade.[16] Some delegates to the Constitutional Convention of 1787 expressed the hope (eventually realized) that the nation's capital would not be the site of an existing state capital.[17] Similar reasoning might call for holding the convention outside Washington, especially if the gathering were seeking a fresh perspective on governmental issues or if it were seeking to distance itself from existing institutions that were thought to have been unresponsive in providing for needed constitutional changes.

There could be great symbolic value in holding an Article V convention, or at least its opening session, in Philadelphia. Similar arguments might be made for Boston, New York, or Williamsburg. It seems unlikely, however, that Independence Hall or even the nearby Constitution Center, whose roles as tourist destinations would be interrupted, could accommodate the entire delegation. Moreover, symbolism would be far less important for a convention designed to formulate a single amendment or set of amendments than for a body actually seeking to rewrite the document as a whole. If a convention were to be largely confined to a summer, it might be held on a college or university campus, although this could end up inadvertently setting an arbitrary deadline for the convention to complete its deliberations.[18] A recently published novel placed its Article V convention in the Yosemite Valley, presumably as a way to isolate participants from public opinion, give them time for reflection, and underline the environmental concerns expressed by the author.[19]

As the United States added states, its population center has progressively shifted westward (in 2010 it was near Plato, Missouri),[20] and many early American states (and former colonies), which initially located their capitals on or near the coast, moved them westward as they expanded largely so that they would be more centrally located for citizen access. Such precedents suggest that the site of a national Article V convention might be a city like St. Louis, Houston, Kansas City, or Chicago.[21] Given sufficient lead time, cities might bid for a convention much as they currently do to host political conventions or Olympic Games.

The author of a recent novel further suggests that there would be great symbolic value in scheduling the opening of the convention for September 17, the day the U.S. Constitution was signed.[22] July 4 might have similar significance. One might imagine scheduling a convention called to deal with taxation or national debt on April 15, the day that income taxes are due, or on Tax Freedom Day, the day on which "the nation as a whole has earned enough money to pay its total tax bill for [the] year."[23]

It might be prudent to locate a convention in an area of the nation generally known for its political moderation. In contemporary terminology, a purple city (and state) might be preferable to a solidly Republican red or Democratic blue one. Especially if the proceedings were televised, cities, like those that host national nominating conventions, would have to have adequate security and disciplined police forces that would avoid chaotic scenes like those at the Democratic National Convention in Chicago in 1968. It would be important to have a plan that could ensure safety for delegates and relative freedom for peaceful demonstrators. Indeed, Jon Elster suggests that "to reduce the scope for threats and attempts to influence the deliberations by mass demonstrations, the assembly should not convene in the capital of the country or in a major city; nor should armed forces be allowed to sojourn in the vicinity of the assembly."[24]

The number of elites was far smaller in 1787 than it is today, but delegates to the Constitutional Convention appear to have succeeded in reaching compromises in part because many of them had previously attended university together, participated in the Revolution, or served in continental legislative bodies, and in part because they associated at inns and restaurants outside of convention deliberations. It might be wise to encourage delegates to stay in the same facility and to eat common meals together. If the convention decided on secrecy, it might further be wise to set aside a single facility that would accommodate convention guests and no others (except perhaps for family members or for individuals invited to testify).

A number of individuals who have proposed conventions have suggested that they could take place in cyberspace.[25] I believe that such ideas are extremely misguided. I think that contemporary delegates, like those who met together in 1787, should be able to meet one another face to face, and that delegates should be able to observe one another's participation and character. The establishment of personal rapport among delegates might ultimately prove essential to formulating compromises that would be acceptable to all; it was certainly important at the Constitutional Convention of 1787. Delegates who have personally participated in and listened to arguments are far likelier to be good spokespersons on behalf of its proposals than individuals who have done little more than e-mail one another or participate in chat rooms!

What Would Be the Likely Staff Needs of the Convention?

A convention would have to have adequate staff, which would include administrative assistants and individuals responsible for securing lodging and authorizing transportation expenses for delegates. Delegates would need access to secure computers and copiers. Committees should have the power to summon and perhaps pay expenses for witnesses, although it seems likely that experts, especially those who had university support to travel to testify, would relish the opportunity to make an appearance. Novelist Tom Donohue suggests that a convention would have nine constitutional experts on hand.[26]

The convention would have to decide whether any such hearings could be shielded from press coverage. Such secrecy could aid candor among delegates and individuals testifying, but it might also breed suspicion of and undermine public support for its work. It seems likely that a convention might ultimately want to print reports of its hearings or deliberations, with explanations of its reasons for deciding to propose or reject various proposals.

What Ceremonial Trappings Would Be Appropriate?

Both houses of Congress employ chaplains who begin each day's deliberations with prayer, and current precedents that point to such long-established practices have permitted public prayers in state legislatures and at town councils and would appear to allow this at a convention.[27] Such prayer, or even a period of silent meditation, would further solemnize the occasion and would have particular meaning for those who believed in God, especially if those who delivered them were sensitive to the religious diversity of the nation and did not use the occasion for proselyting.[28] As odd as it seems, a convention called specifically to modify the First Amendment or its interpretations might forgo public prayers lest they provide a forum for non-elected members of the clergy from inserting their opinions into the proceedings.

When individuals accept public offices in the United States, Article VI, Section 3, of the Constitution requires that they take an oath to support the document. It seems likely that delegates to a convention would also take an oath. Such oaths would further solemnize the occasion and remind members of the importance of their responsibilities. As some of the delegates to the Constitutional Convention of 1787 observed,[29] it might seem odd for delegates to swear to uphold a constitution that they were commissioned to examine for changes, but perhaps no more so than members of Congress who introduce amendments in that body. It would certainly be appropriate for delegates to swear or affirm that they were committed to following existing constitutional procedures for amending the Constitution, which would include submitting any proposals to the states for approval.

Some proponents of a limited convention believe that delegates should swear or affirm that they would not exceed the commissions for which they were called. The effectiveness of such oaths might well depend on the scope of the convention's charge. Delegates could arguably chafe at having to cast a single up-or-down vote on a preformulated amendment (and might well run on a platform that made such opposition clear), but, except under the most extraordinary circumstances, it seems unlikely that many would be selected with a view to considering a single amendment and conclude that the entire Constitution needed to be rewritten.

Delegates to an Article V convention might assure the public of their fidelity to constitutional principles by beginning proceedings by reading the U.S. Constitution, much as members of the 112th Congress did in 2011.[30] One might also imagine a pledge to the flag, a rendition of the national anthem, and other ceremonies designed to remind individuals of the nation they were convened to serve. Such ceremonies might increase public faith in the deliberations and remind delegates of their solemn responsibilities.

Who Would Lead the Convention?

As in the case of the Constitutional Convention of 1787, the success of an Article V convention might well depend on the quality of its leaders. Although contemporary politicians may generally be as capable as many who have served throughout U.S. history,[31] it would be difficult to find another George Washington or James Madison. Under ideal circumstances, an individual like Dwight D. Eisenhower (especially prior to being identified with a political party and selected as president), or someone like Colin Powell (albeit not necessarily from a military background), who was generally known for patriotism rather than for party identification, or Robert Gates, who had served in both Democratic and Republican administrations, might be an ideal chair or president of the convention. A retired president, perhaps someone like George W. Bush or Jimmy Carter at a younger age,[32] might fulfill this role as might a retired member of Congress (Senator George Mitchell, for example). So might a leading university president, a head of the American Bar Association, the League of Women Voters, or a similar professional organization. In anticipating how to lead a Posterity College to make recommendations to Congress with respect to long-term amendments, Edward B. Foley suggested that such a body might be headed by two ex-presidents of different parties.[33]

Conventions traditionally have chosen outsiders to keep the minutes or journal. I believe that the convention should also be permitted to select an individual to preside who was not elected or appointed.[34] If the convention chose a delegate, perhaps the state that selected the delegate should be allowed to seat an alternate, allowing the chair not to cast votes. A scholar, a group of scholars, or a member of the congressional staff who was familiar with such matters would ideally be available to help with parliamentary issues.

Congress might choose to designate or suggest an individual who could open the convention and guide it through the opening days.[35] An ex-president or former Supreme Court justice might be appropriate. Congressional legislation has suggested that the President Pro Tempore of the Senate and the Speaker of the House of Representatives should do this,[36] although such individuals (like a sitting vice president) would almost surely carry partisan baggage. The Chief Justice of the United States, whom the Constitution designates to preside over Senate impeachment trials of presidents, might be a better choice, although there would be advantages in avoiding this lest the Court later have to adjudicate an issue relative to the convention (perhaps the chief justice of the state in which the convention was being held could be a substitute). The highest public official of the city or the governor of the state hosting the convention might also fill this role, though again, such an individual might be too closely identified with a particular position or party. Congress should be particularly wary of designating one of its own officers (for example, the Speaker of the House) to open a convention if the convention were specifically called, as seems likely, in reaction to perceived congressional abuses.

It seems likely that delegates would choose their own leaders at the beginning of the meeting, much as the Constitutional Convention of 1787 chose George

Washington to preside in its opening days. Convention committees would probably select their own chairs. Without seniority to consider, committees would likely have greater flexibility in selecting chairs than would members of Congress or existing state legislatures. They might also be able to select chairs without regard to party affiliations. If delegates run under partisan labels, it would be especially important to have members of both parties on all committees. A convention would likely give some consideration to geographical balance. Discussion of some issues—governmental powers over birth control, for example—would almost cry out for both male and female delegates.

Issues That Would Arise Once the Convention Was Finished

Once the convention decided whether or not it would propose amendments, the head of the convention or members of this individual's staff would presumably forward the amendments to Congress to send to the states for approval. Such a step would be required because Article V provides that Congress specify whether amendments will be ratified by state legislatures or by special conventions called for this purpose.

A number of issues would then arise. These include whether Article V convention proposals should be ratified by state legislatures or by state conventions; by what majorities states would ratify convention proposals; whether the work of the convention would be subject to congressional disapproval; whether the work of the convention would be subject to presidential veto; whether the work of the convention would be subject to judicial review, and how searching it likely would be; and whether there are any limits on the amendments that the convention can propose. This section will also consider unknowns and special considerations as well as the issues of contemporaneousness and state attempts at ratification rescissions.

Should Article V Convention Proposals Be Ratified by State Legislatures or by State Conventions?

Although the Constitutional Convention of 1787 did not follow the wooden state legislative unanimity requirement for amending the Articles of Confederation, it is important to remember that it was not an Article V convention, and that, unlike today's amendments, the Constitution only went into effect among ratifying states. Article V requires that the work of a convention would not become part of the Constitution unless and until three-fourths of the states ratified it. As is the case with other proposed amendments, Congress would have the responsibility of deciding whether ratification would occur by state legislatures or by state conventions.

One area in which the Article V convention mechanism could compare un-
favorably to the method of congressional proposal and state ratification is that
the former mechanism involves deliberation of proposals by two different sets
of bodies (both houses of Congress and the state legislatures) with somewhat
different electoral bases. I suggest that Congress should accordingly consider
requiring ratification by state conventions, thus preventing state legislatures
from both proposing and ratifying the same set of amendments. This could be
especially important if voters perceived that state legislatures were engaged in a
"power grab" with respect to Congress or if the convention were called to take an
up-or-down vote on language of a specific amendment that state legislatures had
already proposed.

By What Majorities Would States Ratify Convention Proposals?

Article V does not specify the majorities by which state legislatures must petition
for conventions. Currently, some states require majority votes and others require
a 65 percent majority.[37] Similarly, Article V does not specify the majorities by
which such legislatures or conventions must ratify amendments. Although uniformity might seem to be desirable, to date Congress has left such matters to
state legislatures, and it should presumably do the same should it call for ratification by state conventions. This would be consistent with a mixed, or federal,
model and with the policy of allowing an Article V convention to establish its
own rules of procedures.

Would the Work of a Convention Be Subject to Congressional Disapproval?

As I have delineated earlier in this book, I believe that states have the right to
limit the agenda of a convention, and, like Weber and Perry, I believe there are a
number of political checks in place that would permit them to do so. Congress
might seek to serve as a final check by refusing to send amendments to the states
for ratification or by refusing to specify how states should ratify them (although
this would not necessarily deter states from attempting to decide this issue on
their own).

I believe that the primary responsibility for limiting the agenda of a convention rests with the states that petitioned it, rather than the Congress that convened it. Especially in close cases, Congress might well be able to defer any responsibility for deciding whether individual proposals exceeded the scope of the
convention's charge to the states.

Would the Work of a Convention Be Subject to Presidential Veto?

The work of an Article V convention would not be subject to a presidential veto.
The Supreme Court's decision in *Hollingsworth v. Virginia* (1798) conclusively

established that the president does not need to sign congressional proposals for amendments to ratify them, although the president has the power to veto other acts of legislation subject to being overridden by two-thirds majorities of both houses.[38] The president would seem to have even less authority to try to veto the work of a convention. A president would, of course, have a position of public prominence to encourage delegates to act on behalf of the common good and either to support or oppose any changes that a convention proposed, but the president's legal authority would be limited, as would that of state governors.

Would the Work of a Convention Be Subject to Judicial Review, and How Searching Would It Likely Be?

The Supreme Court exercises power to decide whether state and federal laws are constitutional. It can invalidate actions that it believes have violated constitutional standards. In early U.S. history, the Supreme Court decided a number of issues related to the adoption of constitutional amendments. Thus, as just mentioned, in *Hollingsworth v. Virginia* (1798) it decided that the president did not have to sign an amendment before it became law of the land. In *Hawke v. Smith I* (1920) it decided that a state could not condition ratification of the Eighteenth Amendment on the approval of a referendum,[39] and in *Hawke v. Smith II* (1920) it applied the same judgment to ratification of the Nineteenth Amendment.[40] In the *National Prohibition Cases* (1920),[41] the Court ruled that the adoption of national alcoholic prohibition did not exceed federal powers. In *Dillon v. Gloss* (1921), the Court decided that the seven-year ratification deadline that the Eighteenth Amendment had specified was reasonable.[42]

The Supreme Court subsequently cast some doubt on such precedents in *Coleman v. Miller* (1939). In that case, after declaring itself to be "equally divided" on the issue of whether a lieutenant governor could cast a deciding vote for an amendment in a state legislature, it decided that the issue of contemporaneousness—in this case a thirteen-year period—was a "political question" for Congress to resolve.[43]

Subsequent decisions, most notably *Baker v. Carr* (1962),[44] have refined the political questions doctrine. In that case, the Court outlined six criteria, none of which it believed came into play to prevent judicial oversight of state legislative apportionment, at least one of which would be required to classify an issue a political question:

[1] a textually demonstrable constitutional commitment of the issue to a coordinate political department; or [2] a lack of judicially discoverable and manageable standards for resolving it; or [3] the impossibility of deciding without an initial policy determination of a kind clearly for nonjudicial discretion; or [4] the impossibility of a court's undertaking independent resolution without

expressing lack of the respect due coordinate branches of government; or [5] an unusual need for unquestioning adherence to a political decision already made; or [6] the potentiality of embarrassment from multifarious pronouncements by various departments on one question.[45]

Moreover, judicial decisions continue to be important. In *Kimble v. Swackhamer* (1978) Justice William Rehnquist (later Chief Justice), acting in the capacity of a circuit court judge, refused to enjoin placing an advisory referendum on a state ballot with respect to ratification of the Equal Rights Amendment (ERA).[46] Another decision, *Idaho v. Freeman* (1981), relative to the proposed Equal Rights Amendment that did not make it to the U.S. Supreme Court,[47] suggests some willingness on the part of a U.S. district court to intervene in amending issues. One difficulty of judicial review is that it often takes years before issues reach the Supreme Court, and by almost any timeline a convention could well have met, have deliberated, and have made recommendations before such time as parties with standing could raise a genuine case or controversy. This could involve criteria 5 and 6 of *Baker v. Carr*.

Because the Constitution specifically authorizes Congress to "call a Convention for proposing amendments," which implicates the first test that the Court articulated in *Baker v. Carr*, both precedents and prudence might dictate that courts should take a fairly deferential posture toward congressional decision-making. Although the Constitution vested states with the right to petition for a convention, it granted Congress the power to call it, and this power must carry some ancillary authority. It would be unfortunate if the public perceived that members of the judiciary were attempting to squash the deliberations of a convention, particularly if the delegates were specifically addressing issues related to the judiciary, such as its exercise of judicial review (this would echo the problems that would be caused if Congress were perceived to be ignoring state requests for a convention).

Are There Any Limits on Amendments That a Convention Could Propose?

Given the limited temporal scope of the original provision related to slave importation and the subsequent elimination of that institution, the only remaining stated limitation on the content of constitutional amendments is the provision in Article V that prohibits states from being deprived of their equal representation in the U.S. Senate without their consent. There is a virtual cottage industry of scholarly writings, many drawing from experiences of foreign constitutions, as to whether there might be unstated implicit limits on this process.[48] I am among those who believe that if the sovereignty of "We the People" is to be meaningful, whatever unstated constitutional limits exist are procedural, prudential, and moral rather than constitutional in nature.[49] As the U.S. Supreme Court observed in *Whitehill v. Elkins* (1967), a case involving state loyalty oaths, "For the Constitution prescribes the method of 'alteration' by the amending process in Article V; and while the procedure for amending it is restricted, there is no restraint on the kind of amendment that may be offered."[50]

In any event, it is difficult to think of a reason that there would be special limits on the content of amendments proposed by constitutional conventions as opposed to those enacted through congressional proposal and state ratification. Indeed, if anything, a convention—especially one with a broad mandate—might have a wider scope. One mechanism might prove better able to filter out unwise proposals than another, and one might be a better way to propose systematic constitutional change than another, but if any implicit limits exist, they would likely cover amendments however proposed and ratified.

Unknowns and Special Considerations

Although individuals study history for patterns, history exhibits numerous apparent contingencies. A mechanism that works well in one circumstance may not work well in others. As chapter 3 demonstrated, the nation adopted ten amendments relatively quickly after ratifying the Constitution, but it adopted no such amendments from 1803 to 1865, when they might have averted the Civil War. One presidential election does not produce as good a set of candidates or as clear a mandate as another. A leader who exercises solid judgment in times of peace may be ill equipped for war. A policy that seems liberal in one time period might appear quite regressive in another.

There are times when emergencies, like hangings, can concentrate the mind.[51] Madison was among those who believed that the sense of emergency contributed positively to the deliberations at the Constitutional Convention in 1787. There are other times when emergencies—the terrorist attacks of September 11, 2001, may prove to have been such an event—leave little time or space for rational deliberation and may elevate passions over rational deliberations. During such emergencies, as, for example, the undeclared war with France in 1798 that resulted in the adoption of the Alien and Sedition Acts, one or another side might be tempted to exploit the occasion for partisan purposes. Unless the Constitution were itself directly implicated as part of the problem, it would generally seem wise for states not to call a convention during an active war.

The United States holds presidential elections every four years. One could argue that to the extent that the states or Congress can control the timing of a convention, it might be best not to schedule one during a presidential election contest, when the issue of constitutional change could become enmeshed with that of electoral politics. There might be similar reasons for avoiding calling a convention during particularly controversial Supreme Court justice confirmation battles, such as those that surrounded Robert Bork or Clarence Thomas. There might be similar reasons for avoiding conventions in even-numbered years, when all members of the U.S. House of Representatives and a third of Senate members are elected, although there is no time that could completely avoid all state and local elections.

On the other hand, if voting districts corresponded with those of congressional districts, it would be far less expensive to hold elections for convention delegates in such election years than to find new times for them. Political scientist Austin Ranney has observed that elections to state constitutional conventions have "very low voter turnouts: 15, 16, 18 percent."[52] One advantage of holding such elections concurrently with those for the president or Congress is that the turnout numbers would likely be much higher, although this would not guarantee that the voters would be any better informed on the issues. Moreover, debates might be better informed if presidential candidates took positions on the agenda of the convention, although it would augur much better for success if leading candidates took the same position on the issue. Although the U.S. Constitution does not include a provision for national referendums, national elections sometimes serve such a purpose. Kart T. Lash thus observes that the key vote on ratification of the Fourteenth Amendment took place on November 6, 1866, when, after both parties ran on the issue, the Republicans secured an overwhelming electoral victory in congressional elections.[53]

Other Issues

Despite more than two hundred years of experience using existing processes, a number of issues remain unresolved with respect to constitutional amendments that parallel similar questions involving state petitions for Article V conventions.

Contemporaneousness

One issue has to do with the amount of time that a proposed amendment, or petition, remains valid. States have ratified most amendments that Congress has proposed within a matter of months or years. In *Dillon v. Gloss* (1921) the Supreme Court decided that ratifications should reflect a contemporary consensus,[54] but *Coleman v. Miller* (1939) described the issue as a political question for Congress to resolve.[55] Beginning with the Eighteenth Amendment and continuing through the Twenty-Second, Congress attached internal seven-year deadlines within amendments where they were presumably self-enforcing (an amendment with a seven-year deadline that was ratified after this limit would presumably self-destruct).[56] In the case of the ERA Congress extended this deadline in an authorizing resolution rather than within the amendment itself, and when the required number of states failed to adopt it within seven years, Congress amid considerable controversy extended this deadline, albeit still without garnering the required number of state votes.[57] Because the required number of states never ratified the amendment, even with the extended deadline, a lower court decision questioning this decision became moot,[58] and the Supreme Court never decided on the issue. Although such provisions arguably "clutter" the Constitution, I believe that experience shows the wisdom of including such amending deadlines within amendments, no matter how they are proposed.

Although some scholars had hypothesized that amendments spread out over decades or centuries were covered by the doctrine of desuetude,[59] Congress chose to accept ratification of the congressional pay amendment in 1992, or 203 years after Congress first proposed it as part of the original Bill of Rights. As discussed in chapter 3, this was a fairly unusual situation, and one reason to suggest that it is not a particularly good precedent is that Congress has never sought to add petitions for conventions that are spread out over such a long time period. Congress, which undoubtedly has a vested institutional interest in remaining the key source of proposed amendments, is relatively disinclined to aggregate petitions for Article V conventions beyond the seven-year period, which proposed congressional legislation on the topic has suggested.[60]

Rescissions and Reconsiderations

Another issue that remains unresolved with respect to amendments in general is whether states can reconsider proposed amendments that they have previously rejected or rescind ratification of proposals that they have previously approved but that the required majority of states has not yet ratified. Historically, Congress has accepted ratification of amendments that states have previously rejected, and there would be no reason to depart from such precedents with respect to amendments proposed by Article V conventions.

Although I have elsewhere argued that precedents that enable states to ratify proposed amendments that they have previously rejected point to the desirability of also allowing them to rescind ratifications of pending amendments,[61] these precedents are far more controversial. Because Congress has allowed states to rescind calls for conventions, however, there might be more reason for it to accept state rescissions of amendments proposed by an Article V convention than to accept those proposed by Congress.

Analysis

Because it remains untried, some aspects of an Article V convention are not as clear as the corresponding process of congressional proposal and state ratification. Still, most answers fall within a fairly narrow and manageable range that would not warrant alarm or create unnecessary instability. If states successfully issue a convention call, they should work together with Congress to ensure that the convention would devote itself to the public good, in the process demonstrating accountability, engaging in deliberation, and doing so in a manner designed not simply with a view to the perceived desirability of the amendment at hand but also with consideration of those that states might propose in the future.

CHAPTER 10

Different Kinds of Conventions

As chapter 2 discussed, when drafting the new Constitution all three authors of *The Federalist* distinguished between calling another convention to revise the document prior to its ratification and proposing individual amendments through such a convention or through what has now become the more traditional means initiated by Congress once the Constitution was ratified. So too, one can distinguish mechanisms designed to introduce a single amendment or amendments from those that are designed to propose a new constitution.

An Extralegal or Illegal Convention

In *A Treatise on Constitutional Conventions*, Judge John Jameson distinguished the revolutionary convention, which met without constitutional sanction, from the constitutional convention, which would meet under the authority of Article V.[1] As chapter 4 of this book further demonstrated, even after the adoption of Article V, there have been a number of extra-constitutional conventions—such as the Hartford Convention, the Seneca Falls Convention, the convention that was called to revise the Rhode Island Constitution, the Nashville Convention, the Peace Conventions, and the Montgomery Convention—that have been called outside the parameters of Article V.[2] Indeed, such conventions, especially those that called for disunion, have arguably tainted the reputation of the still untried Article V convention option.

As Abraham Lincoln indicated in his First Inaugural Address, the people of the United States always have the power to exercise "their constitutional right" to amend the Constitution.[3] Alternatively, if citizens become impatient with legal forms or perceive that existing constitutional mechanisms are unworkable, they can resort to extra-constitutional mechanisms, or what Lincoln called their "revolutionary right" to seek a new government as they did in 1776.[4] The issue of whether states may call for a limited convention is important because it might well affect states' willingness to seek change through legal, rather than through extralegal or unconstitutional, means. I believe that the Constitution permits a range of such conventions and that it is important for states to understand what kind of convention they are requesting. Although the classifications here are largely mine, I believe they are relatively consistent with options that other scholars have considered.

Thinking in Two Dimensions

Article V conventions can be analyzed according to the degree of their scope and deliberativeness. The most limited convention would address a single issue or issues whereas the most general would examine and consider rewriting, or even replacing, the entire document. Similarly, a deliberative convention would seek input from all delegates and be open to compromises, whereas a nondeliberative convention would simply assemble, much like state ratifying conventions, to take a single up-or-down vote on a single issue or set of issues.

As illustrated in figure 1, such a classification scheme would result in four major types of conventions: the single-issue(s) deliberative convention; the single-issue(s) nondeliberative convention; the convention to deliberate about major constitutional changes, including the possibility of a complete rewrite or replacement; and the convention simply designed to concur in a new constitution (perhaps along the order of those formulated by famous lawgivers of antiquity).[5]

Since the American people have yet to utilize the Article V convention process, no prior convention quite fits in among any of the four resulting quadrants. The Mt. Vernon Convention of 1785 came close to what I would describe as a single-issue deliberative convention in that representatives from Virginia and Maryland met to discuss the pressing issues of navigation between them. When a state petitions Congress to call a convention to propose an amendment to permit prayer in public schools or provide equal rights for women, this is the kind of convention that it envisions.

Recent proposals that call for a convention to take an up-or-down vote on an amendment or series of amendments would illustrate the single-issue nondeliberative convention. It would be similar to the individual state conventions that met to ratify the Twenty-First Amendment repealing national alcoholic prohibition, although it would require yet another set of ratifications at the state level.[6]

The Convention of 1787, although not held under the authority of Article V, began its deliberations by considering a new document and assembled it piece by piece through a process of deliberation and debate. It would appear to be the quintessential model of a deliberative convention to examine the entire document.

Similarly, one could imagine a convention called to take an up-or-down vote on a new constitution formulated by a notable individual or blue-ribbon panel

DELIBERATIVE

Mt. Vernon Convention	U.S. Constitutional Convention of 1787

SINGLE-ISSUE — ENTIRE DOCUMENT

Convention similar to ratification of 21st Amendment	Up-or-down vote on new constitution

NONDELIBERATIVE

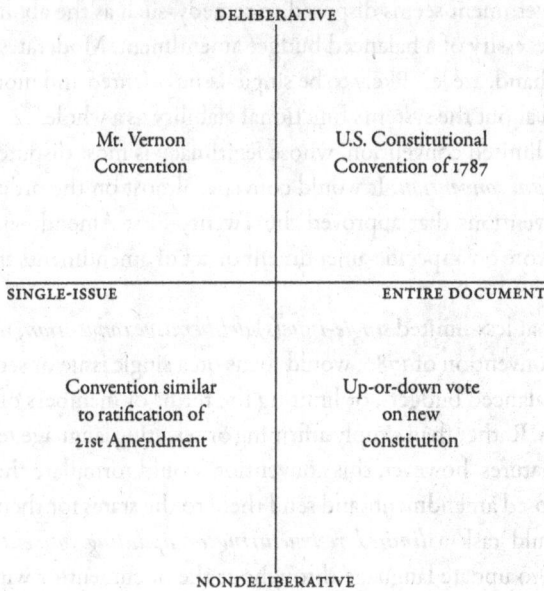

FIGURE 1. *Four types of Article V conventions.*

or commission. Like the single-issue nondeliberative convention, its work would require additional approval by the states.

Four Kinds of Article V Conventions

Because I think that nondeliberative conventions are most appropriate not at the proposing stage but at the ratifying stage, and that it is highly unlikely that states would meet to take a nondeliberative up-or-down vote on a new document, I have divided Article V conventions into four ideal types (with obvious gradations among them), chiefly focusing on the scope of their powers. I designate these as:

- A single-issue referendum convention;
- A single-issue deliberative convention;
- A limited restructuring or updating convention; and
- A convention to rewrite or replace the Constitution.[7]

Different kinds of conventions are appropriate to different circumstances and might resonate better with some groups than others. Writing during the bicentennial year of the Constitution, Michael Kammen thus reflected the central distinction between single-issue and restructuring conventions by observing that "conservatives are more likely to have in mind one or two matters which no branch of government seems disposed to remedy, such as the abolition of abortion or the necessity of a balanced budget amendment. Moderates and liberals, on the other hand, are less likely to be single-issue oriented and more inclined to be concerned about the system's functional viability as a whole."[8]

The most limited convention, whose legitimacy is most disputed, is a *single-issue referendum convention*. It would convene, almost on the order of the state ratifying conventions that approved the Twenty-First Amendment, to take an up-or-down vote on a specific amendment or set of amendments that states had requested.

A somewhat less-limited *single-issue(s) deliberative convention*, not unlike the Annapolis Convention of 1786, would focus on a single issue or set of issues like commerce, balanced budgets, or limiting the terms of members of Congress or federal judges. Rather than simply affirming or rejecting language recommended by state legislatures, however, this convention would formulate the language of its own proposed amendments and send them to the states for their approval.[9]

States would task a *limited restructuring or updating convention* with the power either to update language throughout the document or with the task of examining a position area or areas whose functioning seemed problematic. It might thus focus on the division of power between the legislative and executive branches with respect to foreign policy. Alternatively, it might consider a complete overall of the judiciary, or tweaking the current system of federalism. As with a single-issue deliberative convention, it would formulate its own constitutional language, although it is certainly possible to imagine such a convention meeting simply to debate whether to propose or reject a set of recommendations made by a blue-ribbon committee or commission.

The people would task a fourth type of convention, the *convention to rewrite the Constitution*, perhaps most similar to the Convention of 1787, with examining the entire Constitution and rewriting or replacing it. Although I believe that Article V allows for such a contingency, I do not believe that there is an adequate consensus as to how the document as a whole needs to be altered and accordingly think that the most likely and desirable kind of convention, as well as the one least likely to stir popular fears, is the single-issue deliberative convention. Much of the fear surrounding Article V proceeds from concerns that it might morph from such a single-issue convention into a convention to rewrite the entire document.

Single-Issue Referendum Conventions

Charles Kacprowicz, the founder of a group known as Citizens Initiatives, recently wrote a book in which he advocated calling Article V conventions that would take an up-or-down vote on specific amendments that he has formulated.[10] The Compact for America has recommended a similar approach with respect to calling a state convention to ratify the specific language of a preformulated amendment designed to rein in federal debt.[11]

In a report prepared for the American Legislative Exchange Council (ALEC), Professor Robert G. Natelson, who has elsewhere observed that the Founding Fathers distinguished between what he described as "plenipotentiary and limited-purpose conventions,"[12] both of which he thinks are appropriate, has nonetheless argued that such single-issue referendum conventions are improper. He explains:

> Although applications may limit a convention to one or more subjects, the existing case law strongly suggests that an application may not attempt to dictate particular wording or rules to the convention nor may the application attempt to coerce Congress or other state legislatures. As the courts have ruled repeatedly, assemblies (Congress, state legislatures, and conventions) are entitled to some deliberative freedom when involved in Article V procedures. An application may suggest particular language or rules for the convention, but to avoid confusion, suggestions should be placed only in separate, accompanying resolutions.[13]

Natelson's view receives support from the Supreme Court decision in *Hawke v. Smith* (1920), in which in opposing a state requirement that the people ratify federal amendments through referendums, it observed with reference to ratification of the Constitution that "both methods of ratification, by legislatures or conventions, call for actions by deliberative assemblages representative of the people, which it was assumed would voice the will of the people."[14]

I am not sure that a single-issue ratifying convention would be unconstitutional, but I think that it would almost always be unwise. The most analogous legal precedent indicating that a single-issue referendum convention would be constitutional is the ratification of the Twenty-First Amendment. Acting in the absence of congressional legislation, states called conventions, which acted as plebiscitary bodies, most of which engaged only in perfunctory deliberation. Indeed, the delegates from New Hampshire completed their ratifying work in seventeen minutes![15] Moreover, only one state convention registered significant opposition.[16] After observing these meetings, Edward S. Corwin of Princeton concluded that "the term 'convention,' therefore, it must be presumed, does not today, if it ever did, denote a deliberative body; it is sufficient if it is representative of popular sentiment."[17]

Since the proliferation of primaries, national nominating conventions are another example of conventions that have put far greater emphasis on ratifying the choice of candidates that party primaries, caucuses, and state conventions have already made than on making independent decisions. Presidential scholar Michael Nelson has accordingly observed that "since 1952 all the nominees of the two major parties have been chosen on the first ballot."[18] Moreover, individual members of Congress take similar votes when deciding whether to accept or reject the wording of amendments that committees and subcommittees have largely formulated.

Although I do not believe that the Constitution outlaws such conventions, I can see little to be gained from calling them. Textually, one might argue that Article V summons states to call conventions to "propose" rather than "ratify" amendments, but no one at the Constitutional Convention or during the ratification debates appeared to make, or to rely on, that particular distinction during their proceedings. Moreover, an Article V convention—whose members would differ in composition from those of state legislatures and would thus have a somewhat different perspective from the originating bodies—would still have to decide whether to "propose" or refrain from proposing an amendment that state legislatures had sent to them. Similarly, Congress would determine whether to send such proposals for ratification to the state legislatures that had petitioned for the conventions or to special conventions called in three-fourths or more of the states.

Because it would likely involve fifty state elections as well as costs for delegates, convention proposal of a single amendment would be far more expensive than the mechanism of congressional proposal that has been used to date.[19] Moreover, the idea of requiring delegates assembled from all the states to cast a single up-or-down vote on language that someone else had already proposed calls in heavier artillery than is necessary to get the job done. Indeed, it comes closer to mechanisms for state referenda than for the deliberations typically associated with conventions.

If, as described below, Congress can develop institutional interests that are at odds with the general welfare, it seems just as possible for states as states (even in the aggregate) to have interests that might be separate from those of the nation as a whole. This was arguably the situation under the Articles of Confederation. Consistent with Madison's concerns in *The Federalist*, citizens should rightly view with suspicion any efforts by such governments, or by any groups, to short-circuit deliberation.

According to Madison's storied arguments respecting factions in Federalist No. 10,[20] because of their smaller size and greater homogeneity, states are more likely than the nation to be swept by factions that favor measures that may not be popular at the national level.[21] The fact that states have never collectively mustered the required two-thirds majorities to call a convention is arguably testimony to this. Even if two-thirds of the states decided to call a convention on a particular measure, they might find compatriots in other states to be far less certain of its value, and a negative vote in such conventions might demonstrate this.

One advantage of the national amending processes that have been used to date is that they involve deliberation at both the congressional level, where both houses have to decide what an amendment should say and whether to propose it, and the state level, where state legislatures or state conventions have to ratify. If a convention deliberates simply on whether to cast a yes-or-no vote rather than on the actual language of an amendment, then the only deliberation as to the language of the amendment would ultimately take place not collectively but at the state level, since only states would call for the convention, only states would select delegates who might be pledged to one or the other side, and only states would ratify its results. There is good reason to be wary of such an approach. Professor Michael B. Rappaport has suggested that states should be allowed and encouraged "to deliberate and coordinate with one another" by creating an "advisory convention" to formulate language for states to adopt,[22] but if states have an issue that they cannot get Congress to propose, it seems preferable for them to call a single-issue *deliberative* convention in which they would both formulate and decide whether to propose an amendment or amendments.

Focusing on a more practical matter, the Committee on the Federal Constitution of the New York State Bar Association observed that states take a greater risk of stalemate in proposing "a convention whose agenda is limited to voting up or down a single amendment." The committee reasoned that "the wider the agenda, the greater the probability of a result that is at least partially satisfactory to those state legislatures which applied for the convention."[23] A single-issue ratifying convention would take away such flexibility. Examining proposals by the radio host and author Mark Levin for controlling the federal bureaucracy, the main thrust of which he supports, Thomas E. Brennan observes that they would have profited from "a devil's advocate."[24] Unless one anticipates a modern-day Moses, one would hope that a convention would be permitted to make a nip here and a tuck there rather than be faced with a simple up-or-down vote.

Single-Issue Deliberative Conventions

Even those who deny that *state legislatures* can limit a convention to the consideration of a single issue or set of issues generally agree that the convention itself has the power to limit its focus to a single matter, and then formulate and propose an amendment, or set of amendments to send to the states for consideration. To take some obvious examples, if the Constitution lacked a bill of rights, or if there were a movement to add social and political rights to the Constitution that Congress refused to propose, this might be an appropriate subject for a single-issue deliberative convention called at the request of the states.

Because Congress routinely exercises this function and has successfully done so on thirty-three occasions, the first question that advocates of a new amendment must ask is why they would bypass the established process whereby members of Congress introduce amendments (most as joint resolutions), committees examine them, and if they garner adequate support, both houses of Congress eventually vote on them. One obvious answer is that it is difficult to muster a two-thirds majority of both houses of Congress for an amendment, but this answer is uncompelling because history to this point would suggest that it is even more difficult to get two-thirds of the states to propose a convention for dealing with such a subject. Moreover, the convention option would require considerably more expense and planning.

Three Situations Calling for
Single-Issue Deliberative Conventions

When confronted with the choice of using a mechanism that the nation has successfully employed multiple times over a two-hundred-year period on a variety of subjects, or choosing one that it has yet to utilize, the onus would clearly be on those who favor the second course. There are at least three situations where such an argument for a convention for a single amendment or set of amendments to bypass Congress might be especially persuasive.[25]

When Congress as a Whole Is Seriously Malfunctioning

The first such situation, analogous to the one that American Revolutionaries confronted when they opposed assertions of sovereignty by the British Parliament, would occur where Congress as a whole was clearly malfunctioning with respect to the public good. Having once lived in a state where bumper stickers frequently proclaimed that "No man's life, wife, or property are secure when the legislature is in session," I am aware that some wags (perhaps aligned with those who say that the best way to know whether politicians are lying is whether they are talking) would likewise claim that Congress malfunctions every time it meets, but I am suggesting that there are times when generalized complaints about Congress could be truly warranted. If, for example, districts were so malapportioned that the population lost confidence in whether Congress adequately represented the people and the courts refused to intervene, as they had done before *Baker v. Carr*,[26] if members sought to give themselves life terms, or if Congress were to act in a completely arbitrary way that the other two branches could not counter, then this would clearly call for restructuring that only a convention might propose.[27]

There are individuals who believe that Congress is already at such a stage. For example, in a provocative article, John Davenport, a philosopher at Fordham University, cites the use of the filibuster, the influence of special interests, and what he believes is a "vicious cycle" whereby "the minority party in Congress has more to gain by blocking all significant legislation than by compromising to do something" as indications that "Congress is broken."[28] On the flyleaf of a recent novel, Tom Donohue observes:

> I believe Congress is not capable of creating laws or amendments that will change the endemic problems: fiscal irresponsibility and concentrated power. Mark Meckler, at the September 2011 Harvard Conference on the Constitutional Convention said, "We have a two party system in this country that is part of the problem. Many people will tell you it is Democrats and Republicans. From my perspective, it is incumbents versus citizens." Because Congress is incapable of changing itself, it is up to us, as Citizens, to invoke our inalienable rights.[29]

Others have argued that the present system of campaign financing has thwarted the will of the people.

When Rules Effectively Block All Amendments

A second situation might arise in which Congress adopts rules that effectively block consideration of all constitutional amendments, no matter what their merits. Imagine, for example:

- Congress tabled or refused to examine all motions for amendments, regardless of their subject;
- Leaders announced that they would do all in their power to sidetrack any proposed changes (as, for example, when it adopted a gag motion in the nineteenth century that rejected all antislavery petitions);[30]
- Congress began utilizing filibusters to stop consideration of all proposed amendments, even those with clear popular support; or
- Congress refused to consider any amendments that had not received unanimous committee or subcommittee approval and amendments were clearly needed.

Although these situations address problems in both houses of Congress, since amendments require two-thirds majorities of *both* houses, they might be equally powerful if they applied only to one. Indeed, Professor William J. Quirk has argued that the U.S. Senate "has, for practical purposes, removed the amendment process from the Constitution."[31] He cites proposed amendments that dealt with balanced budgets, prayer in public schools, and declaring war that passed the House of Representatives only to be defeated in the Senate.[32] Similarly, Professor Davenport, who lists elimination of the Senate filibuster among the first of sixteen agenda items for such a convention, argues that "*Congress can no longer pass the amendments needed to fix itself.*"[33]

Under such circumstances, if amendments were needed, it would make sense for the people to pursue alternate channels, and especially the Article V convention process. In examining the origins of the convention mechanism in the Convention of 1787, Professor William W. Van Alstyne thus observed that "the fact that no one could foresee just how responsive the untried 'Congress' might be to the felt necessities for amendment meant, necessarily, that no critical reliance could be placed upon Congress as a plausible sole or even plausible best source for every kind of amendment."[34]

When Institutional Interests Block Needed Amendments

Although one can imagine such a scenario, it seems far more likely that proponents of a single amendment or set of amendments would consider using the convention option in cases where Congress was unwilling because of its own institutional interests or considerations to propose such an amendment on its own. Indeed, this appears to be the primary purpose for which the Founders created this amending alternative. The proposal for direct election of U.S. senators that eventuated in the Seventeenth Amendment remains perhaps the quintessential example. Members of Congress who owed their appointments to state legislatures had little incentive to take their chances with members of the public. Hence, the proposal garnered greatest support among senators who had been selected in states that had adopted the so-called Oregon Plan, where the legislators had already agreed to appoint the individual who had won the popular vote.[35]

However they might rationally assess such issues on their merits, many contemporary members of Congress have similar incentives to oppose proposing amendments limiting the length of their own terms,[36] significantly increasing the number of U.S. representatives,[37] allocating senators according to population (a change that would, under the remaining entrenchment provision in Article V of the Constitution, require the consent of all states), restricting partisan gerrymandering (configuring districts for party advantage) of legislative districts, limiting employment of ex-legislators as lobbyists when they leave office, cutting their health or retirement benefits, trimming their powers over interstate commerce, enacting a line-item veto, eliminating the filibuster in the Senate,[38] or the like. If such amendments are desirable and the people favor them, conventions are far more likely to propose them than are members of Congress themselves unless, as in the case of the Seventeenth Amendment, Congress proposes its own amendment as a means of precluding a state-called convention. To quote Professor Van Alstyne once again: "But insofar as the felt shortcoming was one of Congress' own doing (for instance, in the self-aggrandizement of its powers at the expense of state powers), a check for a specific shortcoming of that kind was the power of states to mount adequate support from like-minded legislatures elsewhere, to convoke a convention where a corrective measure might be approved, subject thereafter only to ratification pursuant to whichever mode of ratification Congress elected."[39] In a similar fashion, Fred Graham observed that "the states may find future opportunities for meaningful participation in the amending process" in situations where Congress failed to propose amendments because "they would detract from congressional prerogatives."[40] Thomas E. Brennan has recently called for a convention because he does not believe that members of Congress, members of the two major political parties, the president, or the courts will otherwise bring needed changes about.[41]

Possible Ambiguity: Where Does the Proposed Balanced Budget Amendment Fit?

Proponents of a balanced budget amendment might also argue that a convention is more likely to formulate a solution than Congress itself. Indeed, they can argue that Congress has already tried a number of solutions that have failed. Critics charge that the current political system appears to offer an incentive for members to gain favor with their constituents by authorizing and spending money whose payment they defer to future generations.[42] If true change is to be made, it may need to be made by those with no interest in the current process.

Contrariwise, it might be that unbalanced budgets (at least at the national level) are simply not susceptible to a constitutional cure. Opponents of balanced budget amendments often suggest both that exceptions for wars, depressions, or other catastrophes could swallow any general rule and that courts would find such an amendment particularly difficult to enforce.[43] Keynesian economics further suggests that governmental deficit spending is actually desirable in times of economic depression.[44] For current purposes, it is unnecessary to settle such issues but only to point out that some issue might not fully fit into any single category, or may be amenable to solutions, if they exist, by either Article V mechanism.

A Limited Constitutional Restructuring or Updating Convention

A third type of convention, a limited constitutional restructuring or updating convention, might likewise be an appropriate remedy if there were similar systemic problems relative to the presidency, the judiciary, or the system of federalism, or if the public simply became convinced that the language of the document needed to be updated to enhance public understanding. Especially since the direct election of senators, which may, while increasing accountability to individual citizens, have undermined ties between senators and state governments, state legislatures might think that they would have a far better chance of redressing perceived imbalances in federal relations through the convention mechanism rather than by going through Congress. Alternately, and with a view to the debilitating state exercises of state sovereignty under the Articles of Confederation, there may be occasions where it would be appropriate to guard against the institutional self-interests of state legislatures.

Conventions to redraw a single institution or set of institutions might be the most difficult for either Congress or the states to cabin in advance since their resolution would be likely to affect multiple provisions of the Constitution. An attempt to increase congressional powers might lessen state powers, while efforts to reduce federal powers might well leave more for the states. One may not be able to trim the powers of Congress without increasing those of the president or the judiciary. A provision weakening or eliminating judicial review would necessarily increase the powers of the other two branches or even of state courts. It is unlikely that one could adjust powers relative to war and peace without dealing with both legislative and executive powers. Even the adoption of an item veto might not only decrease congressional powers of the purse but also increase presidential powers. A proposal allowing states to veto congressional legislation such as that which Randy Barnett and a number of others have advocated[45] might similarly affect both congressional powers and federalism.[46]

The American Constitution is now more than 225 years old, and a number of would-be reformers have argued that the document needs updating, much as one might update translations of the Bible.[47] States could choose to request a convention for this purpose, but if the task were simply that of updating, it might be more appropriate for a smaller group of legal and linguistic experts to propose changes, which Congress could then propose as a group. Alternatively, a convention might assemble, entrust the task of updating to a select committee, confirm such a rewrite in a single vote or series of votes, and then propose its recommendations to the nation as a whole.

A Convention to Rewrite the Constitution

More than 175 individuals throughout U.S. history have proposed massive changes to the Constitution, and more than 50 proponents of change have actually drafted documents for consideration.[48] Rexford Tugwell alone drafted more than forty versions of an alternate constitution for what he called the Newstates of America.[49] Some proponents of change have advocated calling Article V conventions to rewrite the Constitution. This constitutes the fourth such type of convention.[50] There are a number of models that such a convention could follow.

The Convention of 1787

As described in chapter 1, the U.S. Constitution was the product of a convention that, while initially called for "revising" the Articles of Confederation,[51] decided instead to draft a new document. The convention justified its scope not from strict legality but from necessity that had continued to motivate the search for effective government in the aftermath of the Revolution against Great Britain and sealed its legitimacy by providing for ratifications by conventions in each of the states. Apart from the provision in Article V that calls for Congress on the application of two-thirds of the states to "call a Convention for proposing Amendments," the existing Constitution does not specifically outline a procedure to "draft" or "rewrite" the document.

Because the U.S. Constitution rejected the British practice of legislative sovereignty and instead divided powers relatively equally among the legislative, executive, and judicial branches, neither Congress nor the other two branches can adopt a new constitution on their own. Two-thirds majorities of both houses could arguably propose an amendment for state ratification (probably by state conventions rather than by state legislatures) that would begin with a statement to the effect that "We the People of the United States do hereby propose this new constitution to form a more perfect union than that in the Constitution of 1787" and follow with the text of a new document, but this seems fairly unlikely. Moreover, depending on one's view of congressional representativeness, such a procedure might be in tension with the view that the Constitution should originate with "We the People."

Given the role that Congress has taken in proposing individual amendments, conventions appear to be the quintessential mechanism for wholesale reform. Judge Jameson thus contrasted the role of legislatures in proposing individual amendments "of no great extent" with those of conventions, with which he associated more extensive reforms like those that I have associated with either a limited restructuring convention or a convention to rewrite the Constitution: "For amendments of such a stamp, separately considered, the mode by legislative action is well adapted; and it is adapted to no other. It ought to be confined, it is believed, to changes which are few, simple, independent, and of comparatively small importance. For a general revision of a Constitution, or even for single propositions involving radical changes as to the policy of which the popular mind has not been informed by prior discussion, the employment of this mode is impracticable, or of doubtful expediency."[52]

The Continental Congress

Although the Second Continental Congress drafted the Articles of Confederation, there are several reasons to suggest that the current Congress should not follow that precedent but that the states should emulate the example of 1787 by calling a convention if they decided that a new or significantly revised constitution were needed. First, the Continental Congress was acting as a revolutionary rather than as a purely constitutional body; it devoted far greater attention to winning the American Revolution than to drawing up a plan of government. Second, as chapter 1 of this book describes, its actions preceded the pattern of institutional differentiation that subsequently developed at the state level where a convention generally drafted a new constitution, which the people then ratified. Under the circumstances, proposals from Congress would likely lack the legitimacy of those coming from a constitutional convention. Third, Congress already has a full agenda connected to lawmaking, governmental oversight, and constituent service that could make it difficult to concentrate its energies on wholesale constitutional reform. Fourth, voters typically elect members of Congress for their opinions on legislative matters rather than for their views on constitutional change or their expertise in drafting constitutions, whereas delegates to Article V conventions could be selected for the latter qualifications and for these alone. Fifth, members of Congress are clearly identified with political parties and organized with respect to overall leadership and committee tasks according to party identification, and any proposal that reflected such partisanship would likely have a rocky public reception. Sixth, vesting Congress with power to write a new constitution would arguably give inordinate authority to one of three existing branches in the determination of a new government and might tempt members to assume more powers for themselves than might be appropriate. Vesting Congress with the power of initiating wholesale constitutional reform would be like allowing Congress to be a judge in its own case.

Constitutional Commissions

Some states have employed constitutional commissions, often appointed by the state legislature and the governor, to propose constitutional changes. Near the time that President Richard M. Nixon resigned from the presidency, at least one academic association suggested using a similar mechanism at the national level.[53] Although the U.S. Constitution does not explicitly provide for such a body, it does not specifically prohibit it. The president and congressional leaders could probably appoint one, as long as its purpose was simply to make proposals that Congress or an Article V convention would then consider proposing as amendments. At the state level, recent commentary suggests that such commissions might be more effective than they were sometimes considered to be in the past.[54]

Advantages of a Convention

Most organizations seek to balance continuity and change. Members of institutions, however, may be so accustomed and comfortable with keeping the status quo in place that they fail to give due consideration to the need for possible changes. Members of established congressional committees who are accustomed to seeing the same proposed amendments appear over and over again may over time fail to consider that circumstances may have changed in ways that would warrant reconsideration of an amendment that once seemed untimely.

A key advantage of an Article V convention might be that it could look at some old issues through some new eyes. A majority of convention delegates might ultimately conclude, as majorities in Congress have done before, that certain publicly favored proposed amendments were ultimately undesirable, but the people might profit from seeing delegates debate these issues in a fresh light and from new perspectives. If delegates were selected and apportioned in what the people considered to be a fair manner, they might further affirm that a clear national consensus either did or did not exist on the subject. A convention that truly wanted to make a difference would likely end its deliberations, as did the Convention of 1787, by sending its resolutions to Congress and asking it to send them to the states. Although it is not clear that this would be necessary, it would be a way of expressing confidence that a Congress that examined its proposals would come to the same conclusions that it did.

Such considerations suggests that if a national consensus develops either on the need for a new constitution or substantial revisions in the document, then a convention might be the most viable mechanism for accomplishing this. The viability might well depend in part on how some of the issues with respect to the organization of such a body are settled, but the advantages of using a convention to revise the Constitution would largely correspond to the ways that it would differ from an existing Congress.

A convention called under Article V that came close to replicating the features of rational deliberation and consideration for the public welfare that the Convention of 1787 used to create the current Constitution might secure popular legitimacy. Members of a convention could be elected specifically because of their interest in or commitment to constitutional change, their expertise with regard to the subject, or their perceived wisdom and patriotism. The advantages of congressional incumbency would be eliminated. If, as seems likely, the convention were unicameral, it would probably operate more efficiently than the current body. Once elected, delegates could devote their full energies to constitutional change without being distracted by ordinary legislative tasks and constituency services. Delegates would likely be encouraged to pursue their task with a view toward the common good rather than with a view to partisan advantage. Members could include scholars as well as individuals who had experience serving in all three branches of government.

Opposition to Amendments
and Fears of an Article V Convention

However valid or invalid they may be, few political fears are more pervasive than that of a "runaway constitutional convention." It is sometimes difficult to distinguish between those who genuinely fear such a convention and those who merely use this fear to discourage amendments that they think such a convention would introduce, but in my experience, there are few strong advocates of amendments who fear conventions and even fewer strong opponents of amendments who favor calling conventions.

As the diagram in figure 2 indicates, it is possible to place individuals who have written on the subject into one of four categories. The most enthusiastic proponents of change are those who favor a particular amendment or set of amendments and have little or no fear of having states petition for an Article V convention for this purpose. Richard Labunski and Sanford Levinson would be good examples.[55] A second group favors constitutional change but fears using the Article V convention mechanism. Although he appears to have changed his mind, Levin initially appeared to have been in this group.[56] A third group opposes a particular constitutional change but does so on its merits rather than for fear of the convention. Thus, in writing their book arguing that the Article V mechanism itself was safe, Weber and Perry nonetheless opposed adoption of a balanced budget amendment.[57] A fourth group opposes constitutional change and stresses fears of Article V conventions. Frank J. Sorauf has observed that "the enemies of a convention under Article V have considerable interest in perpetuating the fear of a runaway convention."[58] Phyllis Schlafly, who successfully opposed the Equal Rights Amendment and now adamantly opposes an Article V convention, and her Eagle Forum would be good examples of this group. Representative Don Edwards opposed legislation to clarify Article V convention procedures by arguing that "anything that encourages this sort of utilization of Article V is unwise."[59] I have drawn a line illustrating where he believes the most vigorous advocates and opponents of Article V conventions would find themselves.

I find myself at the intersection of the two matrices. Although I think that alternate paths are more appropriate in some circumstances than in others, I do not think there is much more reason to fear an Article V convention than alternate paths to constitutional change. By the same token, I am not an advocate of a particular amendment or set of amendments. I believe, however, that the American Founders were wise to recognize that Congress could become unwilling to propose necessary constitutional changes. There have, moreover, been at least two occasions in U.S. history, one after severing ties to Great Britain in 1776–77, and the other in 1787, when a consensus emerged that the nation needed a new

FAVOR AMENDMENTS

GREAT FEAR OF CONVENTION   NO FEAR OF CONVENTION

OPPOSE AMENDMENTS

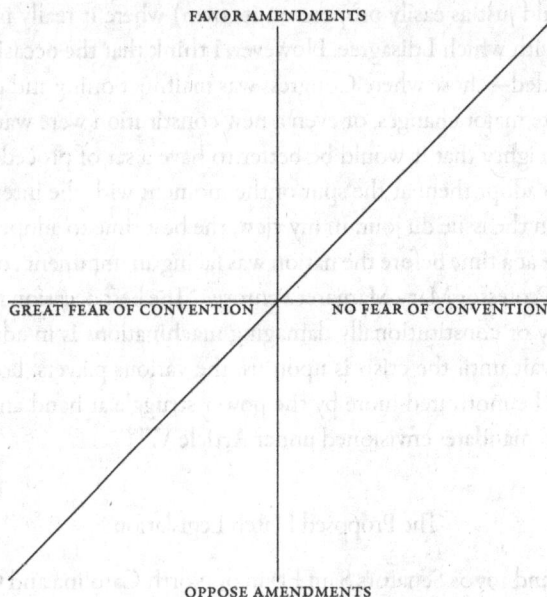

FIGURE 2. *Categories of individuals who have written on Article V conventions. The line shows where Representative Don Edwards thinks the most vigorous advocates and opponents of Article V conventions would fit.*

or substantially revised constitution. Such occasions could emerge again, and the nation should prepare for them.

Much of the opposition to the convention mechanism is inconsistent with faithful adherence to the text. Constitutionally, the Article V convention mechanism is just as valid a method of proposing amendments as the more-regularized method of congressional proposal and state confirmation. It is important to reiterate that an Article V convention is not a revolutionary act but an existing *constitutional* mechanism. Moreover, it is not the only provision in the constitutional toolbox that is primarily suited for rare occasions. The impeachment mechanisms and the provision for expelling wayward members of Congress are other examples of similar provisions.

The Desirability of Legislation

Because I take such a perspective, I favor the adoption of a congressional law on the subject. I recognize that this might increase the chances that the nation might use an Article V convention in situations (single-issue amendments that

Congress could just as easily propose on its own) where it really is not needed or on issues with which I disagree. However, I think that the occasions where it might be needed—those where Congress was malfunctioning and unresponsive or those where major changes, or even a new constitution were warranted—are sufficiently weighty that it would be better to have a set of procedures in place than to try to adopt them at the spur of the moment with the intent of tipping the balance on the issue du jour. In my view, the best time to adopt such legislation would be at a time before the nation was facing an imminent convention. In the words of Professor Mary Margaret Penrose: "The best occasion for curtailing any politically or constitutionally damaging machinations is in advance of any crisis. If we wait until the crisis is upon us, the various players, both local and national, will be motivated more by the power struggle at hand and less by the constitutional mandates envisioned under Article V."[60]

The Proposed Hatch Legislation

In the 1960s and 1970s Senators Sam Ervin of North Carolina and Orrin Hatch of Utah proposed legislation on Article V conventions.[61] Weber and Perry include a copy of the legislation sponsored by Hatch in 1985, known as the Constitutional Convention Implementation Act of 1985, and labeled each section.[62] I have included these labels and a brief summary of each section below:

APPLICATIONS FOR CONSTITUTIONAL CONVENTION

• State petitions would identify the specific subject of the amendment or amendments that they were proposing (Section 2).[63]

APPLICATION PROCEDURE

• State rules would govern the adoption or withdrawal of petitions, except that gubernatorial consent would not be required (Section 3).

TRANSMITTAL OF APPLICATIONS

• State Secretaries of State or equivalents would transmit resolutions to Congress. For transmittal of such resolutions to members of Congress, they would specify, where possible, other state applications that they believe deal with the same subject matter (Section 4). Senate President and House Speaker should send copies of application to each member and to state legislatures.

EFFECTIVE PERIOD OF APPLICATION

• Petitions would be active for seven years, with a provision to extend petitions from the last twelve years for another two; provision for withdrawal of state petitions (Section 5).

CALLING OF A CONSTITUTIONAL CONVENTION

- Congress would within forty-five days of receiving petitions from two-thirds of the states on the same subject issue a concurrent resolution calling for such a convention and designating "the place and time of meeting of the convention," and "the subject matter of the amendments or amendments of which the convention is called" (Section 6).

DELEGATES

- States would elect two at-large members and one from each congressional district; members of Congress would be ineligible; laws would privilege members from arrest while attending the convention (Section 7).

CONVENING THE CONVENTION

- The President Pro Tempore of the Senate and the Speaker of the House would convene the convention until delegates chose a presiding officer and administer oaths to act in accord with the Constitution (Section 8).
- Congress would pay delegates the same salary as members of Congress and cover expenses at the same rate, and the Administrator of General Services would provide facilities and information as was needed (Section 8).

PROCEDURES OF THE CONVENTION

- Delegates would have one vote, would keep records, would end the convention within six months, and transmit records within thirty days of adjourning (Section 9).

PROPOSAL OF AMENDMENTS

- Prohibitions on proposing any amendments different from those stated in the convention call (Section 10).

APPROVAL BY THE CONGRESS AND
TRANSMITTAL TO THE STATES
FOR RATIFICATION

- Congressional transmittal of resolutions that were consistent with the convention call to the state for ratification (Section 11).

RATIFICATION OF PROPOSED AMENDMENTS

- Ratification in accord with the method specified by Congress (Section 12).

RESCISSION OF RATIFICATIONS

- State rescission of proposed amendments and ratification of proposals they had previously rejected (Section 13).

PROCLAMATION OF CONSTITUTIONAL AMENDMENTS

- Proclamation of the amendment by the Administrator of General Services (Section 14).

JUDICIAL REVIEW

- Judicial review of claims filed within sixty days or as prescribed in the Constitution (Section 15).

EFFECTIVE DATE OF AMENDMENTS

- Implementation of the amendment according to when it specified or when the required number of states ratified (Section 16).

Even though such legislation was never adopted and could even be changed by a subsequent Congress if it were adopted, it is a good starting point for those anticipating how a future convention might work. Moreover, it would be a likely starting point were Congress faced with calling such a convention.

The Basic Elements of Legislation

My own recommendations are similar to those in the Hatch legislation, and I will accordingly use the same headings.

APPLICATIONS FOR CONSTITUTIONAL CONVENTION

- Recognize the validity of state convention applications *both* for limited conventions and for general conventions for seven years, unless previously rescinded;
- Provide for the systematic recording of calls both for general conventions and for those on a single subject, but aggregate only the former together and only the latter together in ascertaining whether the necessary three-fourths of the states have petitioned. To the extent possible, determinations of what states want should be determined by a neutral individual such as the administrator of the General Services Administration rather than by a partisan congressional leader.

APPLICATION PROCEDURE

- As in the Hatch legislation, allow states to determine their own rules for applying for conventions, with the continuing understanding that (as in the case of state amendment ratifications) gubernatorial assent is not required.

TRANSMITTAL OF APPLICATIONS

- As in the Hatch legislation, this should be done by the state Secretary of State or equivalent. The General Services Administrator should continually post updated lists of proposed amendments, aggregating similar proposals together for members of Congress and for public scrutiny so that states know whether they are likely to trigger another convention by making another petition. Calling a convention by stealth does not provide the kind of open and robust debate that should be given to matters of fundamental law.

EFFECTIVE PERIOD OF APPLICATION

- Unless the petitions specify otherwise (states could either limit them or declare that they remained in force until repealed), seven years would be an appropriate shelf life for new proposals (this has been proposed as a suitable ratification deadline for a number of constitutional amendments that Congress has proposed);
- Consistent with existing historical practices, the law should recognize the right of states to withdraw applications for conventions. The law should specify whether this rule also applied to the ratification of pending constitutional amendments or not.

CALLING OF A CONSTITUTIONAL CONVENTION

- Provide for calling for a convention in a timely manner (the eight months specified in the Hatch legislation seems reasonable) after the requisite number of state petitions had been received. Congress should further specify whether states had called for a general convention or for a convention dealing with a particular subject or subject area, and, if the latter, the specific subject or subjects intended to be reviewed.

DELEGATES

- Establish minimum standards for delegates, which should be based on the current requirements to be a member of the U.S. House of Representatives. Alternatively, the law could specify that states establish such standards on their own, with due regard to principles of equal protection relative to race and sex;
- Specify that conventions would consist of 436 delegates, apportioned like the current House of Representatives, with the District of Columbia having a single vote. If Congress chose an alternate plan of apportioning the convention like it does the Electoral College, I further propose electing delegates from states with voters qualified to vote for members of the House of Representatives, choosing one per legislative district and two statewide (with D.C. choosing its delegates at large). If Congress chose to divide the number of delegates by three, it could combine districts together for electoral purposes;
- Recommend that voters choose delegates in nonpartisan ballots.

CONVENING THE CONVENTION

- Congress should seek to designate *a nonsitting member*, perhaps the Chief Justice of the state where the convention is being held, the vice president, or a nationally recognized statesperson, to convene the convention;
- Provide for delegates to take an oath indicating that they will support the current U.S. Constitution and its mechanisms for enacting amendments

and that they adhere to the scope of their commission (whether for a single subject or for a general convention);

- Congress should provide for delegate pay and expenses for up to sixty days for a single-issue deliberative convention and up to six months to a year for a convention designed to revise or rewrite the entire document; basing this pay on that of members of Congress should allow individuals to participate regardless of socioeconomic status;
- Congress should seek suitable facilities, with access to transportation and communications, preferably outside the capital and closer to the population center of the nation.

PROCEDURES OF THE CONVENTION

- Each delegate shall have one vote;
- The convention would choose its own officers (specifying whether or not its president would have to be an elected delegate) and set its rules, including the majorities by which it would decide whether or not to propose amendments;
- Current members of Congress would be prohibited from serving. States could decide whether they did or did not want to elect members of their legislatures as delegates.

APPROVAL BY THE CONGRESS AND TRANSMITTAL
TO THE STATES FOR RATIFICATION

- Congressional transmittal of resolutions consistent with the convention call to the state for ratification. If states want to consider alternate amendments, they can call another convention for them or petition members of Congress to introduce them.

RATIFICATION OF PROPOSED AMENDMENTS

- Recognize that the convention's work would require subsequent ratification by three-fourths of the states, in one of the two ways provided by Article V. If the convention wants to include a deadline for ratification, it should include this within the text of the amendment, which would make it self-enforcing.

RESCISSION OF RATIFICATIONS

- States should be permitted to rescind petitions for an Article V convention, up to the point where two-thirds of the states have petitioned for it. The General Services Administrator should duly note these on the list of state petitions.

PROCLAMATION OF CONSTITUTIONAL AMENDMENT

- Recognize this as a possible, but not a necessary step, for amendments that have received approval by three-fourths of the state legislatures. States should be encouraged to submit notices of their ratifications just as they previously submitted notices of their calls for conventions.

JUDICIAL REVIEW

- Recognize that the law, like convention proceedings, would be subject to judicial review (a statement designed to encourage all sides to act reasonably), but with a statement that previous decisions have generally taken a deferential posture toward good-faith congressional efforts to see that amendments reflected a contemporary consensus.

EFFECTIVE DATE OF AMENDMENTS

- If not otherwise specified within the text of proposed amendments, and consistent with existing amending precedents, this would occur on the day that the thirty-eighth state ratified.

Loose Ends

These rules would not cover all contingencies. They thus remain open to criticisms by those, whom I would liken to Antifederalists of a bygone era, who say that the nation cannot afford to take any risks. Although the nation should not undertake constitutional revision for what the Declaration of Independence referred to as "light and transient causes," most ordinary laws require some administrative interpretation and carry risks of unanticipated consequences. Moreover, if constitutional changes are needed, there are additional risks in kicking the can down the road and leaving major issues unaddressed.

Congress can tailor solutions specific to when and where to hold a convention to individual circumstances. A president could further remind delegates of taking their task seriously. In the meantime, legislation like that which I advocate could iron out some of the more problematic issues in advance and give state legislatures reasonable notice of what to expect should they decide to trigger the convention mechanism. If calling a convention is likely to lead to chaos, or if it would lead to a fairly routine procedure, states have the right to know in advance.

The Importance of the First Article V Convention

As this book has amply documented, there have been numerous previous extralegal conventions as well as a few false alarms about the imminence of an Article V convention. With momentum again apparently building for an Article V convention to deal with the issue of balanced federal budgets and campaign financing, however, it is quite possible that a sufficient number of states will submit the requisite number of petitions to trigger such a convention before the congressional passage of legislation on the subject. This would force Congress either to speed up a general convention bill or to make specific arrangements for the convention at hand.

I think that the former course would be wiser. Congress should generally treat conventions equally, and states should know what to expect when they call for a convention. It is especially important for members of Congress to recognize that whatever precedents they establish could be long lasting and could strongly influence the further usefulness of the Article V convention mechanism. It would be particularly unfortunate if states began electing delegates before Congress decided how to apportion them or if the convention were to begin with a dispute between Congress and the states over whether state delegates were to cast votes as states or whether delegates would cast individual votes.

Although I have chalked out what I believe to be generally wise guidelines that are based on the best available precedents and arguments, this is likely a situation where, in the words of Justice Oliver Wendell Holmes Jr., "A page of history is worth a volume of logic."[64] Once the first Article V convention meets, its precedents are likely to trump prior constitutional speculation (though if such a convention failed, it might serve as a warning about how not to proceed). In such circumstances, both proponents and opponents of the particular subject of the convention should proceed as patriots, not simply with a partisan eye to the outcome of the first convention but with a view toward possible future conventions.

For reasons that the first chapter of this book outlines, the Constitutional Convention of 1787 remains paradigmatic. At the outset of the convention, George Washington is reported to have admonished: "Let us raise a standard to which the wise and honest can repair; the event is in the hands of God."[65] Similarly, as the nation's first president, Washington, and his immediate successors, later acted with the recognition that whatever he did could become a future precedent.[66] Just as those who planned and organized the 1787 convention largely took the long view of how to enhance overall deliberation rather than simply how to advance their own agendas, so too should those who follow in their footsteps.

Does Article V Need Amending?

Although scholars have frequently criticized Article V for being overly difficult, it is possible that some of this difficulty would be overcome if states began to exercise the power to call for Article V conventions. There are three ways that this could probably be facilitated. The first, which would not require an amendment to current language, would be for Congress simply to post a running track of Article V convention petitions that grouped them according to whether they favored a general convention or a convention on a single subject or subjects and what these were. Such a checklist might thus indicate that twelve states had requested a general convention, twenty favored an amendment dealing with deficit spending, and twenty-five specifically wanted an amendment to limit tax increases. This would enable states to know whether their own petitions were likely to trigger a convention.

A second relatively minor reform would clarify whether calls for limited conventions are permissible, and whether states could confine convention discussion to an up-or-down vote on a single preformulated amendment or a single topic area. I believe that states already have power to do both, but this may be a case where the public would be reassured by the presence of both belts and suspenders. In any event, I do not see the wisdom in calling a convention essentially to serve as a referendum on a preformulated language, which may or may not have been the subject of adequate deliberation, and I believe that this could be a sufficient evil against which to guard if such proposals became increasingly popular.

A third more fundamental reform that would apply to Article V in general, rather than to the convention mechanism in particular, might involve lowering the threshold of amendments, perhaps to three-fifths of both houses of Congress and the states. A more palatable alternative, which could allay fears that amendments might be adopted with less than majority support, might be to require that ratification involve states with at least 60 percent of the population. If, as it would appear, public opinion now regards referendums as clearer indicators of the public will than conventions, it might even be appropriate to specify a national referendum on proposed amendments, with due safeguards for the principles of national stability that Madison articulated in Federalist No. 49.

A Review of First Principles

Having surveyed various issues connected to the Article V convention mechanism, it is now time to revisit the central issue. For those who accept the cardinal tenets of American constitutionalism, namely that the Constitution is the nation's fundamental law that embodies natural law principles and that guides all other laws, the processes for amending this document must be taken quite seriously. A constitutional mistake is far more costly than most errors by one of the three branches of government, in part because the Constitution is foundational law.[67] As such, it can only be formally modified (as in the case of the Eighteenth and Twenty-First Amendments) by yet another constitutional change, which is necessarily difficult to enact.

A constitution should embody both the vision and the wisdom of a society. A well-designed constitutional amending process will necessarily seek both to preserve what is best about the existing constitutional system and provide mechanisms for changing provisions that need alterations. Ideally, it should do so in as peaceful, orderly, and deliberative a manner as possible.

Although formal amending processes have their critics,[68] there is little doubt that the nation has used the current amending mechanisms on a number of occasions and that many of the changes they have enacted have been consequential. As chapter 3 illustrated, the process has reaffirmed individual rights, dealt with unintended consequences and filled in gaps, voided Supreme Court decisions that the public did not think were true to the spirit of the document, outlawed slavery, and expanded suffrage. Although three amendments were largely the product of civil war, the amending process itself was carried out without further bloodshed or violence. This is a worthy heritage.

Because mechanisms that have been used to date depend on Congress to initiate them, they depend on the continued proper functioning of this body, and yet the American Revolution began in part because of the abuses of a similar legislature, and the Framers wisely recognized that something similar could happen in the future. Similarly, the current Constitution is not the nation's first but is a successor to the Articles of Confederation. If that document needed to be replaced within less than a decade, it would not be surprising to find that this one, which has lasted for more than 225 years, might also one day need to be updated or superseded.

In assessing what he perceived to be the relative success of the Constitutional Convention of 1787 versus what he feared from an immediate successor that would convene without constitutional guidelines even before states ratified the document, James Madison argued that the first had successfully channeled or subordinated popular passion to reason.[69] If the nation ever decides to call an Article V convention, whether to introduce an individual initiative or set of initiatives or to rewrite or propose a completely different constitution, this should again be the central goal. As much as possible, the nation should so choose delegates to such a convention, and its proceedings should be so structured that it will be most likely to promote reasoned deliberation and debate or what Alexander Hamilton called "good government from reflection and choice."[70] I believe that the nation is far likelier to achieve this objective by detailing convention procedures in advance when such reflection is possible than in leaving them to the last minute when members of Congress would be less influenced by general considerations than by their desire to facilitate or thwart a particular convention based on what they perceived to be its agenda.

Timeline

1215	King John of England signs the Magna Carta, which becomes a beacon for the liberties of English-speaking peoples.
1492	Christopher Columbus discovers America.
1619	The Virginia House of Burgesses is formed.
1620	Puritans and others aboard ship sign the Mayflower Compact before they debark from their ship to settle in the New World.
1650s	Cromwell, the Lord Protector, calls convention parliaments.
1683	William Penn devises an amending process by which to change one of the charters he has issued to govern his colonies.
1689	A Convention Parliament invites William and Mary to take over the English throne.
1754–1763	The French and Indian War rekindles British concern with her American colonies.
1765	The Stamp Act Congress meets to discuss colonial opposition to parliamentary taxes.
1775	The First Continental Congress meets to discuss colonial grievances.
	Fighting breaks out between the Americans and British at Lexington and Concord.
1776	Thomas Paine authors *Common Sense*, questioning America's continuing ties with Britain.
	Second Continental Congress calls on states to write new constitutions, and many of them do so.
	The Second Continental Congress declares independence from Great Britain; Thomas Jefferson writes the Declaration of Independence.
1777	Congress proposes the Articles of Confederation.
1781	The last state ratifies the Articles of Confederation.
	British troops under Cornwallis surrender to Washington at Yorktown.
1783	The Treaty of Paris brings the Revolutionary War to an official end.
1785	Delegates from Virginia and Maryland meet at Mt. Vernon, Virginia, to discuss common navigation problems.

1786   Delegates from five states meet at Annapolis, Maryland, to discuss issues related to commerce and call for a convention to consider wider matters.

1787   The Federal Convention meets in Philadelphia and decides to propose a new constitution, which Congress sends to state conventions for ratification.

1787–1788   Publication of *The Federalist* by Alexander Hamilton, James Madison, and John Jay.

1788   The required number of state conventions ratifies the U.S. Constitution.

1789   The new Constitution goes into effect with the election of George Washington as president and the assembling of the new Congress, which proposes a Bill of Rights. Congress decides to add new amendments to the end of the document.

1791   The states ratify the first ten amendments.

1798   The Eleventh Amendment becomes the first to reverse a U.S. Supreme Court decision.

            Hollingsworth v. Virginia decides that a presidential signature is not needed for constitutional amendments.

            The adoption of the Alien and Sedition Acts spurs the backing of the Virginia and Kentucky Resolutions challenging their constitutionality.

1800–1801   The presidential election, while peacefully passing power from the Federalists to the Democratic-Republicans, exposes flaws in the Constitution.

1803   In *Marbury v. Madison* the U.S. Supreme Court declares its power to invalidate unconstitutional federal legislation.

            The Twelfth Amendment is ratified to address problems with the election of 1800.

1815   The Hartford Convention meets in New England to discuss opposition to the War of 1812 and various constitutional reforms.

1819   The Supreme Court recognizes the existence of implied powers in upholding the constitutionality of the national bank in *McCulloch v. Maryland*.

1820s   Numerous states call conventions to revise their constitutions, most favoring increased democracy.

1828–1832   The Nullification Crisis ensues when southern states question the legitimacy of federal tariffs.

1831   *Smith v. Union Bank of Georgetown* suggests Supreme Court acceptance of limited conventions.

            The Anti-Mason Party holds the first national nominating convention, which soon becomes the norm for others.

1833   *Barron v. Baltimore* decides that the Bill of Rights only limits the national government.

1841   A peoples' convention meets in Rhode Island and proposes a new state constitution.

1848   The Seneca Falls Convention calls for woman suffrage.

1849   The Supreme Court articulates the political questions doctrine in *Luther v. Borden*.

1850   The Nashville Convention seeks compromise to avoid civil war.

1855–1858   A series of irregular conventions in Kansas stirs rising sectional tensions over slavery.

1857   The Supreme Court decides in *Dred Scott v. Sandford* that blacks are not, and cannot become, U.S. citizens.

1860   Abraham Lincoln is elected as the first Republican president.

1861   Twenty-one states send delegates to the Peace Convention in Washington, D.C.

Congress proposes the Corwin Amendment, which would have prohibited Congress from abolishing slavery within individual states.

Southern delegates meet in Montgomery to draft a provisional Confederate constitution.

Southern troops fire on Fort Sumter in South Carolina, triggering the Civil War.

1862   Sidney George Fisher advocates allowing Congress to exercise sovereignty in providing for constitutional changes.

1865   Abraham Lincoln is assassinated shortly after the end of the Civil War.

The ratification of the Thirteenth Amendment eliminates slavery.

1868   The Fourteenth Amendment provides citizenship to all persons born or naturalized in the United States, thus overturning the Dred Scott Decision.

1870   The Fifteenth Amendment forbids discrimination in voting on the basis of race or previous condition of servitude.

1867   Judge John Jameson publishes the first edition of his *Treatise on Constitutional Conventions* in which he argues that constitutional conventions are subaltern to the bodies that call them.

1865–1877   Congress attempts to "reconstruct" the South, leading to new state constitutions.

1876   United States celebrates the centennial of the Declaration of Independence.

1887   United States celebrates the centennial of the U.S. Constitution.

1893   Nebraska petitions Congress to call a convention to initiate direct election of U.S. senators. Since that time, most proposals have called for such limited conventions.

1896   Herman V. Ames publishes the first comprehensive list of proposed amendments.

U.S. Supreme Court upholds racial segregation under the doctrine of separate but equal.

1910   Walter Dodd publishes *The Revision and Amendment of State Constitutions*.

1913   The Sixteenth Amendment legitimizes the national income tax.

Congress proposes the Seventeenth Amendment, providing for direct election of senators after receiving numerous state calls for an Article V convention on the subject.

1917   Roger Sherman Hoar publishes his *Constitutional Conventions: Their Nature, Powers, and Limitations*.

1919   The Eighteenth Amendment provides for national prohibition of alcohol.

1920   States ratify the Nineteenth Amendment, which prohibits voting discrimination on the basis of sex.

The Supreme Court rules in the *National Prohibition Cases* that the power to prohibit national alcoholic consumption is within the powers of Article V.

The Supreme Court decides in *Hawke v. Smith* that states cannot require federal amendments to be ratified by popular referendum.

1921   In *Dillon v. Gloss*, the Supreme Court decides that Congress can establish reasonable time limits on the ratification of amendments that were designed to reflect a contemporary consensus.

1925   Congress proposes a child labor amendment.

1929   A stock market crash signals the beginning of the Great Depression.

1930   In *Coleman v. Miller*, the U.S. Supreme Court decides that issues of contemporaneousness of state ratifications of amendments were "political questions" for Congress to decide.

1932   Franklin D. Roosevelt is elected to his first term as U.S. president.

1933   States repeal national alcoholic prohibition in conventions called by Congress for this purpose.

1937   The U.S. Supreme Court gives greater deference to congressional exercises of power.

Roosevelt proposes legislation to "pack" the Supreme Court. His proposal fails, but the Court becomes more deferential to New Deal legislation.

1942   Lester B. Orfield publishes *The Amending of the Federal Constitution*.

1953   Earl Warren becomes Chief Justice of the United States.

1954   *Brown v. Board of Education* declares an end to the doctrine of "separate but equal" accommodations for blacks and whites.

1961   The Twenty-Third Amendment provides representation for the District of Columbia in the Electoral College.

1962   The Supreme Court's decision in *Baker v. Carr* and subsequent decisions lead numerous states to call for an Article V convention.

U.S. Supreme Court decision in *Engel v. Vitale* stirs numerous proposals for amendments permitting prayer in schools.

1963   President John F. Kennedy is assassinated in Dallas, Texas.

1964   The Twenty-Fourth Amendment prohibits the use of poll taxes in national elections.

Relying on its power to control interstate commerce, the Civil Rights Act prohibits discrimination in places of public accommodation.

1965   The Supreme Court decision in *Griswold v. Connecticut* striking down a Connecticut birth control law announces a right to privacy.

1967   States ratify Twenty-Fifth Amendment, providing for presidential disabilities and vice-presidential vacancies.

1968   Dr. Martin Luther King Jr. and Senator Robert Kennedy are both assassinated.

1971   The Twenty-Sixth Amendment prohibits discrimination in vote on the basis of age over eighteen.

1972   Congress proposes the Equal Rights Amendment.

1973   The American Bar Association issues a study arguing for the permissibility of limited Article V conventions.

In *Roe v. Wade*, the Supreme Court allows for wider use of abortion under its expanding privacy doctrine.

1974   Under threat of impeachment in the wake of the Watergate break-in, Richard M. Nixon becomes the first individual to resign the U.S. presidency. Gerald Ford, appointed as vice president under provisions outlined in the Twenty-Fifth Amendment, peacefully succeeds him.

1976   The United States celebrates the bicentennial of the Declaration of Independence.

1978   Congress proposes an amendment to treat the District of Columbia as though it were a state.

1979   Project 87 sponsors a conference in Houston on the constitutional convention as an amending device.

1981   Publication of *The Constitutional Convention as an Amending Device* (Kermit L. Hall, Harold M. Hyman, and Leon V. Sigal, eds.).

1987   United States celebrates the bicentennial of the U.S. Constitution.

1988   Russell L. Caplan publishes *Constitutional Brinkmanship*.

1989   Paul Weber and Barbara Perry publish *Unfounded Fears*.

1992   States finally ratify the Twenty-Seventh Amendment, which was first proposed in 1789 as part of the original Bill of Rights.

1994   Republican Contract for America promises to work for a number of amendments, including congressional term limits.

2000   Richard Labunski publishes *The Second Constitutional Convention: How the American People Can Take Back Their Government*.

2008   Barack Obama is elected, and he becomes the first African American president.

2011   Harvard University hosts a Conference on a Constitutional Convention (ConConCon) in September that brings together convention advocates from both the right and the left ends of the political spectrum.

2013   Nearly one hundred state legislators from thirty-two states meet at Mt. Vernon, Virginia, to discuss the possibility of an Article V convention.

Radio commentator Mark R. Levin publishes *The Liberty Amendments: Restoring the American Republic*.

2014   A second group of state legislators meets in Indianapolis to plan for a "Convention for Proposing Amendments."

Thomas E. Brennan publishes *The Article V Amendatory Constitutional Convention: Keeping the Republic in the Twenty-First Century*.

2015   States continue to petition Congress to call constitutional conventions.

NOTES

Preface

1. Vile, *Rewriting the United States Constitution*, and Vile, *Re-Framers*.
2. See Caplan, *Constitutional Brinkmanship*, and Weber and Perry. *Unfounded Fears*. See also Hall, Hyman, and Sigal, eds., *Constitutional Convention as Amending Device*.
3. Brennan, *Article V Amendatory Constitutional Convention*.
4. See "Articles of Freedom," http://www.articlesoffreedom.org/ArticlesofFreedom/ReadtheArticlesHTML.aspx. Accessed October 21, 2014.
5. Lessig, *Republic, Lost*. Also see Lessig, "Real Step to Fix Democracy."
6. Warren Mass, "Amendment Resolution Complements Wolf-PAC Con-Con Plan," *New American*, July 2, 2014. http://www.thenewamerican.com/usnews/constitution/item/18609-amendment-resolution-complements-wolf-pac-con-con-plan. Accessed October 26, 2014.
7. Kacprowicz, *Reclaiming America*.
8. Rodenkirch, *Constitutional Balance Amendment*.
9. Albert, "Constitution Disuse or Desuetude."
10. Fukuyama, *Political Order and Political Decay*, 488–505.
11. Barber, *Constitutional Failure*.
12. Toobin, "Our Broken Constitution."
13. Main, *Is the American Constitution Obsolete?* It should be noted, however, that Main's book does not end with a positive affirmation but with pro and con discussions of major proposals for constitutional reform. A French writer, Jean-Philippe Immarigeon, who thinks that the U.S. president should be able to call elections to resolve controversies with Congress, has weighed in by saying that America's response to recent economic crises "suggests that the country's institutional dysfunction is no longer a consequence of perpetual crisis but rather its cause" ("Dissolve Congress," 51). For the argument that much of this kind of criticism is based on a misunderstanding of Congress, see Rosenthal, Loomis, Hibbing, and Kurtz, *Republic on Trial*.
14. Jessica Mason, "ALEC's Jeffersonian Project Pushes to Amend Constitution," PR Watch, http://www.prwatch.org/news/2014/07/12554/alecs-jeffersonian-project-pushes-amend-us-constitution. Accessed October 25, 2014.
15. Natelson, *Proposing Constitutional Amendments*. As I indicate later in this book, although I agree with Natelson in believing that states can propose single-issue conventions,

I believe that the primary responsibility for calling, and therefore governing, the convention rests first with Congress and then with convention delegates themselves and that much of Natelson's otherwise fine historical work is otherwise wide of the mark.

16. State Legislators Article V Caucus, "About," http://articlevcaucus.com/about/. Accessed June 21, 2014.

17. Citizens for Self Government, *Convention of States: A Handbook for Legislators and Citizens*, 3rd ed., found at SelfGovern.com. Accessed June 20, 2014.

18. Taken from website "The Madison Coalition: Restoring a Balance of State and Federal Power," at http://www.madisoncoalition.org/.

19. Compact for America, http://www.compactforamerica.org/about-2/. Accessed June 28, 2014. The Board of Directors consists of Nick Dranias, the Director of Policy Development and Constitutional Government at the Goldwater Institute, Harold R. ("Chip") DeMoss, III, Managing Director of Tanglewood Capital Partners, and Kyle McAlister, CEOP of the Questor Pipeline Company.

20. Levin, *The Liberty Amendments*.

21. Lauer, *I Overthrew the Government*; Howard Strassner, *Bill of Rights for Our Posterity: Journal of the Second Constitutional Convention* (Amazon Digital Services, 2014); Hambleton, *The Convention*; Andrews, *Convention* (chapter 25 includes the text of a proposed new constitution); Rudomanski, *Article V*; Strout, *Restoration*; O'Kane, *Constitutional Convention of 2022*; Enns, *Sword of Liberty*; and Donohue, *Capitol Bypass*. Rudomanski appears to be under the mistaken impression that Article V contains only the convention mechanism, although he does recognize that the convention method is a way of bypassing Congress.

22. John Michelthwait and Adrian Woolridge, *The Fourth Revolution: The Global Race to Reinvent the State* (New York: Penguin Press, 2014).

23. Rob Natelson, "Momentum for an Amendments Convention Accelerates Even More," June 15, 2014, http://constitution.i2i.org/2014/06/15/momentum-for-an-amendments-convention-accelerates-even-more/. Accessed June 20, 2014.

24. For a similar observation, see Byron DeLear, "Fiver Movement Splits into Two Camps: Tea Party and Open-Convention Supporters," Examiner.com, February 24, 2014, http://www.examiner.com/article/fiver-movement-splits-into-two-camps-tea-party-and-open-convention-supporters. Accessed July 31, 2014.

25. Language used in a website titled "Secure Arkansas," on December 9, 2013, and purposing to list numerous organizations that both favor and disfavor a convention, that the website believes would be dangerous. See http://securetherepublic.com/arkansas/2013/12/09/exposing-the-convention-of-the-states-cos-as-an-article-v-constitutional-convention/. Accessed July 5, 2014).

Thomas E. Brennan has documented strong opposition to a convention on the part of such diverse groups and individuals as the John Birch Society, former chief justice Warren Burger, Phyllis Schlafly's Eagle Forum, former congressman Ron Paul, the pseudonymous Publius Hulda, Professor Louis Michael Seidman, and others. See *Article V Amendatory Constitutional Convention*, 43–63.

26. See, for example, Schlafly, "Mischief-Making about the Constitution."

27. Thomas E. Brennan discusses many of these critics in a chapter titled "The Yeas and Nays," in *Article V Amendatory Constitutional Convention*, 43–63.

28. Vile, *Constitutional Convention of 1787*; Vile, *Writing and Ratification*; Vile, *Men Who*

Made the Constitution; Vile, *"Wisest Council in the World"*; and Vile, Pederson, and Williams, eds. *James Madison*.

29. These include Vile, *Constitutional Amending Process*; Vile, *Contemporary Questions*; Vile, ed., *Theory and Practice of Constitutional Change*; Vile, *Constitutional Change*.

30. Vile, ed. *Proposed Amendments*; Vile, *Encyclopedia of Constitutional Amendments*.

31. These have been compiled in Contiades, ed., *Engineering Constitutional Change*. For a similar book, see Dawn Oliver and Carlo Fusaro, eds., *How Constitutions Change: A Comparative Study* (Oxford: Hart Publishing, 2013).

32. Vile, *Companion*; Vile, *United States Constitution*; and Vile, *Essential Supreme Court Decisions*.

33. Vile, "The Supreme Court and the Amending Process." I followed up a second seminar at Princeton under Walter Murphy with "Judicial Review of the Amending Process."

34. Vile, *Contemporary Questions*, 55–73.

Chapter 1. The Constitutional Convention of 1787 and Its Origins

1. Article V of the U.S. Constitution.

2. Friends of the Article V Convention, "Congressional Records," http://foavc.org/file. php/1/Amendments. Accessed April 23, 2014. The report credits Boughey and Sickle, "Lawful and Peaceful Revolution," as its primary source. The report cautions that some of the petitions may be redundant, and the list appears to include state rescissions of convention calls. In 1993 the appendix to Paulsen, "General Theory of Article V," listed 399 state applications for Article V conventions and includes one or more petition from each state.

3. In "A General Theory of Article V," Michael Stokes Paulsen argued that thirty-four states had called for a general Article V convention and that Congress was therefore obligated to call one, but in "How to Count to Thirty-four," he concluded that enough states had rescinded earlier calls that only thirty-three of the needed thirty-four had current applications before Congress.

4. Lutz, *Origins of American Constitutionalism*.

5. This has not eliminated some continuing role for customs and usages that supplement constitutional language. See Foley, *Silence of Constitutions*.

6. Willi Paul Adams, *First American Constitutions*, 59.

7. *Lutz, Origins of American Constitutionalism*, 133. Lutz further identified eighty-six "constitution-like documents" written in America that preceded these, and another forty-two that were written in Great Britain for the colonies; see 129–33.

   Although state conventions had an important influence on subsequent constitutional development, the nature of state and federal constitutions subsequently took different routes, with state documents being considerably more detailed than the federal counterpart and subject to considerably more changes. For an explication of such differences, see Morton Keller, "The Politics of State Constitutional Revision, 1820–1930," in Hall, Hyman, and Sigal, eds., *Constitutional Convention as Amending Device*, 67–86.

8. Dodd, *Revision and Amending of State Constitutions*, 24.

9. *Notes on the State of Virginia*, 115–19. Jefferson had previously informed the state legislature that it "should elect deputies" to write a state constitution, although this had

not prevented him from sending the legislature a proposed draft of such a document. See Cheney, *James Madison*, 60–61. For further reflections on the transition from legislative to convention ratification of constitutions, see Kay, "Constituent Authority."

10. Dodd, *Revision and Amending of State Constitutions*, 24–25.

11. For information on Kent, see Johnson, "Kent, James," in Vile, ed., *Great American Judges*.

12. Street, *Council of Revision of the State of New York*, 390.

13. Ibid., 391.

14. Ibid., 393.

15. Samuel Johnson had defined the word "convention" as 1. "The act of coming together; union; coalition; junction"; 2. "An assembly"; and as 3. "A contract; an agreement for a time, previous to a definitive treaty." *Dictionary of the English Language*.

16. Robert G. Natelson thus observes that "the founding generation employed the word convention in the political context to denote an assembly that, unlike a legislature, was assembled for a particular project, to be dissolved once its work was complete. In other words, a sort of ad hoc committee." "James Madison," 432.

17. Caplan, *Constitutional Brinkmanship*, 5. Also see Braxton, "Powers of Conventions," 83.

18. Henry Baldwin, *General View of the Origin and Nature of the Constitution and Government of the United States*, 56. Italics in this and the following quotation are from the original.

19. Ibid., 56–57.

20. J. Franklin Jameson, "Early Political Uses of the Word Convention," 485.

21. Natelson, "Founding-Era Conventions," 1–2. Natelson concluded that the structure of such conventions, which fairly consistently included a call establishing the time and place of the gathering but allowed states (usually the legislatures) to choose their delegates and decide on how many delegates to send, pay them, decide whether to instruct them or not, was so well established by 1787 that Article V conventions are necessarily bound by the same requirements.

    In my judgment, the adoption of both the Fourteenth and Seventeenth Amendments, and their increased emphasis on equality and democratic accountability, suggest that today's public would not be satisfied with such requirements. Moreover, as discussed in a subsequent chapter, debates at the Constitutional Convention of 1787 indicated some serious questions about the operation of *constitutional* conventions, suggesting that Natelson has overstated the degree of consensus on the subject.

22. Quoted in John Alexander Jameson, *Treatise on Constitutional Conventions*, 304.

23. Ibid.

24. See John R. Vile, "John Alexander Jameson's Enduring Constitutional Legacy," intro. to John Alexander Jameson, *Treatise on Constitutional Conventions*, v–xxi.

25. Ibid., 4.

26. Ibid., 6 (all three quotations from this page).

27. Ibid., 10.

28. Thorpe, *Federal and State Constitutions*, 5:3053–54.

29. Ibid., 5:3052.

30. Traynor, *Amending System of the United States Constitution*, 61–62.

31. For these resolutions, see Solberg, ed., *Federal Convention*, 32.

32. For further information on Dickinson, see Vile, *Men Who Made the Constitution*, 48–60.

33. "Circular Letter of Congress Recommending the Adoption of the Articles of Confederation, In Congress, Yorktown, November 17th, 1777," appendix 1 of George

Ticknor Curtis, *History of the Origin, Formation, and Adoption of the Constitution of the United States; with Notices of Its Principal Framers* (New York: Harper and Brothers, 1861), 1:492.

34. Quoted from Jarred Sparks, *The Life of Benjamin Franklin* (Boston: Tappan, Whittemore and Mason, 1840), chap. 9 n.62, by Walter Isaacson, *Benjamin Franklin: An American Life* (New York: Simon and Schuster, 2003), 313.

35. See his "Vices of the Political System of the United States," which he wrote in April 1787. Madison, *Mind of the Founder*, 83–92.

36. Solberg, ed., *Federal Convention*, 42.

37. Ibid., 51.

38. Clark, "Eleventh Amendment," 1840–42.

39. "Attempts to Revise the Articles of Confederation," Department of History, University of Wisconsin–Madison, Center for the Study of the American Constitution, http://history. wisc.edu/csac/documentary_resources/attempts_to_revise.thm.

40. Ibid.

41. Richard B. Morris, "Mount Vernon Conference," 38–40.

42. Quoted from the Resolution of the General Assembly of Virginia, January 21, 1786, in Solberg, ed., *Federal Convention*, 54.

   In a contemporary update, about a hundred delegates from 32 states met against at Mt. Vernon in December 2013 and again in Indianapolis in June 2014, to discuss an Article V convention. See Thomas Lifson, "Indiana to host meeting for planning Constitutional Convention," *American Thinker*, May 5, 2014. http://www.americanthinker.com/ blog/2014/05/indiana_to_host_meeting_for_planning_constitutional_convention_ comments.html. Accessed May 29, 2014.

43. Rakove, "Gamble at Annapolis," 5–10.

44. I acknowledge consulting the work of Van Sickle and Boughey, "Lawful and Peaceful Revolution," in refining the analysis in this chapter.

45. Solberg, ed., *Federal Convention*, 64.

46. Robert A. Feer, "Shays's Rebellion and the Constitution." Fritz presents a very sympathetic reading of this event, in which he argues that the regulators who participated in the event that closed down local courthouses drew from revolutionary rhetoric of the rights of the people to control government. See *American Sovereigns*, 80–116.

47. Solberg, ed., *Federal Convention*, 64.

48. See his essays, "Of Ancient and Modern Confederacies" (1786), and "Vices of the Political System" (1787), in Meyers, ed., *Mind of the Founder*, 69–81 and 82–92.

49. Rutland, "Virginia Plan of 1787," 23–30.

50. See Kammen, *Machine That Would Go of Itself*.

51. Hamilton, Madison, John Jay, *Federalist Papers*, 315.

52. Ibid.

53. For prominent analyses of the Articles, see Hoffert, *Politics of Tensions*; McDonald and McDonald, eds., *Confederation and Constitution*; and McLaughlin, *Confederation and Constitution*.

54. Hendrickson, *Peace Pact*; Marks, "Foreign Affairs."

55. Thus, on June 30 Gunning Bedford Jr. of Delaware stirred considerable alarm when he observed, "The Large States dare not dissolve the confederation. If they do the small ones will find some foreign ally of more honor and good faith, who will take them by the hand and do them justice." See Farrand, ed., *Records of the Federal Convention*, 1:492.

56. Alexis DeTocqueville, *Democracy in America*, ed. J. P. Mayer (Garden City, N.Y.: Anchor Books, 1969). Huq, "Function of Article V," stresses the role of Article V, and its "formal rigidity," as one of the catalysts in the early years of the Republic to develop institutions, like political parties, that have subsequently provided for "informal flexibility" that has supplemented Article V processes of change.

57. Thomas Paine, *Common Sense and Other Writings*, ed. with an introduction by Gordon Wood (New York: Modern Library, 2003), 5.

58. Richard S. Patterson and Richardson Dougall, *The Eagle and the Shield: A History of the Great Seal of the United States* (n.p.: University Press of the Pacific, 2005).

59. Hamilton, Madison, and Jay, Federalist No. 49, 315.

60. Vile, *Wisest Council in the World*.

61. See Vile, *Men Who Made the Constitution*.

62. Hamilton, Madison, and Jay, Federalist No. 49, 315.

63. Gilhooley, "Framers Themselves."

64. Edward J. Larson has recently reemphasized the importance of Washington to the writing of the U.S. Constitution in *Return of George Washington*.

65. Garry Wills, *Cincinnatus: George Washington and the Enlightenment* (New York: Doubleday, 1984).

66. In Federalist No. 10, p, 82, James Madison, thus lauded representative democracy over pure democracy because the former sought "to refine and enlarge the public views by passing them through the medium of a chosen body of citizens, whose wisdom may best discern the true interest of their country and whose patriotism and love of justice will be least likely to sacrifice it to temporary or partial considerations."

67. Natelson, "Founding-Era Conventions."

68. Vile, "Wythe, George," in *Great American Lawyers: An Encyclopedia*, ed. John R. Vile, 2 vols. (Santa Barbara, Calif.: ABC-CLIO, 2001), 2:735.

69. Vile, *Constitutional Convention of 1787*, 2:683.

70. Farrand, *Records of the Federal Convention*, 1:11–12.

71. Webb, "Original Meaning of Civility," 190.

72. Dellinger, "1787," and Finkelman, *Slavery and the Founders*.

73. Roche, "Founding Fathers," does a particularly good job of demonstrating all the groups that the convention attempted to please with the development of the Electoral College.

74. Farrand, *Records of the Federal Convention*, 2:137.

75. Graber, *New Introduction to American Constitutionalism*, 194.

76. Elster, "Arguing and Bargaining," 411.

77. Mansbridge et al., *Negotiating Agreement in Politics*, 106–14.

78. Joseph Ellis, *Founding Brothers*, 51.

79. See, for example, Alexander, *Selling of the Constitutional Convention*.

80. Historian Cecelia Kenyon was particularly known for describing the Antifederalists as "men of little faith." See Kenyon, *Men of Little Faith*. For a more appreciative view, see Lim, *Lovers' Quarrel*.

81. The best collection of Antifederalist writings continues to be Herbert J. Storing, ed., *Complete Anti-Federalists*.

82. There is growing commentary on ratification of the Constitution. See Maier, *Ratification* and Jurgen Heideking, *Constitution before the Judgment Seat*.

83. Vile, *Constitutional Convention of 1787*, 1:274.

84. Catherine Drinker Bowen, *Miracle at Philadelphia*.

85. On this subject, see Kay, "Illegality of the Constitution," and Rakove, "Super-Legality of the Constitution."

86. Adams was serving in a diplomatic role in England and Jefferson in France. Henry said that he "smelt a rat."

87. Hamilton, Madison and Jay, *Federalist Papers*, 33.

Chapter 2. The Establishment of the Amending Provisions in Article V and the Ratification Provisions in Article VII

1. Farrand, ed., *Records of the Federal Convention*, 1:22.

2. Professor William J. Quirk, *Courts and Congress*, believes that this was an important part of the Virginia Plan and of its system of checks and balances. He explains that "if the central government started to exceed its powers, the states by amendment could call it back. Of course, the government that was exceeding its powers would not consent to limit itself" (204).

3. Farrand, *Records of the Federal Convention*, 1:121.

4. See Weber and Perry, *Unfounded Fears*, 32–33.

5. Farrand, *Records of the Federal Convention*, 1:122.

6. Ibid., 1:202–3.

7. Ibid., 1:242.

8. Ibid., 1:475–76. King's notes further record that Madison had observed that "the Defects of the Amphictionick League were acknowledged, but they never cd. Be reformed." See ibid., 1:478.

9. Ibid., 1:476.

10. Ibid., 2:87, 88. In a fascinating update to this issue, James W. Lucas, an attorney and entrepreneur, has recently proposed a number of amendments to the U.S. Constitution, one of which would require that "upon any amendment of this Constitution, all judicial Officers of the United States shall renew their Oath or Affirmation to support this Constitution." See Lucas, *Timely Renewed*, 229. Also see "The Faith to Change: Reconciling the Oath to Uphold with the Power to Amend," *Harvard Law Review* 109 (May 1996): 1747–64.

11. Farrand, *Records of the Federal Convention*, 2:88.

12. Ibid., 2:133, 159, 468.

13. Ibid., 2:557–58.

14. Ibid., 2:558.

15. Ibid.

16. Ibid., 2:558–59.

17. Schwartzberg, *Counting the Many*, 148.

18. Farrand, *Records of the Federal Convention*, 2:559.

19. Ibid.

20. Ibid., 2:629. The spaces are in the original because the final configuration of sections had yet to be decided.

21. Ibid.

22. What is less clear is whether Mason would have equated the people with state legislatures, with state conventions, or with both. Mason had on June 7 favored the appointment of

U.S. Senators by state legislatures on the basis that "the State Legislatures also ought to have some means of defending themselves agst. Encroachments of the Natl. Govt." Ibid., 1:155. Acknowledging that "we have only seen the evisl arising on the side of the State Govts.," he commented that "those on the other side remain to be displayed." Ibid, 1:156.

23. Ibid., 2:629. Mason thereby clearly distinguished the people from Congress, but it is unclear whether his generic reference to "the people" referred to state legislatures or whether it referred to the people of the states as represented in conventions. Natelson's analysis (*State Initiation of Constitutional Amendments*) essentially avoids this issue by equating state conventions to *instruments* of the state legislatures rather than possible *substitutes* for them.

24. Ibid., 2:629n8.

25. Ibid., 2:629.

26. Ibid., 2:629–30. Madison's comments call into question Natelson's view that widespread precedents had already settled such issues.

27. In opposing the idea of limited conventions, Walter Dellinger, argues that the acceptance of this change indicated that delegates did not think that state legislators should "be given authority to propose amendments without the involvement of some national body in the formulation of such amendments," and that "to permit the state legislatures to dictate to the convention the exact terms of its proposal is to short-circuit the carefully structured division of authority between state and national interests" ("Recurring Question," 1:632). William W. Van Alstyne responds that "the question is the extent of the check this provided" and believes that even a limited constitutional convention would fit the bill ("Limited Constitutional Convention," 993).

28. Farrand, *Records of the Federal Convention*, 2:630–31.

29. Ibid., 2:631.

30. U.S. Constitution, Article V. The article consists of a single sentence. One of the more exotic treatments of this Article provides a Reed-Kellogg diagram of the sentence designed to show "that the Article makes itself absolutely clear without interference of 'constitutionalists,' Constitutional lawyers, judges, or politicians." See Ruff, The Constitution According to English: Article V., Published by The Sherman Institute on a website entitled "Managing an Article V Constitutional Convention: The Con-Con." http://www.slideshare.net/nikihannevig/article-v-public-version. Accessed 6/1/2014. This extensive site consists of numerous articles largely devoted to arguing against the wisdom of calling such a convention.

31. Because the Great Compromise represented states on the basis of population in one house and in the other equally, the bicameral requirement gives weight to both factors in proposing amendments. The two-thirds majority required of both houses is what the Constitution requires to override presidential vetoes. This likely accounts for the provision's failure to mention the president in the amending process.

32. Because this language is so similar to that of the necessary and proper clause in Article I, Section 8, which John Marshall interpreted so capaciously in *McCulloch v. Maryland*, 4 Wheaton (17 U.S.) 316 (1819) by distinguishing "necessary" from the corresponding language in Article I, Section 10 limiting inspection duties to those which were "absolutely necessary," one might doubt that the Framers intended for the words "shall deem it necessary" to serve as significant limits. This might, however, be an anachronistic reading based on an interpretation with which the authors of *The Federalist* would have been unaware.

33. This, like the Framers' decision to submit the Constitution to state conventions rather than to state legislatures for approval, indicates that the Framers recognized that the two institutions might not have identical interests, especially with respect to institutional interests. One of the great difficulties in interpreting Article V, and especially in interpreting the convention mechanism, is that of understanding whether the Framers anticipated that state conventions would largely *echo* state calls for amendments or whether they would act differently than state legislatures might have done had it been possible to convene them.

34. Jack Rakove has pointed out that Madison thought the original intent of those who ratified the Constitution was even more important than those who wrote it. *Original Meanings*, 17–18.

35. Hamilton, Madison, and Jay, *Federalist Papers*, 246.
    Madison's terminology is potentially confusing because, as Nicholas Aroney explains: "In Madison's day, the terms 'federal' and 'confederal' were used more or less interchangeably, and were contrasted to 'national' or 'consolidated' systems of government." See Aboney, "Formation, Representation and Amendment," 306.

36. Hamilton, Madison, and Jay, *Federalist Papers*, 246. One oddity of Madison's argument is that it seems to attribute the need for supermajorities to amend or replace constitutions to federalism rather than to the need for adequate deliberation or the necessity of protecting minority rights. This may indicate that Madison necessarily equated unitary (or national) governments, like that of Great Britain, with parliamentary sovereignty.

37. Ibid., 279–80. There is ambiguity in Madison's use of the word "originate" in his statement that Article V "equally enables the general and the State government to originate the amendment of errors"; does this mean that states, like Congress, have the same power to propose texts of proposed amendments (as in a single-issue constitutional convention), or does it simply vest states with the ability to call Article V conventions that will propose such amendments on their own?

38. Bailey, "Should We Venerate That Which We Cannot Love?," 733.

39. Hamilton, Madison, and Jay, *Federalist Papers*, 313–14.

40. Ibid., 314.

41. Ibid., 315, 317.

42. For a discussion of this mechanism, see Meador, "Council of Censors."

43. Hamilton, Madison, and Jay, *Federalist Papers*, 314.

44. Matthew Spalding and Trent England, *Article V: Congress, Conventions, and Constitutional Amendments* (Washington, D.C.: Heritage Foundation), 2011, 4, observe that the only subsequent time that Madison advocated a national convention was "during the Nullification Crisis of 1832 as a last-ditch effort to prevent the wholly unacceptable and unconstitutional alternative of nullification and secession that then threatened the continued existence of the United States." They further note that Lincoln advocated a similar convention during the Civil War because it "allows amendments to originate with the people themselves, instead of only permitting them to take or reject propositions originated by others, not especially chosen for the purpose" (*Article V*, 4).

45. For a modern study examining the influence of constitutional amending processes and other factors on constitutional stability, see Ginsburg, Elkins, And Melton, *Endurance of National Constitutions*.

46. See, for example, Epstein, *Political Theory of "The Federalist,"* 133–36.

47. See Weber and Perry, *Unfounded Fears*, 31–32. They cite a letter from Madison to George

Lee Turberville dated November 2, 1788: "If a General Convention were to take place for the avowed and sole purpose of revising the Constitution, it would naturally consider itself as having a greater latitude than the Congress appointed to administer and support as well as to amend the system; it would consequently give greater agitation to the public mind; and election into it would be courted by the most violent partizans on both sides; it would probably consist of the most heterogeneous characters; would be the very focus of that flame which had already too much heated men of all parties; would no doubt contain individuals of insidious views, who under the mask of seeking alterations popular in some parts but inadmissible in other parts of the Union might have a dangerous opportunity of sapping the very foundation of the fabric. Under all these circumstances it seems scarcely to be presumable that the deliberations of the body could be conducted in harmony, or terminate the general good. Having witnessed the difficulties and dangers experienced by the first Convention which assembled under every propitious circumstance, I should tremble for the result of a Second."

48. In a letter to Edmund Randolph dated January 8, 1788, Washington wrote: "To my judgment, it is more clear than ever, that an attempt to amend the Constitution which is submitted, would be productive of more heat, & greater confusion than can well be conceived." See Farrand, *Records of the Federal Convention*, 3:242.

49. Hamilton, Madison, and Jay, *Federalist Papers*, 470.

50. Paul C. Light discussed this essay in "Federalist No. 85: Has the National Government Become an 'Awful Spectacle'?" *Public Administration Review* 72, supp. 1 (December 2011): S155–S159, but he did not focus on Hamilton's view with respect to limiting such a convention.

51. Hamilton, Madison, and Jay, *Federalist Papers*, 523.

52. Farrand, *Records of the Federal Convention*, 2:641–43. Franklin had observed that "when you assemble a number of men to have the advantage of their joint wisdom, you inevitably assemble with those men, all their prejudices, their passions, their errors of opinion, their local interests, and their selfish views" (2:642). He had gone on to observe that: "It therefor astonishes me, Sir, to find this system approaching so near to perfect as it does" (2:642), and noted that "I consent, Sir to this Constitution because I expect no better, and because I am not sure, that it is not the best" (3:643).

53. Hamilton, Madison, and Jay, *Federalist Papers*, 523–24.

54. After having said that "the chances are as thirteen to nine in favor of subsequent amendment, rather than of the original adoption of an entire system," Hamilton added a † with the correction that "it may rather be said TEN, for though two thirds may set on foot the measure, three fourths must ratify" (ibid.).

55. Ibid.

56. Ibid., 525.

57. Ibid.

58. Ibid. In addition to believing that national officials would be likely to propose "any amendments which may, upon mature consideration, be thought useful," Hamilton also believed that the necessity of governing thirteen states would "constantly *impose* on the national rulers the *necessity* of a spirit of accommodation to the reasonable expectations of their constituents."

59. Ibid., 526. Hamilton goes on to repeat Madison's assertions that the amending process will not be too difficult by observing, on the same page, "Nor however difficult it may be supposed to unite two thirds or three fourths of the State legislatures in amendments

which may affect local interests can there be any room to apprehend any such difficulty in a union on points which are merely relative to the general liberty or security of the people. We may safely rely on the disposition of the State legislatures to erect barriers against the encroachments of the national authority."

60. Ibid., 525.

61. Moreover, the argument was repeated at the state ratifying conventions. See Lash "Rejecting Conventional Wisdom," 210n80, 213.

62. Hamilton, Madison, and Jay, *Federalist Papers*, 526.

63. Ibid., 527.

64. Lash, "Rejecting Convention Wisdom," 211.

65. Elliot, *Debates in State Conventions*, 4:477.

66. Ibid., 3:49–50.

67. Ibid., 3:101, 102. In quoting this passage, Lash, "Rejecting Conventional Wisdom," notes that "It was not clear whether Nicholas was expressing his *hope*, or whether he believed conventions under Article V could be limited" (213n102).

68. For their correspondence on the subject, see James Morton Smith, ed., *Republic of Letters*, 1:518–90.

69. Weber and Perry, *Unfounded Fears*, 31–54.

70. For Madison's work, see Labunski, *Madison and the Struggle for the Bill of Rights*; and Goldwin, *From Parchment to Power*. For Madison's (and other representatives') arguments in the House of Representatives, see Kurland and Lerner, eds., *Founders' Constitution*, 5:20–40.

71. Kobach, "Rethinking Article V," 1985. The U.S. Supreme Court further affirmed this in *Dodge v. Woolsey*: "It [the Constitution] is supreme over the people of the United States, aggregately and in their separate sovereignties, because they have excluded themselves from any direct or immediate agency in making amendments to it, and have directed that amendments should be made representatively for them, by the congress of the United States, when two thirds of both houses shall propose them; or where the legislatures of two thirds of the several states shall call a convention for proposing amendments, which, in either case, become valid, to all intents and purposes, as part of the constitution, when ratified by the legislatures of three fourths of the several States, or by conventions in three fourths of them, as one or the other mode of ratification may be proposed by Congress" (348).

72. Moore, "Variable Constitutional Authority," 232.

73. Sanford Levinson, "Twenty-first Century Rediscovery," 43.

74. Platz, "Article Five of the Federal Constitution," 37.

75. One of the more bizarre proposals that I have encountered for amending today's Constitution provides that "nothing in the Constitution prevents two-thirds of the states from ratifying the Constitution (including 27 amendments) with the Constitutional Balance Amendment added at the end. As soon as this happens, the Constitutional Balance Amendment will be in full effect for every state that completes this ratification and cannot be re-interpreted or blocked by Congress." See Rodenkirch, *Constitutional Balance Amendment*.

76. Farrand, *Records of the Federal Convention*, 1:22. I have not figured out why the resolution does not, at this point, specifically identify such assemblies as conventions, although this might simply confirm that the latter term originated from the former.

77. Ibid., 1:122–23.

78. Ibid., 1:123.
79. Ibid., 1:335.
80. Ibid., 2:87, 88, 89.
81. Ibid.
82. Ibid., 2:90.
83. Ibid.
84. Gordon Wood, *Creation of the American Republic*, 306–43. Notably, when James Madison introduced the Bill of Rights in the first Congress, he was met by the objection that the Congress had far more pressing matters at hand connected to the establishment of the new government.
85. Farrand, *Records of the Federal Convention*, 2:91.
86. Ibid., 2:91, 92.
87. Ibid., 2:92.
88. Ibid., 2:93. This motion, which would have gone even farther than that under consideration in emphasizing the consolidated nature of the new government, did not get a second.
89. Ibid., 2:468. At this point the provision still left the number of state conventions blank.
90. Ibid., 2:468, 469.
91. Ibid., 2:476.
92. Ibid.
93. Ibid., 2:477.
94. Ibid., 2:478.
95. Ibid., 2:479.
96. Ibid., 2:560.
97. Ibid., 2:561. Randolph thus distinguished a "General Convention" from mere ratifying conventions.
98. Ibid., 2:561, 562.
99. Ibid., 2:631, 632.
100. Ibid., 2:632, 633.
101. Article VII, U.S. Constitution thus specifies that "The Ratification of the Conventions of nine States shall be sufficient for the Establishment of this Constitution between the States so ratifying the Same."
102. Moore, "Variable Constitutional Authority," 229.
103. Hamilton, Madison, and Jay, *Federalist Papers*, 243–44.
104. Ibid., 248. For the resolution from which Madison was quoting, see Solberg, ed., *Federal Convention*, 64.
105. Hamilton, Madison, and Jay, *Federalist Papers*, 251, 252.
106. Ibid., 253. The phrase Madison was attempting to quote (apparently from memory) from the Declaration of Independence had said "that whenever any Form of Government becomes destructive of these ends, it is the Right of the People to alter or to abolish it, and to institute new Government, laying its foundation on such principles and organizing its powers in such form, as to them shall seem most likely to effect their Safety and Happiness."
107. Ibid.
108. Ibid., 279, 280.
109. Farrand, *Records of The Federal Convention*, 1:335, 2:632.

110. Letter found in Hammond, Wardwick, and Lubert, *Classics of American Political and Constitutional Thought*, 1:962.

111. Vile, "Ann Diamond," 177–83. This was in partial response to Diamond, "A Convention for Proposing Amendments."

Chapter 3. The History of Constitutional Amendments in the United States

1. For lists of these proposals, which reprint earlier treatments of the subject, see Vile, ed., *Proposed Amendments*.

2. See, for example, Kyvic, *Explicit and Authentic Acts*; Bernstein, *Amending America*; Grimes, *Democracy and the Amendments*; Grossman, *Constitutional Amendments*; Palmer, ed., *Constitutional Amendments*; Pendergast, Pendergast, and Sousnir, *Constitutional Amendments*; and Anastaplo, *Amendments to the Constitution*.

3. Vile, *Constitutional Convention of 1787*, 2:657. This compromise chiefly originated during the ratification debates over the Constitution in Massachusetts.

4. *Marbury v. Madison*, 5 U.S. 137, 176 (1803).

5. Steven Brown, "Mirroring Madison," in Vile, Pederson, and J. Williams, eds., *James Madison*, 164.

6. Hartnett, "A 'Uniform and Entire' Constitution"; Payandeh, "Constitutional Aesthetics."

7. See Vile, Hudson, and Schultz, eds., *Encyclopedia of the First Amendment*.

8. *District of Columbia v. Heller*, 5554 U.S. 570 (2008) and *McDonald v. Chicago*, 566 U.S. 3025 (2010). The first decision applied to the national government and the second to the states.

9. Vile and Hudson, eds., *Encyclopedia of the Fourth Amendment*.

10. *Weeks v. United States*, 232 U.S. 383 (1914).

11. *Mapp v. Ohio*, 367 U.S. 643 (1961).

12. Akhil Reed Amar, *Bill of Rights*, 78. It seems just as likely, however, that the Framers would have thought that a provision against arbitrary governmental takings was closely tied to the general protection of "life, liberty, and property" listed in the same amendment.

13. *Kelo v. City of New London*, 545 U.S. 469 (2005), thus permitted a city to condemn a private home to enhance economic development.

14. *Gideon v. Wainwright*, 372 U.S. 335 (1963).

15. Bessler, *Cruel and Unusual*.

16. Barnett, ed., *Rights Retained by the People*; and Massey, *Silent Rights*.

17. 32 U.S. 243 (1833).

18. For a detailed development of this process of "incorporation," see Abraham and Perry, *Freedom and the Court*.

19. Chipman, *Sketches*.

20. Ibid., 286. Here, and in other quotations, I have changed old-style elongated s's that can like like f's to modern s's where appropriate.

21. Ibid., 289–90.

22. Ibid., 291.

23. Ibid.

24. 2 U.S. (2 Dal.) 419 (1793).

25. Kurt T. Lash, *The Lost History of the Ninth Amendment* (New York: Oxford University Press, 2009).

26. Vose, *Constitutional Change*, xxiii.

27. Kuroda, *Origins of the Twelfth Amendment*; Hawley, "Transformative Twelfth Amendment."

28. This statement was from Lincoln's "House Divided Speech," delivered in Springfield, Illinois, on June 16, 1858. "House Divided" speech by Abraham Lincoln, http://www.abrahamlincolnonline.org/lincoln/speeches/house.htm. Accessed May 7, 2014.

29. Allen C. Guelzom, *Lincoln's Emancipation Proclamation: The End of Slavery in America* (New York: Simon and Schuster, 3005).

30. Vorenberg, *Final Freedom*.

31. 60 U.S. (19 How.) 393 (1857).

32. For an illuminating discussion of this elusive phrase, see Lash, *Fourteenth Amendment*.

33. William E. Nelson, *Fourteenth Amendment*; Maltz, *Civil Rights, the Constitution, and Congress*; and Meyer, *Amendment That Refused to Die*.

34. Gillette, *Right to Vote*.

35. Thus, in the *Slaughterhouse Cases*, 16 Wallace (83 U.S.) 36 (1873), the Court narrowly interpreted the privileges and immunities clause of the Fourteenth Amendment; in the *Civil Rights Cases*, 109 U.S. 3 (1883), it limited the scope of the Civil Rights Act of 1875 by narrowly defining state action; and in *Plessy v. Ferguson*, 163 U.S. 537 (1896), it endorsed racial segregation under the separate but equal doctrine. In a recent book, Chinn argues that it has been common in U.S. history for periods of reforms to be compromised in intervening years. See his *Recalibrating Reform*.

36. The most important of these cases was, of course, *Brown v. Board of Education*, 347 U.S. 483 (1954), which reversed the decision upholding racial segregation in *Plessy v. Ferguson*.

37. Chin and Abraham thus point out that states have continued their post-ratification adoption of amendments so that all three Reconstruction Amendments as well as the Nineteenth Amendment have been unanimously ratified. See "Beyond the Supermajority."

38. See his *We the People: Foundations*; *We the People: Transformation*; and *We the People: The Civil Rights Revolution*. Ackerman argues that three transformative events in U.S. constitutional history (the writing of the Constitution in 1787, the ratification of the Reconstruction Amendments, and the institution of the New Deal), which he identifies as major "constitutional moments," all proceeded apart from Article V processes.

39. Vile, *Constitutional Amending Process*, 137–56.

40. 158 U.S. 601 (1895).

41. Rossum, *Federalism, the Supreme Court, and the Seventeenth Amendment*; Hoebeke, *Road to Mass Democracy*. However, for the view that the amendment has made little difference in this respect, see Schiller and Stewart, *Electing the Senate*.

42. See Okrent, *Last Call*; Kyvig, ed. *Alcohol and Order*.

43. Baker, ed., *Votes for Women*.

44. Brown, "Ratification of the Twenty-First Amendment." Whereas the Founders chiefly designed the Article V convention mechanism for proposing amendments to bypass an unresponsive Congress (the primary engine of the national government), the convention method for ratifying amendments chiefly bypasses unresponsive state legislatures (the

main engines of state governments), which in the case of the Twenty-First Amendment had not been recently reapportioned and were considerably to be considerably "drier" than popular sentiment within their states.

45. Tiedeman, *Unwritten Constitution.*
46. Stathis, "Twenty-Second Amendment."
47. Feerick, *Twenty-Fifth Amendment.*
48. 400 U.S. 112 (1972). The opinion had upheld provisions of a federal law that lowered requirements in national elections but ruled that Congress had no authority to do so in state and local elections.
49. See Bernstein, "Sleeper Wakes."
50. 256 U.S. 368 (1921).
51. See Carol Berkin, *Wondrous Beauty: The Life and Adventures of Elizabeth Patterson Bonaparte* (New York: Alfred A. Knopf, 2014), 74–75.
52. As a subsequent chapter details, twenty-one states sent 132 delegates to the Willard Hotel in Washington, D.C., for the Peace Convention, which proposed a number of compromises similar to those of the Crittenden Compromise. See Gunderson, *Old Gentleman's Convention.*
53. R. Alton Lee, "Corwin Amendment."
54. Stephen B. Wood, *Constitutional Politics in the Progressive Era.*
55. Contrast support for this action in Held, Herndon, and Stager, "Equal Rights Amendment," with Denning and Vile, "Necromancing the Equal Rights Amendment."
56. See, for example *Reed v. Reed*, 404 U.S. 71 (1971), giving women an equal right to serve as state executors as men and *Frontiero v. Richardson*, 411 U.S. 677 (1973), mandating that the military provide equal benefits for dependents of both males and females.
57. One common link is the leadership of Phyllis Schlafly, the head of the conservative Eagle Forum, who is most credited with stopping ratification of the Equal Rights Amendment and who has been equally opposed to the calling of an Article V convention. See Critchlow, *Phyllis Schlafly.*
58. Mansbridge, *Why We Lost the ERA*; Mary Francis Berry, *Why ERA Failed.* For the larger context, see Kerber, *No Constitutional Right to be Ladies.*
59. Vose, "When District of Columbia Representation Collides."
60. Committee on the Federal Constitution, New York Bar Association, "Article V," 543.
61. Caplan, *Constitutional Brinkmanship*, 63–64.
62. Ibid., 65.
63. 369 U.S. 186 (1962). This case decided that issues of state legislative apportionment were justiciable.
64. 377 U.S. 533 (1964). This case applied the one-person, one-vote standard to both houses of state legislatures.
65. 376 U.S. 1 (1964). This case applied the one-person, one-vote standard to congressional districts.
66. Caplan, *Constitutional Brinkmanship*, 76.
67. Ibid., 75.
68. Vile, 2014. *Re-Framers*, 109–11. Interestingly, a number of such proposals continue to find their way onto lists of proposed amendments to secure liberty or rebalance the federal system.

69. Swindler, "Current Challenge."
70. Black, "Proposed Amendment of Article V."
71. Mason, *States Rights Debate.*
72. Thomas B. Morgan, "Seventeen States Vote to Destroy Democracy."
73. Caplan, *Constitutional Brinkmanship*, 76.
74. Ibid.
75. Ellis, et al., "Article V Constitutional Conventions," 667.
76. Caplan, *Constitutional Brinkmanship*, 81.
77. Ibid.
78. Ibid., 178.
79. I have gleaned these from the "appendix" to Paulsen, "General Theory of Article V." A 1987 report singled out six proposals as garnering the most petitions. In addition to the three identified here, they included twenty-five applications from the turn of the century to 1930 for an amendment to outlaw polygamy, twenty-seven proposals from 1939–57 to limit national taxing powers, and nineteen petitions in the late 1970s to restrict the right to abortion. See U.S. Department of Justice, Office of Legal Policy, Report to the Attorney General, *Limited Constitutional Conventions*, 30.
80. Vile, *Constitutional Change*, 63.
81. Glendon, "Rights in Twentieth-Century Constitutions." For further distinctions between "modern" liberal constitutions and "contemporary" constitutions, see Graber, *New Introduction to American Constitutionalism*, 35–39.
82. Guerra, *Perfecting the Constitution.*

Chapter 4. The Late Eighteenth Century and Nineteenth Century
Provide a Rival Set of Convention Precedents

1. Jonathan Israel, *Revolutionary Ideas: An Intellectual History of the French Revolution from The Rights of Man to Robespierre* (Princeton, N.J.: Princeton University Press, 2014).
2. Banner, *To the Hartford Convention.*
3. Vile, *Encyclopedia of Amendments, Proposed Amendments, and Amending Issues*, 1:230.
4. Fritz observes that while the delegates to the convention often cited the Virginia and Kentucky Resolutions, which Madison and Jefferson had drafted in the state legislatures to rally resistance to the Alien and Sedition Acts, which they believed violated both the First and Tenth Amendments, those who did so often had a far less sophisticated understanding of the relation between state legislatures and the people (a distinction that I have tried to accentuate in the previous chapter on the deliberations of the U.S. Constitutional Convention). See *American Sovereigns*, 210–18. The advocates of nullification later repeated, and arguably magnified, these mistakes.
5. Vile, *Constitutional Amending Process*, 79–93. Also see John R. Vile, "John C. Calhoun on the Guarantee Clause," *South Carolina Law Review* 50 (Spring 1989): 667–92.
6. Calhoun, *Works*, 1:131.
7. Ibid., 178. Emphases omitted. For modern writers who take an almost identical approach, see Mobley and Mobley, *We the People: Whose Constitution Is It Anyway?*, 391–93.
8. Calhoun, *Works*, 2:208. I have elaborated on Calhoun's views at greater length in *Constitutional Amending Process*, 79–93.

9. Calhoun, *Works*, 6:180.

10. Pullen, *Applications of State Legislatures to Congress*, 39.

11. Cited in Ames, *Proposed Amendments*, 282. This is a decidedly mixed bag. South Carolina is clearly calling for a convention on a broad, but limited subject, but it does not appear to be calling for a convention that completely fits Article V guidelines.

12. Ames, *Proposed Amendments*, 282.

13. Michael Nelson, ed. *Guide to the Presidency*, 1:323.

14. Where the first Anti-Mason convention had only 116 delegates, the first Democratic Convention had only 283. Democrats had 4,233 delegates at their 2004 convention and Republicans had 2,380. Calhoun, *Works*, 1:323–24. Jarvis critiques the nondeliberative aspect of modern conventions, which he associates in large part with the increased power of incumbent nominees, see *United States of Dysfunction*.

15. For the argument that such conventions were far preferable to modern ones and that the nation should consider using primaries to select electors who would exercise independent judgment rather than the actual candidates, see Jarvis, *United States of Dysfunction*.

16. Schlafly, "Is Article V in Our Future?"

17. Raven, *Dorr War*.

18. See Peterson, ed., *Democracy, Liberty, and Property*.
   There has been a series of waves of reform at the state level, which distinguish their experiences from that of the national government and, in my judgment, therefore make it difficult to draw lessons for an Article V convention (a difficulty compounded by the fact that state constitutions are always recognized as subordinate to the U.S. Constitution and do not therefore raise similar fears over denigration of rights like those found in the first ten amendments). Morton Keller, 69, observed that "in a sense this constant, endless process of amendment is for state constitutions what judicial review has been for the federal charter. Between 1776 and 1976 some 226 state constitutional conventions were convened, 136 constitutions ratified, and more than 5,000 amendments adopted." He further went on to note that waves of state constitutional reform occurred at the time of the U.S. Revolution, after the writing of the U.S. Constitution, in the 1820s, just prior to the Civil War, during Reconstruction, during the Southern Redeemer period, and during the Progressive Era. See Morton Keller, "The Politics of State Constitutional Revision, 1820–1930," in Hall, Hyman, and Sigal, eds., *Constitutional Convention as Amending Device*.

19. 7 How. (48 U.S.) 1 (1848).

20. Palmer, *Constitutional Amendments*, 429.

21. Bernhard and Fox-Genovese, *Birth of American Feminism*, 10. Also see McMillen, *Seneca Falls and the Origins*.

22. Jennings, *Nashville Convention*.

23. Waugh, *On the Brink of Civil War*.

24. See Finkelman, *Dred Scott v. Sandford*.

25. Etcheson, *Bleeding Kansas*.

26. John A. Jameson, *Treatise on Constitutional Conventions*, 204–8.

27. Richardson, *Compilation of the Messages and Papers of the Presidents*, 6:10.

28. In 1866, as the Fourteenth Amendment was widely debated, southern Loyalists held a five-day convention in Philadelphia in which they endorsed the proposed Fourteenth

Amendment. See Lash, *Fourteenth Amendment*, 204–8. For the proceedings, see *The Southern Loyalist's Convention: Call for a Convention of Southern Unionists, to Meet at Independence Hall, Philadelphia, on Monday, the Third day of September, 1866*, YA Pamphlet Collection, Library of Congress, DLC Southern Loyalists Convention, Philadelphia, September 3–7, 1866.

29. Lash, *Fourteenth Amendment*.

30. See Wooster, *Secession Conventions of the South*. After the war, there was another set of conventions designed to reconstruct the South in the aftermath of its defeat in the Civil War. See Hume and Gough, *Blacks, Carpetbaggers, and Scalawags*.

31. See Chittenden, *Report on the Debates and Proceedings*, 453.

32. Quoted in Charles Robert Lee, Jr., *Confederate Constitutions*, 116, from *The American Annual Cyclopedia and Register of Important Events*, 15 vols. (New York: D. Appleton and Company, 1869), 1, 564.

33. Keogh, "Formal and Informal Constitutional Lawmaking."

34. "Confederate States of America—Constitution for the Provisional Government," http://avalon.law.yale.edu/19th_century_csa_caapro.asp.

35. Charles Robert Lee Jr., *Confederate Constitutions*, 70.

36. For a recent discussion, see Tsai, *America's Forgotten Constitutions*, 118–51.

37. Charles Robert Lee Jr., *Confederate Constitutions*, 196.

38. In this respect, the provision resembled the provision in the original Virginia Plan providing "that provision ought to be made for the amendment of the Articles of Union whensoever it shall seem necessary, and that the assent of the National Legislature ought not to be required thereto." Farrand, *Records of the Federal Convention*, 1:22.

39. I do not know whether to interpret this as expressing a lack of confidence in state legislatures or chiefly as an outgrowth of the fact that such state conventions had initially declared state independence and ratified the Confederate Constitution, but I am inclined to accept the latter explanation.

40. Charles Robert Lee Jr., *Confederate Constitutions*, 118, notes this link.

41. Currie, "Through the Looking-Glass," 1386, quoting from "Smith's Address to the Citizens of Alabama" (1861), in *Southern Pamphlets on Secession, November 1860–April 1861*, ed. John L. Wakelyn (Chapel Hill: University of North Carolina Press, 1996), 205. Brackets included in Currie.

42. Quoted in Charles Robert Lee Jr., *Confederate Constitutions*, 119.

43. Quoted in ibid.

44. In 2010 several members of the U.S. Congress introduced H.J. Res. 95, an amendment that would have provided that "the Congress, on application of the legislatures of two-thirds of the several states, which all contain an identical amendment, shall call a convention solely to decide whether to propose that specific amendment to the States, which, if proposed, shall be valid to all intents and purposes as part of this Constitution when ratified pursuant to Article V."

45. Caplan, *Constitutional Brinkmanship*, 58, thus observed that "the journals of the Montgomery Convention reveal only that Alexander De Clouet of Louisiana inserted the phrase 'at the time when the said demand is made' to ensure that the agenda of the convention would be, in the words of Alabama delegate Robert H. Smith, 'confined to action on propositions put forth by three States.' The journals do not indicate whether De

Clouet's addition was meant to confirm an existing understanding of the original article V or to establish a departure from it." Charles Robert Lee Jr., *Confederate Constitutions*, 118, suggested that the new provision might have been inserted to avoid the possibility that a convention would exceed its mandate, but he offered no specific evidence for this view.

46. One reason for accepting this interpretation is that the framers of the Confederate Constitution stressed that they were seeking to return to the original understandings of the U.S. Constitution. See Currie, "Through the Looking-Glass," 1267.

In explaining the amending clauses in a letter to Stuart Rhett, probably written in 1867 but transcribed the following year, Rhett stressed that the Confederate Constitution had been "simply the Constitution of the United States, as the south had always interpreted its powers, with only such alterations, as would remove ambiguity, and better carry out its plain intents." Davis, ed., *Fire-Eater Remembers*, 119n19.

In this letter, he prefaced the actual language of Article V of the Confederate Constitution with the following comments, which speak to the difficulty of the U.S. Constitution's Article V provision and the postbellum amendments but did not specifically address whether the convention mechanism had been designed to allow states to limit the scope of Article V conventions:

Amendments to the Constitution of the United States proved to be so difficult in the course of its administration before the War, that it amounted to prohibition. Since the War, the country has been in a condition of Revolution; and practically with no Constitution, but the despotic will of a Congress, of a part only of the States. I proposed in the committee, the Article V Article of the Confederate States Constitution, which both by them, and the Convention afterwards, was unanimously adopted as part of the Constitution of the Confederate States. If it had been a part of the Constitution of the United States, the vast discontents which preceded the War, and made it inevitable, would have been easily arrested and allayed; and the States assembled in Convention, would have settled amicably all their differences. (Ibid., 122)

47. Currie, "Through the Looking-Glass," 1386n547 observes that "resolving an issue left dangling by the U.S. Constitution, the Confederate version, by limiting the authority of the Convention to pass amendments to those amendments that the states might unanimously propose, undertook to deal with the persistent fear of a runaway convention, a fear which has allegedly inhibited invocation of the comparable provision in the United States." Currie is incorrect in alleging that states had to propose amendments unanimously, but because he does not cite specific evidence, I am unsure whether the fear of runaway conventions was actually the trigger for this mechanism or if Currie is largely mistaking the cause for the effect; it is possible that much of this fear developed later, perhaps in partial response to the way that state conventions had called for secession.

48. Tsai, *American's Forgotten Constitutions*, 141.
49. White, *Robert Barnwell Rhett*, 237.
50. Herman Belz, *The Webster-Hayne Debate on the Nature of the Union* (Indianapolis: Liberty Fund, 2000).
51. Virginia Commission on Constitutional Government, *Reconstruction Amendments Debates*.

52. Haynes, *James Baird Weaver*, 358.
53. These proposals are analyzed in Vile, *Re-Framers*, 64–67.

Chapter 5. A Survey of Early Commentary on Article V

1. Hoebeke asserts in *Road to Mass Democracy*, 149, that proponents of direct election were willing to hazard general conventions, but an alternate explanation is that they believed that they had the right to call limited conventions that did not pose such a hazard. Similarly, Rossum, *Federalism, the Supreme Court, and the Seventeenth Amendment*, 193, quoted Hoebeke in arguing that "the states seemed willing 'to risk opening Pandora's box for the sake of securing the popular election of senators'" without showing that they actually thought they were taking such a risk. Is it possible that both writers are reading back subsequent fears into the convention mechanism? This seems an area that is ripe for further research.
2. Cheney, *James Madison*, 160.
3. Jefferson, *Writings*, 1:323.
4. Jefferson, *Works*, 2:441.
5. Ibid., 12:13.
6. Ibid., 9:179.
7. Ibid., 11:218–19. By suggesting that he was playing on Federalist fears, Jefferson may have been indicating that he thought a convention might exceed the specific purpose(s) for which it was called, but in the aftermath of a clear Democratic-Republican victory in the election of 1800 (Jefferson was not tied with his Federalist opponent, John Adams, but with his own running mate, Aaron Burr, because of a quirk in the Electoral College system) may simply have been indicating that any changes would likely have been more democratic than Federalist opponents would have preferred.
8. See John R. Vile, "James Madison's Report of 1800," in Vile, Pederson, and Williams, *James Madison*, 133–56.
9. Natelson, "James Madison," 446, citing James Madison, *The Writings of James Madison*, ed. Galliard Hunt (New York: G. P. Putnam's Sons, 1900), 6:403.
10. Ibid., quoting Hunt, 6:404. Significantly, although Madison does not say that the convention was to be limited, he appeared to anticipate that it might formulate a single amendment.
11. Ibid., 447, quoting Hunt 9:398.
12. Tucker, *View of the Constitution*, 121, 122.
13. Ibid., 306.
14. Ibid., 307.
15. Ibid., 307–9. I regret that I failed to include these in *Re-Framers*.
16. Tucker, *View of the Constitution*, 307.
17. Ibid., 310.
18. Story, *Commentaries*, 678, 680.
19. Ibid., 680, 681, 682.
20. See John R. Vile, "Of Catechisms, Religious and Constitutional," intro. to Stansbury, *Elementary Catechism*, v–xx.
21. Stansbury, *Elementary Catechism*, 67. Stansbury thus observed: "When two thirds of the

members both of the Senate and of the House of Representatives shall agree in opinion that an alteration would be proper, they may state such alteration and propose it to be considered by the people of all the States. The alteration must then be considered by the Legislature of each of the States, or by a Convention in each State (which is a meeting of persons chosen by the people for this particular purpose); and if three fourths of the States agree to the amendment, it then becomes a part of the Constitution" (67).

By contrast to Stansbury, Furey, *Explanation of the Constitution*, 128, did inform readers about the Article V convention mechanism, although he did not address the issue of how it would operate or whether its agenda could be limited.

22. Caplan, *Constitutional Brinkmanship*, 45–46.

23. *Smith v. Union Bank of Georgetown*, 30 U.S. (5 Pet.) 518 (1831), 30.

24. Caplan, *Constitutional Brinkmanship*, 46.

25. Johnson had written: "But such an arrangement could only be carried into effect by a reciprocal relinquishment of the right of granting administration to the country of the domicile of the deceases exclusively, and the mutual concession of the right to the administrator, so constituted, to prosecute suits everywhere in virtue of the power so locally granted him, both of which concessions would most materially interfere with the exercise of sovereign right, as at present generally asserted and exercised." *Smith v. Union Bank*, 30.

26. In 1831 Peter S. Du Ponceau, the provost of the Law Academy of Philadelphia published his analysis of the U.S. Constitution with a single paragraph on the amending process:

> It is the duty of congress to propose amendments to the constitution, whenever two-thirds of both houses deem it necessary; and on the application of the legislatures of the several states, they are bound to call a convention for proposing amendments. In either case, when the amendments proposed are ratified by the legislatures of three-fourths of the several states, or by conventions in three-fourths thereof, as the one or the other mode may be proposed by congress, they become parts of the constitution. No state, however, without its consent, can be deprived of its equal suffrage in the senate.

See Ponceau, *Brief View of the Constitution*, 46.

27. Duer, *Course of Lectures*, 342–43. Despite the quotation marks, Duer is not quoting directly from Article V.

28. Ibid., 343. This suggests that Duer regarded state legislatures [state governments], rather than Article V conventions, as having equality with Congress.

29. Ibid., 344. Although states had expressed their clear preferences for adding a bill of rights, there were "recommendatory" only. See Cheney, *James Madison*, 169.

30. Duer's assertion that states offered such amendments "as conditions of their accession to the Constitution," is not completely accurate (unless he is referring to North Carolina and Rhode Island) since the Constitution was not ratified conditionally, even though Federalists had indicated that they would push for the ratification of amendments once the states had approved the document.

31. Vile, *Constitutional Amending Process*, 98–105.

32. Fisher, *Trial of the Constitution*, 33.

33. Ibid., 27.

34. Ibid., 30.

35. Ibid., 34.

36. Ibid.

37. Ibid., 34–35.
38. Ibid., 387.
39. Ibid., 387, 388, 389.
40. Ibid., 389. This discussion of illegal or extra-constitutional conventions suggested that Fisher formed a negative view of conventions based on those that southern states had called to secede and to draw up the Confederate Constitution.
41. Ibid. The reference to a "popular vote" is not altogether clear, but it may simply indicate that Fisher anticipated that convention deliberations would be submitted to state conventions, rather than to state legislatures, for ratification.
42. Vile, "Francis Lieber."
43. Lieber, *Amendments of the Constitution*, 6, 8, 35.
44. Farrar, *Manual of the Constitution*, 391.
45. Ibid., 392.
46. The book is subtitled *A Philosophical Inquiry into the Fundamentals of American Constitutional Law*.
47. Tiedeman, *Unwritten Constitution*, 102.
48. 198 U.S. 45.
49. Tiedeman, *Unwritten Constitution*, 108.
50. Jameson, *Treatise on Constitutional Conventions*, 10.
51. Ibid.
52. Borgeaud, *Adoption and Amendment of Constitutions*, 135.
53. Ibid., 183.
54. Ibid., 185.
55. Ibid., 186.
56. 2 Hill (S.C.) 222.
57. Braxton, "Powers of Conventions," 80.
58. Ibid., 93–94.
59. Ibid., 98.
60. Cooley, *Treatise on the Constitutional Limitations*, 41. After citing Jameson's *Treatise*, Cooley observed that "This work is so complete and satisfactory in its treatment of the general subject, as to leave little to be said by one who shall afterwards attempt to cover the same ground" (41n1).
61. Israel Ward Andrews, *Manual of the Constitution of the United States*, 252.
62. Bryce, "Flexible and Rigid Constitutions."
63. Bryce, *American Commonwealth*, 1:365.
64. Ibid., 1:370. An astute anonymous reviewer of *Conventional Wisdom* observed that one of the difficulties of the Continuity in Government Amendment (designed to provide for contingencies in which large numbers of governmental representatives were killed or incapacitated) is that fairly sensible suggestions have been thwarted precisely because they were largely apolitical and thus did not generate partisan enthusiasm.

 More recently, Elster, "Forces and Mechanisms," 394, has observed two central paradoxes of constitution making. The first is that "the task of constitution-making generally emerges in conditions that are likely to work against good constitution-making." The second is that "the public will to make major constitutional change is unlikely to be present unless a crisis is impending."

65. Bryce, *American Commonwealth*, 1:371.
66. Burgess, *Selections from Political Science*, 17.
67. See Vile, *Constitutional Amending Process*, 139.
68. Burgess, *Political Science and Comparative Constitutional Law*, 1:143.
69. Vile, *Constitutional Amending Process*, 143–44.
70. Wolfe, "Woodrow Wilson."
71. Woodrow Wilson, *Constitutional Government*, 56.
72. Ibid., 192.
73. Ibid., 193.
74. Ibid.
75. Quoted in Corwin, *Constitution and What It Means*, 5.
76. It would, however, take considerable argument to establish that the work of the Court, which consists of appointed justices who serve for life rather than for limited terms, and whose work is not (like that of a convention) subject to subsequent ratification by either state legislatures or state conventions, is, in fact, equivalent either in power or authority to that of the meeting held in Philadelphia in 1787.
77. Ames, *Proposed Amendments*, 281–84. M. A. Musmanno, a lawyer and member of the Pennsylvania legislature, later authored a similar monograph, entitled *Proposed Amendments to the Constitution: A Monograph on the Resolutions Introduced in Congress Proposing Amendments to the Constitution of the United States of America* (Washington, D.C.: United States Government Printing Office, 1929), but it did not address the Article V convention mechanism.
78. Dodd, *Revision and Amendment of State Constitutions*, 80.
79. Ibid.
80. Ibid.
81. Hoar, *Constitutional Conventions*, 89. Hoar is specifically quoting Dodd.
82. Ibid., 225.
83. J. Allen Smith, *Spirit of American Government*, 346.
84. Ibid., 346–47.
85. Ibid., 348.
86. Orfield, *Amending of the Federal*, 40.
87. Ibid., 40.
88. Ibid., 42.
89. Ibid.
90. Ibid., 43.
91. Ibid., 44. Interestingly, Orfield does not specifically say that this precedent *should* be followed.
92. Ibid., 45. The more relevant question would appear to be whether this Constitution, which created the state mechanism, permits the limited option!
93. Ibid.
94. Ibid., 46.
95. Ibid.
96. Cyril F. Brickfield, *Problems Relating to a Federal Constitutional Convention*, 18.
97. Ibid., 20.
98. Ibid.

Chapter 6. The Modern Debate over Limiting Conventions

1. Committee members included C. Clyde Atkins (chair), Warren Christopher, David Dow, John D. Feerick, Adrain M. Foley Jr., Sarah T. Hughes, Albert M. Sacks, William S. Thompson, and Samuel W. Witwer.

2. American Bar Association, *Amendment of the Constitution*, 11.

    A Committee on the Federal Constitution, New York State Bar Association, subsequently issued another report in 1982, which also affirmed the right of the states to call for a limited constitutional convention. See "Article V and the Proposed Federal Constitutional Procedures Bills," *Cardozo Law Review* 3:529–61.

3. Ibid.

4. Ibid., 14, 15. Italics in ABA report. This argument could, of course, cut both ways since one could argue that the difference in wording between this provision and Article V of the U.S. Constitution was intentional.

5. Ibid., 16.

6. Ibid., 17. I have added the numbers in brackets to identify separate arguments.

7. Charles L. Black Jr., "Amending the Constitution: A Letter to a Congressman," *Yale Law Journal* 83 (December 1972), 189–215.

8. Charles L. Black Jr., "Amendment By National Constitutional Convention: A Letter to a Senator," *Oklahoma Law Review* 21 (1979): 628.

9. Ibid., 628, 629, 630, 631. Italics in the original.

10. Ibid.

11. Ibid., 635. The Framers were, of course, also seeking a way to bypass state legislatures, whose members would lose power vis-à-vis the national government under the proposed Constitution.

12. Ibid., 633, 638–41.

13. Ibid., 642. The best answer may have been provided in John M. Harmon's 79-75 Memorandum Opinion, "Constitutional Conventions," 417. Focusing on the earliest applications and observing that "both Virginia and New York expressed a general concern over the adequacy of the Constitution," he argued that "these applications do not support the contention that the applicants believed that they could ask for a general convention only. Instead, he suggested that "the inclusion in these applications of language specifying that the requested convention should have 'full' or 'general' powers suggests rather clearly that the powers of an Article V convention were not thought to be invariably general but were thought to be dependent on the terms of the applications of the States."

14. Black, "Amendment by National Constitutional Convention," 644.

15. Charles Black Jr., "Proposed Amendment of Article V."

16. Dellinger, "Recurring Question," 1630. The first such principle arguably emerges from the debates more forcefully than the second, as might be evident were the second principle to be rephrased to say that state legislatures should have the power to call a convention to check federal excesses!

17. Ibid.

18. Ibid., 1631, 1632.

19. Ibid., 1635.

20. Ibid., 1638–39, 1640.

21. U.S. Department of Justice, Office of Legal Policy, Report to the Attorney General,

Limited Constitutional Conventions under Article V, 5. As the report indicates (14–15), this contrasts with the argument made by Black that *the convention* is equal to Congress.

22. Ibid., 20–21.

23. Ibid., 28.

24. Weber and Perry, *Unfounded Fears*, 105. Italics in original. For an article that takes a similar approach, see Stern, "Reopening the Constitutional Road to Reform."

25. Weber and Perry, *Unfounded Fears*, 106, 97.

26. They observed that as the required majority drew near, states often engaged in what they described as "a 'fourth-quarter cautiousness.'" Ibid., 109.

27. Ibid., 114.

28. Ibid., 117.

29. Lessig, *Republic, Lost*, 298.

30. Harmon, "Constitutional Conventions," 409.

31. Ibid., 409.

32. Weber and Perry, *Unfounded Fears*, 109.

33. See, for example, Levinson, *Our UnDemocratic Constitution*; Sabato, *More Perfect Constitution*; and Labunski, *The Second Constitutional Convention*. Also see Dahl, *How Democratic Is the American Constitution?*

34. Guerra, *Perfecting the Constitution*.

35. Manne, "Good Intentions, New Inventions, and Article V Constitutional Conventions," 169.

36. After making much the same argument, Michael B. Rappaport has proposed changing Article V specifically to recognize the states' right to call advisory conventions, to allow states to ratify according to their electoral votes, and to require that the results of any such conventions would be approved either by state conventions or by state ballot measures. See his "Renewing Federalism by Reforming Article V," 9.

Chapter 7. Using Criteria and Ideal Types to Think about the Big Picture

1. At the time, a number of scholars were concerned about the increasing number of amendments that members of Congress were introducing. See, for example, Kathleen M. Sullivan, "Constitutional Constancy: Why Congress Should Cure Itself of Amendment Fever," *Cardozo Law Review* 17 (1996): 691. Adrian Vermuele, "Constitutional Amendments and the Common Law," in Richard W. Bauman and Tsvi Kahana, *The Least Examined Branch: The Role of Legislatures in the Constitutional State* (New York: Cambridge University Press), 229–72, cautions, however, that it is also important to recognize that changes that are initiated by judicial review rather than by constitutional amendments have their own drawbacks that need to be considered.

2. Citizens for the Constitution, *"Great and Extraordinary Occasions."*

3. A study listed the following factors that it thought would be needed "to ensure a [Pennsylvania] convention serves the public interest:
   - Representative delegate selection;
   - Openness of debate;
   - Use of experts without consideration of political position;
   - Ongoing public input;
   - Access to information held by government agencies and statewide organizations;

- Using technology to foster public interest and interaction with the convention;
- Access to public officials at all levels to help and advise the public and delegates, and direct them to sources of additional information;
- Efforts to keep media attention high to ensure transparency and to promote public awareness and participation;
- Periodic sharing of convention materials with the public, associations, and interest groups along with feedback to the delegates; and
- Follow up to help the electorate prepare for their approval or rejection vote to the recommendations of the convention.

Kerry L. Moyer and Mark W. Podvia, *Citizens' Guide to a Modern Constitutional Convention*, 25. All the above material is quoted and formatted as in the original.

4. Hamilton, Madison, and Jay, *Federalist Papers*, 78.
5. Ibid., 80.
6. Gutmann and Thompson, *Why Deliberative Democracy?*
7. Lincoln, *Works*, 4:269nn270–71. Italics in original.
8. Oliver Wendell Holmes Jr., *The Common Law* (Boston: Little, Brown and Company, 1881), 1.
9. Story, *Commentaries on the Constitution*, 680.
10. This would, of course, have to be weighed against the idea that the Constitution would be even more stable if greater barriers were increased to use of this mechanism.
11. Vile, "Proposals to Amend the Bill of Rights," 62–67. With the possible exception of the Eighteenth Amendment, which has since been repealed, no amendments adopted to date have restricted individual liberties.
12. Hamilton, Madison, *and* Jay, *Federalist Papers*, 246.
13. Orfield, *Amending of the Federal Constitution*, 154.
14. Radin, "Intermittent Sovereign."
15. Quoted in Jameson, *Treatise on Constitutional Conventions*, 304. I am uncertain as to how, under this understanding, "the people" would call such a convention to account unless it would be by failing to ratify a convention's proposals since, unlike legislators, convention delegates do not typically run for reelection.
16. Brennan, *Article V Amendatory Constitutional Convention*, 11, 26.
17. I recognize the ambiguity of using the word "state," which can refer either to a nation-state, or to an entity within a federal system, but consistent with the language of the U.S. Constitution, I am using the word in the latter sense.
18. Natelson, *Amending the Constitution by Convention*. Also see Natelson, *Proposing Constitutional Amendments*. Natelson does, however, recognize the right of Congress to specify "the initial time and place of meeting" in his *State Initiation of Constitutional Amendments* (55).
19. Natelson, *Proposing Constitutional Amendments*, 16. Although he notes that "the convention may change both rules," it is difficult to imagine them making such a change once they arrived with potentially equal numbers of delegates.
20. Ibid., 16, 34. For discussion of the instruction and recall mechanism, see Kobach, "May 'We the People' Speak?" On a related issue, See Vikram David Amar, "People Made Me Do It."
21. Natelson, *Proposing Constitutional Amendments*, 34.
22. This mode of interpretation can be problematic. What elements were critical to the

definition and which were not? If the Framers wanted to incorporate a particular common-law understanding of a mechanism, then they might just as easily have included it. Perhaps most importantly, this model does not take into account the transition from a confederal to a federal system or the subsequent democratization of Congress.

23. Lising, *Remember Roscoe Filburn*, 170. This analysis ignores the fact that Article V specifically provides that "the Congress," at the request of two-thirds of the states, "shall call a Convention for proposing Amendments."

24. Pulitzer, *Repair Washington*, 10.

25. Romney, *Rule of Law*, 121. In his proposed Twenty-Eighth Amendment, Romney thus specifies that "Congress shall have no power to regulate the state conventions, applications or ratification process in any manner" (124).

26. See http://www.compactforamerica.org/about-2/. Accessed June 28, 2014.

27. See, for example, Citizens for Self Governance, *Convention of States: A Handbook for Legislators and Citizens*, 3rd ed. Self-govern.com.

28. 307 U.S. 433 (1939).

29. Daniel T. Young thus observes: "If we take Hamilton's insistence that Congress ought to have no discretion in calling a convention once Article V's requirements are fulfilled as representative of the sentiments of his fellow delegates, then the principle of Congressional non-interference in convention politics seems critical to a proper functioning of the Article V machinery." *Disarming the Constitutional Time Bomb*, 24.

30. KirsAnne Hall, the author of *Sovereign Duty* (which urges the states to reassert their sovereignty), while thus acknowledging that Article V gives a role in the process to Congress, is nonetheless quite concerned that Congress would so completely dominate the process as to frustrate the will of the states. See "Article V Convention," in *Sovereign Duty*, 89–118.

31. Hamilton, Madison, and Jay, *Federalist Papers*, 246.

32. For the variability of legislative sessions from state to state (some of which meet only in alternate years), see National Conference of State Legislatures, "Legislative Session Length," http://www.ncsl.org/research/about-state-legislatures/legislative-session-length. aspx. Accessed June 18, 2014.

33. Jack A. Wilson, *Republic Lost*, 161.

34. Akhil Reed Amar, *America's Unwritten Constitution*, 474.

35. Foley, "Posterity Project," 19.

36. Davenport, "New American Constitutional Convention," 15.

Chapter 8. The Selection and Likely Characteristics of Delegates

1. For a recent critique by two leading political scientists, see Mann and Ornstein, *It's Even Worse Than It Looks*.

2. Howard, *Rule of Nobody*. Howard observes that "the Constitution has a design flaw. . . . It is almost impossible to amend or repeal old laws. Our founders were concerned about *preventing too many laws* but never debated *how to undo laws that didn't work out*" (136).

3. Elizabeth Mendes, "Americans Down on Congress, OK with Own Representative," May 9, 2013, http://www.gallup.com/poll/162362/americans-down-congress-own-representative.aspx?version=print, accessed June 18, 2014.

4. Citizens for the Constitution, "*Great and Extraordinary Occasions*," 6.

5. Chris DeRose, *Founding Rivals*.

6. Vikram David Amar, "People Made Me Do It," 1060.

7. Jack A. Wilson, *Republic Lost*, 127.

8. Vile, *Writing and Ratification*, 19.

9. Frank J. Sorauf, "Political Potential of an Amending Convention," in Hall, Hyman, and Sigal, eds., *Constitutional Convention as Amending Device*, 125.

10. Marvin Meyers thus titled his edited volume on James Madison *The Mind of the Founder* rather than the "Mind of the Legislator" or "President." The book is subtitled *Sources of the Political Thought of James Madison*.

11. Jameson, *Treatise on Constitutional Conventions*, 561.

12. Bryce, "Flexible and Rigid Constitutions," 62.

13. Dodd, *Revision and Amendment of State Constitutions*, 80n13.

14. Burgess, *Recent Changes in American Constitutional Theory*, 114.

15. Jack A. Wilson, *Republic Lost*, 123.

16. Ibid.

17. Hamilton, Madison, and Jay, *Federalist Papers*, 317.

18. "Disadvantages of a Federal Convention," 925. Carson went on to argue that "its membership would be chiefly composed of political partisans, aligned in accordance with the economic forces, the racial or religious affiliations, and the ideologies which in more or less degree the great historic parties serve" (926).

19. If current members of Congress were excluded, the chief difference would probably be that convention delegates would be less experienced and have fewer ties to existing governmental arrangements. This might be a good thing or a bad thing depending on national needs.

20. Webster, *Sketches of American Policy*.

21. Quoted in Kay, "Constituent Authority," 746.

22. Elmer E. Cornwell Jr., "The American Constitutional Tradition: Its Impact and Development," in Hall, Hyman, and Sigal, eds., *Constitutional Convention as Amending Device*, 29.

23. Ibid., 29–30.

24. Strout, *Restoration*, 265.

25. For an argument that time limits unduly infringe on Article V, see Kalfus, "Why Time Limits on the Ratification of Constitutional Amendments Violate Article V." For an argument that Article V should include such limits, see Hanlon, "Note."

26. I believe the weight of the evidence should allow it, but I am not sure that mine is the majority opinion. See Vile, "Permitting States to Rescind Ratifications."

27. Hamilton, Madison, and Jay, *Federalist Papers*, 526.

28. One might argue that proponents of such an amendment might favor the affirmation that state conventions might give and the momentum they might build, but requests for conventions by two-thirds of the states followed by proposal by two-thirds of both houses of Congress would arguably have a similar impact.

29. Robert Berry, *Amendments without Congress*, unpaginated e-book.

30. 4 Wheat (17 U.S.) 316.

31. Natelson, *State Initiation of Constitutional Amendments*.

32. Jon Elster observes: "The mechanism by which delegates are elected or selected must also be in existence prior to the assembly itself" ("Arguing and Bargaining," 358–59).

With specific reference to the French Assembly, Elster further described the relationship between the assembly and the institution that convened it in two opposing slogans: "'Let the kingmaker beware of the king' versus 'Let the king beware of the kingmaker.'"

33. Rees, "Amendment Process and Limited Constitutional Conventions."

34. The amendment consists of seven sections. The first would provide for outlays that exceed receipts to be financed exclusively by debt. The second would limit such debt to 105 percent of the current debt unless approved by the states. The third would require state legislatures to approve such increases by simple majorities, without receiving any inducements to do so within sixty days of receiving the request. The fourth would provide for the president to impound debts over such amount subject to impeachment for refusing to do so. The fifth requires a two-thirds vote of both houses of Congress to add "a new or increased general revenue tax" except for a new "end user sales tax which would completely replace every existing income tax," or "for the reduction or elimination of an exemption, deduction, or credit allowed under an existing general revenue tax." The sixth would provide operational definitions, and the seventh related to enforcement. Found under "Omnibus Concurrent Resolution," at http://www.compactforamerica.org/about-2/; accessed June 28, 2014. For an excellent analysis and defence of the compact provision, see Nick Dranias. *Introducing "Article V 2.0": The Compact for a Balanced Budget*, Policy Study No. 134 for Chicago, Ill.: The Heartland Institute.

35. George F. Will, "Amend the Constitution to Control Federal Spending," *Washington Post*, April 9, 2014, http://www.washingtonpost.com/opinions/george-will-amend-the-constitution-to-control-federal-spending/2014/04/09/00fa7df6-bf3c-11e3-bcec-b71ee10e9bc3_story.html, accessed June 29, 2014.

36. Similarly, John Marshall Cogswell has proposed an amendment to establish a "Board of Governors (State governors) to assist States in the exercise of their powers under the Constitution." *Fix the System*, 113.

37. For recent discussions of this provision relative to the "National Popular Vote" initiative designed to reform the Electoral College, see Pincus, "When Should Interstate Compacts Require Congressional Consent?" and Green, "National Popular Vote Compact." For a more general discussion of the compact clause, see Duncan R. Hollis, "Unpacking the Compact Clause," 741–806.

38. 148 U.S. 503 (1893).

39. 434 U.S. 452 (1978).

40. *Leser v. Garnett*, 258 U.S. 130, 137 (1922).

41. Natelson, *Amending the Constitution by Convention*, thus argues that "Congress may not determine how delegates shall be chosen, what districts they are to represent, or how many a state can send. Nor may Congress establish rules under which the convention is to operate." Such a view almost necessarily assumes, which I do not, that states must have equal votes at such a convention.

42. Fruth, *10 Amendments for Freedom*, 218.

43. Hamilton, Madison, and Jay, *Federalist Papers*, 342. In a similar vein, Jon Elster has observed, "The dynamics of large assemblies, small *bureau*, and small specialized committees are likely to be very different. In a large assembly, it is not possible to pursue an argument in a coherent and systematic fashion. The debates tend to be dominated by a small number of skilled and charismatic speakers, a Mirabeau or a Lamartine, who count on rhetoric rather than argument. The outward form of the debates is that of

deliberation, but the force motivating the decisions is passion rather than reason." See Elster, "Deliberation and Constitution Making," 109.

44. Alice Slu, "Deliberative Polling," http://www.pgexchange.org/index.php?option=com_content&view=article&id=132&Itemid=121. Accessed July 22, 2014.

45. Kristin D. Burnett, "Congressional Apportionment: 2010 Census Briefs," United States Census Bureau, U.S Department of Commerce, November 2011, 1.

46. See, for example, George W. Will, "Congress Just Isn't Big Enough," *Washington Post*, January 14, 2001, who suggested increasing the number to 1,000.

47. Congressional Quarterly, *Guide to Congress*, 4th ed. (Washington D.C.: Congressional Quarterly, 1991), 741–42.

48. Brennan, *Article V Amendatory Constitutional Convention*, 28. Brennan does not specify which delegates would physically attend and which would stay tuned through cyber space.

49. See http://www.thirty-thousand.org/. The site includes the twenty-three-page brochure "Taking Back Our Republic."

50. Schumaker, *Constitutional Convention 2doto*, unpaginated e-book.

51. This could, however, complicate how such delegates were selected, probably by combining groups of three congressional districts together in single elections.

52. Brown, "Ratification of the Twenty-First Amendment," 1006.

53. Farrand, ed., *Records of the Federal Convention*, 1:10–11, notes that Madison observed that "previous to the arrival of a majority of the States, the rule by which they ought to vote in the Convention had been made a subject of conversation among the members present. It was pressed by Gouverneur Morris and favored by Robert Morris and others from Pennsylvania, that the large States should unite in firmly refusing to the small States an equal vote, as unreasonable, and as enabling the small States to negative every good system of Government, which must in the nature of things, be founded on a violation of that equality. The members from Virginia, conceiving that such an attempt might beget fatal altercations between the large & small States, and that it would be easier to prevail on the latter, in the course of the deliberations, to give up their equality for the sake of an effective Government, than on taking the field of discussion, to disarm themselves of the right & thereby throw themselves on the mercy of the large States, discountenanced & stifled the project."

54. See comments by Charles Fried in Penello, ed., *Electing Delegates to a Constitutional Convention*, 15.

55. Natelson, *Proposing Constitutional Amendments*, 14–15.

56. Miller, *True Democracy*, 418.

57. Ibid.

58. Lessig, *Republic, Lost*, 303.

59. Thorvaldur Gylfason, "Democracy on ice: a post-mortem of the Icelandic constitution," openDemocracy, June 19, 2013, https://www.opendemocracy.net/can-europe-make-it/thorvaldur-gylfason/democracy-on-ice-post-mortem-of-icelandic-constitution. Accessed September 22, 2014. This method of amending constitutions was favorably referenced by Peter Sagel in *Constitution USA*, a documentary aired on Public Television in 2013. Note, however, that the proposed constitution was ultimately rejected by the Icelandic parliament. See Tom Ginsburg, "Iceland: End of the Constitutional Saga?" *Huffington Post*, April 5, 2013, http://www.huffingtonpost.com/tom-ginsburg/iceland-end-of-

the-consti_b_3018127.html. Accessed May 1, 2015. This raises the possibility that more seasoned delegates might have been able to develop a document more palatable to existing elites.

60. Cain, *Democracy More or Less*, 83. Cain proceeds to explain on the same page that "to create a common baseline of citizen competence, the new citizen governance institutions all build expert instruction into their model." It would be difficult to keep such instructions from predetermining outcomes.

61. Ibid.

62. Brown, "Ratification of the Twenty-First Amendment," 1010. Also see Schaller, "Democracy at Rest." Schaller argues that "the primary reason for the lopsided convention outcomes in the ratification of the repeal amendment [the Twenty-First] was the decision by many states to use at-large elections to select their convention delegates" (88). Schaller believes that proponents of this method correctly thought that it would make the convention less deliberative and more plebiscitary. Such characteristics seem far more appropriate for conventions designed to ratify amendments than for those designed to propose them.

63. Cain, *Democracy More or Less*, 6, observes that the statewide gubernatorial recall election in California in 2003 was chaotic and included "135 candidates, including a porn actress and the former child actor Gary Coleman." He further observes that this memory "tempered the enthusiasm for a constitutional convention of citizens chosen by lottery."

64. American Bar Association, *Amending of the Constitution*, 15.

65. Sara Johnson, "Diversity in the 113th Congress Looks Pathetic when You Plot It on a Map," *The Atlantic Cities*, http://www.citylab.com/politics/2013/01/diversity-113th-congress-looks-pathetic-when-you-plot-it-map/4348/. Accessed March 14, 2014.

66. In *Wesberry v. Sanders*, 376 U.S. 1, 17 (1964), the Court observed that "other rights, even the most basic, are illusory if the right to vote is undermined." Similarly, in *Reynolds v. Sims*, 377 U.S. 533, 561 (1964), it declared that "any alleged infringement of the rights of citizens to vote must be carefully and meticulously scrutinized." In *Crawford v. Marion County*, 128 S. Ct. 1610 (2008), however, the Court did uphold Indian's Voter ID laws that critics charge have a disproportionate impact on the poor and on minorities.

67. Rappaport, "Reforming Article V," 1523, also raises this possibility.

68. Pulitzer, *Repair Washington*, 11, proposes that they should be at least forty years of age.

69. See *Powell v. McCormack*, 395 U.S. 486 (1969).

70. U.S. Constitution, Article I, Section 6, clause 2. In outlining the Electoral College for selecting the president and vice president, Article II, Section 1 also provides that "no Senator or Representative, or Person holding an Office of Trust or Profit under the United States, shall be appointed an Elector."

71. American Bar Association, *Amending of the Constitution*, 37.

72. Weber and Perry, *Unfounded Fears*, 90.

73. In proposing his plan for a convention, however, Sidney Pulitzer specifies that "no person shall be eligible to serve as a Delegate if he or she is serving or has been in the Federal Government in any elected, judicial, appointed or employed position; nor has ever been convicted as a felon, declared bankruptcy, or been employed as a lobbyist." See *Repair Washington*, 11. Grouping individuals who have previously served in government in the same category as felons undoubtedly expresses Pulitzer's sentiment about the current ineffectiveness of government but seems otherwise unhelpful.

74. Feerick, *Twenty-fifth Amendment*, 38.

75. In 1972 Montana prohibited state legislators from serving in the state constitutional convention, and other states have followed this example. See Tarr and Williams, *State Constitutions for the Twenty-First Century*, 1:197–98.

76. Weber and Perry, *Unfounded Fears*, 113.

77. Lawrence Lessig, "A Real Step to Fix Democracy," *The Atlantic*, May 30, 2014, http://www.theatlantic.com/politics/archieve/2014/05/a-real-step-to-fix-democracy/371898/. Accessed July 4, 2014.

78. Carson, "Disadvantages of a Federal Constitutional Convention," 926, however observed that New York sought to select delegates to its 1967 convention on a nonpartisan basis, but "this failed; delegates were chosen by the electoral process, and the convention was organized on party lines with the Democratic speaker of the State Assembly as chairman."

79. Sabato, *More Perfect Constitution*, 15.

80. Jonathan Turley, "Real Political Reform Should Go beyond Campaign Finance," *Los Angeles Times*, February 11, 2010, http://articles.latimes.com/2010/feb/11/opinion/la-oe-turley//-2010Feb11. Accessed January 7, 2014.

81. Michael B. Rappaport has suggested that one protection against a "runaway" convention would be for delegates to "take pledges to oppose nonconforming amendments" (14) meaning amendments that were not on the agenda for which states called. See "Renewing Federalism by Reforming Article V."

82. Weber and Perry, *Unfounded Fears*, 114.

83. By contrast, Brennan, *Article V Amendatory Constitutional Convention*, 170, has called for a permanent convention in which delegates would be elected every two (odd-numbered) years.

84. Foley, "Posterity Project," 8.

85. Advocates of the creation of an interstate compact to create a convention to propose a single preestablished amendment thus propose limiting such a convention to twenty-four hours. See Dranias, *Introducing "Article V 2.0,"* 7.

Chapter 9. Organizational and Logistical Issues Related to Article V Conventions

1. Cox, *American Safeguard*, includes a section titled "Political Conventions," 365–66. It presents a political convention as synonymous with "a mass meeting" and is not otherwise relevant to constitutional conventions.

2. Robert Berry, *Amendments without Congress*, unpaginated e-book.

3. Robert Berry, *Constitutional Coup*, unpaginated e-book.

4. The latter convention, followed by another that was held in Philadelphia in 2003, was based on deliberative polling and was covered by PBS's *NewsHour*. See "National Issues Conventions: Past (1996) and Future (2003), http://www.nifi.org/news/news_detail.aspx?itemID=3026&catID=440. Accessed July 16, 2014.

5. Labunski, *Second Constitutional Convention*, 220–21. This proposal might, of course, feed expectations that states would also be equally represented at an Article V convention.

6. Rappaport, "Renewing Federalism by Reforming Article V," 10.

7. Vile, "Critical Role of Committees," 147–76.

8. The Constitutional Convention of 1787 frequently appointed committees consisting of a delegate from each state. If a modern Constitution followed this practice, the size of

such committees (fifty) would approximate the total number of delegates (fifty-five) who attended the 1787 gathering.

9. Miller, *True Democracy*, 420, thus believes that all participants should be sworn to "a policy of strict non-disclosure."

10. Hooper, *Next American Revolution*, 10.

11. Davenport, "A New American Constitutional Convention," 16.

12. Thirty-three states currently require supermajorities of between 60 and 75 percent in both houses of their state legislatures in order to petition Congress for an Article V Convention. See Hill and Wright, eds. *Amending the Constitution by an Article V Convention*, 19.

13. For rules of the Federal Convention, see Farrand, *Records of the Federal Convention of 1787*, 1:8–10, 17.

14. This would be consistent with a U.S. District Court decision in *Dyer v. Blair*, 390 F. Supp. 1291 (1975), in which John Paul Stevens, who later became a Supreme Court justice, ruled that state ratifying bodies would decide the majorities by which they would approve amendments.

15. Oliphant, "Amending the U.S. Constitution," 9.

16. Sara Ellis et al. thus note that "given current public opinion of Washington and the perceived disconnectedness between the federal government and the people, a convention, as a source of government expressly and intentionally alternative to Congress, may be better off assembling in one of the nation's other metropolitan centers," ("Article V Constitutional Conventions," 686).

17. See, for example, George Mason's comments at the Constitutional Convention on July 26, 1787. Farrand, *Records of the Federal Convention*, 2:127.

18. In a passage that was obviously written tongue in cheek, Professor Michael Stokes Paulsen, "How to Count to Thirty-four," 860, suggested that Minneapolis might make a good site: "It is in the middle of the country, an airport hub city, has good convention facilities, nice summer weather, and beautiful lakes. The loom of impending bitterly cold winter weather would tend to impose a natural, implicit, unmonitored, unimposed time limitation on the length of the convention. Everyone would get cold and want to go home." Paulsen also suggested that the convention might think of finding an "eminent law professor, preferably from the host state, who is familiar with the relevant Article V constitutional issues" to preside (861)!

   In the spirit of Paulsen's own suggestions, I suggest that it would be wise for delegates to meet in the summer in un-air-conditioned buildings in the Deep South in hope that this would facilitate their deliberations.

19. Strassner, *Bill of Rights for Our Posterity*.

20. "2010 Center of Population," U.S. Census. See http://www.census.gov/newsroom/releases/archives/facts_for_features_special_editions/cb11ff10.html. Accessed June 2, 2014.

21. In his novel *Restoration*, 264, Wayne Strout has Congress consider Philadelphia, Dallas–Ft. Worth, Chicago, and Atlanta before settling on Dallas–Ft. Worth, where they meet in the Irving Convention Center. In his novel *The Convention*, 204, C. W. Hambleton places the site of a projected convention of the states in Houston. Tom Donohue's novel, *Capitol Bypass*, 154, sets his convention in Detroit. Thomas E Brennan, in *The Article V Amendatory Constitutional Convention*, 37–38, proposes that the convention should be

held in St. Louis, which he notes, has previously hosted a World's Fair and which is near the population center of the United States. Believing that delegates "will have to find common ground," he observes that "they will have to meet figuratively, at least, in Saint Louis" (38). The racial divisions evident in the aftermath of the shooting of Michael Brown by Officer Darren Wilson on August 9, 2014, in nearby Ferguson, Missouri, would seem to call into question the suitability of this city for an Article V convention.

22. Hambleton, *The Convention*, 203.

23. In 2014 this was on April 21. See "Tax Freedom Day° 2014 is April 21, Three Days Later Than Last Year," http://taxfoundation.org/article/tx-freedom/day-2014-april-21-three-days-later-last-year. Accessed October 3, 2014.

24. Elster, "Forces and Mechanisms in the Constitution-Making Process," 395.

25. "Friends of the Article V Convention," http://www.foave.org/ (accessed May 7, 2014), for example, suggested that "it is likely the convention will ... turn to a much cheaper, more universal method of communication—internet teleconferences, which will allow delegates to 'meet' on a single website, conduct business, exchange ideas, speeches, documents, debate the issues and vote all while remaining in the comfort of their own homes, still attending to their daily lives." Also see Mobley and Mobley, *We the People: Whose Constitution is it Anyway?*, 400.

26. Donohue, *Capitol Bypass*, 197.

27. See *Marsh v. Chambers*, 463 U.S. 783 (1983), and *Town of Greece v. Galloway*, No. 12–696 (2014).

28. At the Constitutional Convention of 1787, the delegates apparently ignored a request by Benjamin Franklin on June 28, 1787 (*The Records of the Federal Convention*, 1:451), to begin each day with prayer in part because they feared that, coming in the middle of the convention, this would send a signal to the outside public that the convention was in a period of crisis. Because of this context, this precedent seems largely irrelevant to whether an Article V convention would open with prayer.

29. See, for example, the comments of James Wilson, quoted in Farrand, *Records of the Federal Convention*, 2:87.

30. Jennifer Steinhauer, "Constitution Has Its Day (More or Less) in House," *New York Times*, January 6, 2011, http://www.nytimes.com/2011/01/07/us/politics/07constitution.thml. Accessed May 16, 2014. Steinhauer observed that on the recommendation of the Congressional Research Service, House leaders chose to read a version that omitted references to sections (like those dealing with slavery) that had been superseded by subsequent amendments.

31. Ackerman, *We The People: The Civil Rights Revolution*, 16.
    Moreover, after commenting that "the caliber of people" at an Article V convention would not match that of Madison and Hamilton, Antonin Scalia observed that "on the other hand, they will be people who can examine 200 years' worth of experience under the existing Constitution. You trade a little bit of smarts for a little bit of experience" (Daly et al., *Constitutional Convention*, 20).

32. Seeking to bridge the party divide, Thomas E. Brennan, *The Article V Amendatory Constitutional Convention*, 82, suggests that former presidents Bush II and Clinton could cochair the convention. He does not discuss what effects the election of Hillary Clinton or Jeb Bush as president might have on this plan.

33. Foley, "Posterity Project," 6–7. Coming from a somewhat different perspective, in his novel J. B. Andrews anticipates a group of "Founding Partners" calling a meeting to reconsider constitutional reforms. See his *Convention*, unpaginated e-book.

34. Natelson, *State Initiation of Constitutional Amendments*, 60, observes that "the presiding officer always has been elected from among the commissioners rather than from outside the convention."

35. I do not think that Congress should dominate the proceedings, but I cannot figure out a way that Congress could choose its own initial president or chairperson without some predesignated individual calling the session to order.

36. Weber and Perry, *Unfounded Fears*, 149.

37. Durbin, *Amending the U.S. Constitution*.

38. 3 U.S. (3 Dal.) 379 (1798).

39. 253 U.S. 221 (1920).

40. 253 U.S. 231 (1920).

41. 253 U.S. 350 (1920).

42. 256 U.S. 368 (1921).

43. 307 U.S. 433 (1939).

44. 369 U.S. 186 (1962).

45. Ibid. at 217. I have added the numbers.

46. 439 U.S. 385 (1978).

47. 529 F. Supp. 1107 (1981).

48. I have reviewed many of these in "Constitutional Amendments, Limits On," in Vile, *Encyclopedia of Constitutional Amendments*, 1:112–13.

49. John R. Vile, "The Case against Implicit Limits on the Constitutional Amending Process," in Levinson, ed., *Responding to Imperfection*, 191–214.

50. *Whitehill v. Elkins*, 389 U.S. 54 (1967).

51. Johnson observed that "when a man knows he is to be hanged in a fortnight, it concentrates his mind wonderfully." For the background story, see James Boswell, *Boswell's Life of Johnson*, ed. George Birkbeck Hill, rev. L. F. Powell, vol. 3, *The Life (1776–1780)*, (Oxford: Clarendon press, 1971), 165–67.

52. Daly et al., *Constitutional Convention*, 38. Elmer E. Cornwell Jr. has further observed that nonpartisan elections tend to decrease turnout. See his comments in Hall, Hyman, and Sigal, eds., *Constitutional Convention as Amending Device*, 143.

53. Lash, *Fourteenth Amendment*, 176.

54. 256 U.S. 368 (1921).

55. 307 U.S. 433 (1939).

56. Dellinger, "Legitimacy of Constitutional Change," 408–9.

57. See Denning and Vile, "Necromancing the Equal Rights Amendment."

58. For a U.S. District Court decision holding that the congressional extension was unconstitutional, see *Idaho v. Freeman*, 529 F. Supp. 1107 (1981).

59. Dellinger, "Legitimacy of Constitutional Change," 425. Dellinger observed: "The amendments proposed in 1789, 1810, and 1861 raise no problems: they simply died. A court troubled by the existence of amendments proposed over a hundred years ago could invoke the doctrine of desuetude and declare the amendments dead. No such need, however, is likely to arise."

60. Weber and Perry, *Unfounded Fears*, 147.
61. Vile, "Permitting States to Rescind Ratifications."

Chapter 10. Different Kinds of Conventions

1. John Alexander Jameson, *Treatise on Constitutional Conventions*, 3–11. As indicated previously, Jameson also described what he called spontaneous conventions and general assemblies or legislative bodies. Also see "Powers of Constitutional Conventions."
2. In 2009 Bob Schultz, a graduate engineer with a particular concern for the assembly and petition provisions of the First Amendment to the Constitution, called a Continental Congress in which 116 delegates from 48 states met from November 11 to November 22 in St. Charles, Illinois, to discuss constitutional issues. Although the convention was attempting to restore what it believed to be original understandings of the document rather than to write a new one, many of its proposals would have brought about major changes in current constitutional understandings. For a brief description of the event, see Brennan, *Article V Amendatory Constitutional Convention*, 75–76. For resolutions adopted by the Congress, see Articles of Freedom, http://www.articlesoffreedom.org/ArticlesofFreedom/ReadtheArticlesHTML.aspx. Accessed October 21, 2014.
3. Richardson, *Compilation of Messages and Papers*, 6:10.
4. Ibid. Indeed, working from what I believe is a mistaken idea of popular sovereignty, Akhil Reed Amar of Yale University has argued that a majority of people could effectively obligate Congress to call a conventional convention and that such a convention could in turn allow a majority of citizens to ratify its recommendations. See his "Philadelphia Revisited," 1065, 1061. For my critique of this position, see Vile, *Contemporary Questions*, 97–125.
5. Vile, "Three Kinds of Constitutional Founding and Change," 883–85.
6. Jon Elster observes that "there is another sense in which a constituent assembly might be democratic and yet not deliberative, namely if the delegates are sent with bound mandates and obey them rigorously." See "Deliberation and Constitution Making," 99.
7. Mobley and Mobley, *We the People: The Strategy to Convene a Convention*, 37, argue that a convention should be called for neither of these purposes but for what they call "Republic Review." As they explain: "This 'Republic Review' is the process of comparing and contrasting the enumerated powers within the existing Constitution to the functioning RRPs [roles, responsibilities, and powers] within the existing government." Mobley and Mobley liken this convention to the process of nullification, and in my judgment, their vision comes closer to that of John C. Calhoun than that of James Madison. Alternatively, one might compare it to the Council of Censors that some states used before the adoption of the U.S. Constitution.
8. Kammen, *Machine That Would Go of Itself*, 390.
9. Citizens for Self-Government have distinguished between what they call "a convention for a particular *subject* rather than a particular *amendment*." The group explains that "instead of calling a convention for a balanced budget amendment (though we are entirely supportive of such an amendment), we want to call a convention for the purpose of limiting the power and jurisdiction of the federal government." See Citizens for Self-Governance, *Convention of States: A Handbook for Legislators and Citizens*, SelfGovern.com, 8.

10. Similarly, Charles Kacprowicz advocates this kind of convention in *Reclaiming America*.

11. Check home page of Compact for America, Inc., at http://www.compactforamerica.org/about-2/. Accessed June 28, 2014. Also see Dranias, *Introducing "Article V 2.0."*

12. Natelson, "James Madison," 434.

13. Natelson, *Proposing Constitutional Amendments*, 12–13.

14. Hawke v. Smith, 253 U.S. 221, 226–27 (1920).

15. Palmer, ed. *Constitutional Amendments*, 474.

16. Indiana, which held the largest convention, registered 246 ayes and 83 nays. No other state registered more than 4 nays, and thirty-two were unanimous. See *Ratification of the Twenty-First Amendment*, 15.

17. Corwin, *The Constitution and What It Means Today* (Princeton, N.J.: Princeton University Press, 1948), 146.

18. Michael Nelson, ed., *Guide to the Presidency and the Executive Branch*, 1:327.

19. With a particular view toward state constitutional conventions, Dale A. Kimball observed that "one definite disadvantage to constitutional conventions is their expense. Conventions require expenditures for elections, for the payment of delegates and clerical assistants, for research, and for other miscellaneous expenses." "Constitutional Convention, Its Nature and Powers."

20. Hamilton, Madison, and Jay, *Federalist Papers*, 77–84.

21. Fred Graham has noted that "a large percentage of the state applications Congress has received called for amendments which had very little national support and which would have had no chance of approval by two thirds of both houses of Congress." "Role of the States," 1176.

22. Rappaport, "Reforming Article V," 1514.

23. Committee on Federal Constitution, "Article V and the Proposed Federal Constitutional Convention Procedures Bill," 541.

24. Brennan, *Article V Amendatory Constitutional Convention*, 121.

25. Taking a somewhat different tact, Bruce E. Cain has observed, "It is odd and somewhat anomalous in the modern era that the most frequently used path for U.S. constitutional amendment involves approval by elected officials at both the state and national level. It certainly makes sense that critical rule and institutional changes require supermajority votes, but giving a monopoly over reform to elected officials is problematic to say the least, and expecting conventions to work in the modern era is unrealistic." His solution is that "at least some part of the federal constitutional amendment process could be given over to direct popular vote: such as a majority national advisory vote that triggers automatic congressional consideration of a proposed constitutional amendment followed by the current process of state ratification." See *Democracy More or Less*, 210. Cain does not offer a plan to bring about such an amendment.

26. See *Colegrove v. Green*, 328 U.S. 549 (1946). America's Founding Fathers were especially concerned with what they believed to be the "corruption" of the British parliamentary system. They considered the existence of so-called "rotten boroughs," where a few people had disproportionate representation, to be one example of this. See James D. Savage, "Corruption and Virtue at the Constitutional Convention," *Journal of Politics* 56 (February 1994): 176–86.

27. For a recent symposium that presents the views of a number of scholars on current perceptions of congressional gridlock, see the *Notre Dame Law Review* 88 (June 2013). It

is especially useful to compare the views of Magliocca, "Don't Be so Impatient," 2157–65, with those of Teter, "Gridlock, Legislative Supremacy, and the Problem of Arbitrary Inaction," 2217–32.

28. Davenport, "New American Constitutional Convention," 3, http://faculty.fordham.edu/davenport/convention.html. Accessed July 4, 2014.

29. Donohue, *Capitol Bypass*.

30. See William Lee Miller, *Arguing about Slavery: The Great Battle in the United States Congress* (New York: Alfred A. Knopf, 1996).

31. Quirk, *Courts and Congress*, 194.

32. Ibid., 194–202. One could, of course, counter that this only proves that the Senate, whose members have longer terms, is a more deliberative body.

33. Davenport, "New American Constitutional Convention," 3. Italics in original.

34. Van Alstyne, "Does Article V Restrict the States?," 1304.

35. See Hoebeke, *Road to Mass Democracy*, 146.

36. As Kris W. Kobach has shown, this incentive might well have changed had states been permitted to impose such limits individually, as they were attempting to do before the Supreme Court's decision in *U.S. Term Limits v. Thornton*, 514 U.S. 779 (1995), in which it decided that the age, citizenship, and residency restrictions for members of Congress set forth in the Constitution were exclusive. "Rethinking Article V," 1999.

37. In advocating one representative in the U.S. House for every fifty thousand inhabitants, the website of Thirty-thousand.org (http://www.thirty-thousand.org/) observes that "because Congress will never place such an amendment before the people for consideration, *Thirty-Thousand.org* believes it will be necessary for the state legislatures to call a convention (in accordance with Article V of the Constitution) *solely* for the purpose of proposing this amendment."

38. Aaron-Andrew Bruhl, "The Use of the Filibuster and Potential Senate Reform: The Senate: Out of Order?" *Connecticut Law Review* 43 (May): 1041–58.

39. Van Alstyne, "Does Article V Restrict the States?," 1999.

40. Graham, "Role of the States," 1178.

41. Brennan, *Article V Amendatory Constitutional Convention*, 3–19. Brennan argues that states should call an Article V Convention with or without congressional approval. He further argues that its proposals might be either ignored, that they might be introduced in Congress, that congress might belatedly call a convention, or that "the convention might send the proposal directly to the states" (19).

   However effective or ineffective such a convention might be, in my judgment, a convention convened directly by the states, without initial congressional approval, would not be an *Article V* amendatory constitutional convention.

42. Goidel, *America's Failing Experiment*.

   For an analysis of the movement for a balanced budget amendment in the 1970s, see Iwan Morgan, "Unconventional Politics." For one of the most comprehensive analyses see Saturno and Lynch, *Balanced Budget Constitutional Amendment*. Saturno and Lynch point out that Congress has adopted numerous joint resolutions and held numerous hearings on the subject (13–14). They further detail floor considerations of such measures (15–24). For their discussion of past attempts to solve unbalanced budgets through statutes, like the Balanced Budget and Emergency Deficit Control Act of 1985 (usually known as the Gramm-Rudman-Hollings Act) and the Budget Enforcement Act of 1990, see 27–28.

43. See Saturno and Lynch, *Balanced Budget Constitutional Amendment*, 29–41, for a summary of key issues and approaches that Congress has considered.

44. For a discussion of such issues, see James W. Bowen, "Enforcing the Balanced Budget Amendment," and "The Balanced Budget Amendment: An Inquiry into Appropriateness."

45. Barnett, "Bill of Federalism."

46. Vile, "Case against a 'Repeal Amendment,'" 38–39.

47. For discussion of such proposals, see Vile, *Re-Framers*, 323.

48. Ibid., 340–41. For texts of some of these proposals, see Boyd, ed., *Alternative Constitutions*.

49. Tugwell, *Emerging Constitution*. Opponents of constitutional conventions often cite Tugwell's extensive plans as examples of what "runaway" conventions might propose.

50. I identify approximately 35 advocates of such conventions in the last chapter of *Re-Framers*, 342, and I have since discovered a number of others, some of which I have included in my *Encyclopedia of Constitutional Amendments* (2015).

51. Proceedings in Congress, February 21, 1788. See Solberg, ed., *Federal Convention*, 64.

52. Jameson, *Treatise on Constitutional Conventions*, 562.

53. Dillon, "Recommendation for the Establishment of a Permanent Commission."

54. Compare Williams, "Are State Constitutional Conventions Things of the Past?" with Rich, *Major Problems in State Constitutional Revision*, 99.

55. Labunski, *Second Constitutional Convention*; Levinson, *Our UnDemocratic Constitution*.

56. Levin, *Liberty Amendments*.

57. Weber and Perry, *Unfounded Fears*, 127–43.

58. Frank J. Sorau, "Political Potential of Amending Convention," in Hall, Hyman, and Sigal, eds. *Constitutional Convention as Amending Device*. This does not necessarily mean, of course, that those who oppose a convention are dissembling. Many undoubtedly believe that a convention could become a dangerous body.

59. Quoted by Sorauf in "Political Potential of Amending Convention."

60. Penrose, "Conventional Wisdom," 797. Penrose, 804–5, goes on to "recommend that Congress create an Article V sub-committee, with equal House and Senate membership, to work in concert with the American Law Institute and the American Bar Association to create balanced and moderate procedures that would govern any Article V State Convention."

61. For an analysis of such legislation, see "Proposed Legislation on the Convention Method of Amending the United States Constitution." Also see Pritchett, "Congress and the Article V Convention," and Ervin, "Proposed Legislation."

62. Weber and Perry, *Unfounded Fears*, 145–52.

63. If I read the law correctly, it was not designed to deal with proposals for a "general" convention to reconsider or rewrite the document as a whole. I further believe this is a weakness of the legislation, which I think should provide for this contingency as well.

64. *New York Trust Co. v. Eisner*, 256 U.S. 335, 343 (1921).

65. Howard B. Lee, *The Story of the Constitution* (Charlottesville, Va.: Michie Company, 1932), 25.

66. See Bruff, *Untrodeen Ground*.
67. Kyvig, *Unintended Consequences*.
68. See, for example, Strauss, "Commentary." But also see Denning and Vile, "Relevance of Constitutional Amendments." Albert, "Constitutional Disuse or Desuetude," 1029–81. Observing the way that politicians continue to invoke the convention mechanism, Albert noted that "though it has not been used successfully for over 220 years, Article V's convention process has not actually remained unused" (1057).
69. Hamilton, Madison, and Jay, *Federalist Papers*, 315.
70. Ibid., 33.

Updates

After this manuscript was typeset, I discovered three additional resources that should interest readers.

Biggs, Andy 2014. *The Con of the ConCon: The Case Against the States Amending the U.S. Constitution*. Gilbert, Az.: FreeMan Press. Biggs is a Republican Arizona state legislator who opposes calling an Article V convention now because he does not believe that the Constitution is the cause of current problems and because he doubts the fallibility of proposed constitutional solutions. His introduction, pp. 1–4, gives a particularly vivid description of a worst-case scenario involving a convention.

Elster, Jon. 2008. "The Optimal Design of a Constituent Assembly." Prepared for the colloquium on Collective Wisdom, College de France, May 2008. Available on the Internet. Elster addresses many of the practical issues relative to convention size and its effects on deliberation that I address in this book.

Tillman, Seth Barrett. 2014. "Originalism and the Scope of the Constitution's Disqualification Clause," *Quinnipiac Law Review* 33:59–126. Tillman presents evidence, relevant to the discussion on pp. 143–44 of this book, indicating that members of Congress do not "hold office under the United States" and would not therefore be constitutionally barred from serving as delegates to a Constitutional Convention.

SELECTED BIBLIOGRAPHY

Articles and Books

Aboney, Nicholas. 2006. "Formation, Representation and Amendment in Federal Constitutions." *American Journal of Comparative Law* 54 (December): 277–336.

Abraham, Henry J., and Barbara A. Perry. 2003. *Freedom and the Court: Civil Rights and Liberties in the United States.* 8th ed. Lawrence: University Press of Kansas.

Ackerman, Bruce. 2014. *We the People: The Civil Rights Revolution.* Cambridge, Mass.: Belknap Press of Harvard University Press.

———. 1991. *We the People: Foundations.* Cambridge, Mass.: Belknap Press of Harvard University Press.

———. 1996. *We the People: Transformations.* Cambridge, Mass.: Belknap Press of Harvard University Press.

Adams, Frederick U. 1896. *President John Smith: The Story of a Peaceful Revolution.* Chicago: Charles H. Kerr and Company. Reprint. New York: Arno Press, 1970.

Adams, Willi Paul. 2001. *The First American Constitutions: Republican Ideology and the Making of the State Constitutions in the Revolutionary Era.* Expanded ed. Lanham, Md.: Rowman and Littlefield.

Albert, Richard. 2014. "Constitution Disuse or Desuetude: The Case of Article V, Part of Symposium: What Are We to Do about Dysfunction?" *Boston University Law Review* 94 (May): 1029–81.

Alexander, John K. 1990. *The Selling of the Constitutional Convention: A History of News Coverage.* Madison, Wis.: Madison House.

Amar, Akhil Reed. 2012. *America's Unwritten Constitution: The Precedents and Principles We Live By.* New York: Basic Books.

———. 2000. *The Bill of Rights: Creation and Reconstruction.* New Haven, Conn.: Yale University Press.

———. 1988. "Philadelphia Revisited: Amending the Constitution Outside Article V." *University of Chicago Law Review* 55 (Fall): 1043–104.

Amar, Vikram David. 2000. "The People Made Me Do It: Can the People of the States Instruct and Coerce Their State Legislatures in the Article V Constitutional Amendment Process?" *William and Mary Law Review,* 1037–92.

American Bar Association. Special Constitutional Convention Study Committee. 1973. *Amending of the Constitution by the Convention Method under Article V.*

Ames, Herman V. 1960 [1896]. *The Proposed Amendments to the Constitution of the United States during the First Century of Its History*. New York: Burt Franklin.

Anastaplo, George. 1995. *The Amendments to the Constitution: A Commentary*. Baltimore: Johns Hopkins University Press.

Andrews, Israel Ward. 1900. *Manual of the Constitution of the United States*. Rev. Homer Morris. New York: American Book Company.

Andrews, J. B. 2012. *Convention: A Fairy Tale for America*. N.p.: Silas N. Dugudd Publishing. E-book.

Armor, John C. 1984. *The Right of Peaceful Change: Article V of the Constitution*. Washington, D.C.: Tax Limitation Research Foundation.

Bailey, Jeremy D. 2012. "Should We Venerate That Which We Cannot Love? James Madison on Constitutional Imperfection." *Political Research Quarterly* 65 (December): 732–44.

Baker, Jean H., ed. 2001. *Votes for Women: The Struggle for Suffrage Revisited*. New York: Oxford University Press.

Baldwin, Henry. 1837. *A General View of the Origin and Nature of the Constitution and Government of the United States*. Philadelphia: John C. Clark.

Banner, James M., Jr. 1970. *To the Hartford Convention: The Federalists and the Origins of Party Politics in Massachusetts, 1789–1815*. New York: Alfred A. Knopf.

Barber, Sotirios A. 2014. *Constitutional Failure*. Lawrence: University Press of Kansas.

Barnett, Randy. 2009. "A Bill of Federalism." *Forbes*, May 20, http://www.forbes. com/2009/05/20/bill-of-federalism-constitution-states-supreme-court-op.

———, ed. 1989. *The Rights Retained by the People: The History and Meaning of the Ninth Amendment*. Fairfax, Va.: George Mason University Press.

Benson, Allan L. 1914. *Our Dishonest Constitution*. New York: B. W. Huebsch.

Bernhard, Virginia, and Elizabeth Fox-Genovese. 1995. *The Birth of American Feminism: The Seneca Falls Woman's Convention of 1848*. St. James, N.Y.: Brandywine Press.

Bernstein, Richard B. 1992. "The Sleeper Wakes: The History and Legacy of the Twenty-Seventh Amendment." *Fordham Law Review* 56 (December): 497–557.

Bernstein, Richard B., with Jerome Agel. 1996. *Amending America: If We Love the Constitution So Much, Why Do We Keep Trying to Change It?* New York: Random House.

Berry, Mary Francis. 1986. *Why ERA Failed: Politics, Women's Rights, and the Amending Process of the Constitution*. Bloomington: Indiana University Press.

Berry, Robert. 2012a. *Amendments without Congress: A Timely Gift from the Founders*. Kindle book.

———. 2012b. *Constitutional Coup: America's New Lease on Liberty (The Amendments Agenda)*. Kindle book.

Bessler, John D. *Cruel and Unusual: The American Death Penalty and the Founders' Eighth Amendment*. Lehman, N.H.: Northeastern.

Black, Charles, Jr. 1963. "The Proposed Amendment of Article V: A Threatened Disaster." *Yale Law Journal* 73 (April): 957–66.

Borgeaud, Charles. 1895. *Adoption and Amendment of Constitutions in Europe and America*. Trans. Charles D. Hazen. Intro. John M. Vincent. New York: Macmillan and Co.

Bowen, Catherine Drinker. 1966. *Miracle at Philadelphia: The Story of the Constitutional Convention, May to September 1787*. Boston: Little, Brown.

Bowen, James W. 1983. "The Balanced Budget Amendment: An Inquiry into Appropriateness." *Harvard Law Review* 96:1600–1620.

———. 1994. "Enforcing the Balanced Budget Amendment." *Constitutional Law Journal* 4 (Spring): 565–620.

Boyd, Steven R., ed. 1992. *Alternative Constitutions for the United States: A Documentary History*. Westport, Conn.: Greenwood Press.

Braxton, A. Caperton. 1901. "Powers of Conventions." *Virginia Law Register* 7 (June): 79–99.

Brennan, Thomas E. 2014. *The Article V Amendatory Constitutional Convention: Keeping the Republic in the Twenty-first Century*. Lanham, Md.: Lexington Books.

Brickfield, Cyril F. 1957. *Problems Relating to a Federal Constitutional Convention*. Washington, D.C.: Government Printing Office.

Brown, Everett S. 1935. "The Ratification of the Twenty-First Amendment." *American Political Science Review* 29 (December): 1005–17.

Bruff, Harold H. 2015. *Untrodeen Ground: How Presidents Interpret the Constitution*. Chicago: University of Chicago Press.

Bryce, James. 1906. *The American Commonwealth*. 2 vols. 3rd ed. New York: Macmillan.

———. 1980. "Flexible and Rigid Constitutions." In *Constitutions*. Germany: Scientia Verlag Aalen. Orig. pub. New York, 1905.

Burgess, John W. 1890. *Political Science and Comparative Constitutional Law*. Vol. 1, *Sovereignty and Liberty*. Boston: Ginn & Company.

———. 1972. *Recent Changes in American Constitutional Theory*. New York: Arno Press. Orig. pub. 1922.

———. 1978. *Selections from Political Science and Comparative Constitutional Law*. Farmingdale, N.Y.: Dabor Social Science Publications.

Cain, Bruce E. 2015. *Democracy More or Less: America's Political Reform Quandary*. New York: Cambridge University Press.

Calhoun, John C. 1968. *The Works of John C. Calhoun*. Ed. Richard K. Cralle. New York: Russell and Russell. Orig. pub. 1851–56.

Caplan, Russell L. 1988. *Constitutional Brinkmanship: Amending the Constitution by National Convention*. New York: Oxford University Press.

Carson, Ralph M. 1968. "Disadvantages of a Federal Constitutional Convention." *Michigan Law Review* 66 (March): 921–30.

Cheney, Lynne. 2014. *James Madison: A Life Reconsidered*. New York: Viking.

Chin, Gabriel J., and Anjali Abraham. 2008. "Beyond the Supermajority: Post-Adoption Ratification of the Equality Amendments." *Arizona Law Review* 50 (Spring): 25–47.

Chinn, Stuart. 2014. *Recalibrating Reform: The Limits of Political Change*. New York: Cambridge University Press.

Chipman, Nathaniel. 1792. *Sketches of the Principles of Government; by Nathaniel Chipman, Judge of the Court of the United States for the District of Vermont*. Rutland, Vt.: J. Lyon. ECCO Print Editions.

Chittenden, L. E. 1964. *A Report on the Debates and Proceedings in the Secret Sessions of the Conference Convention for Proposing Amendments to the Constitution of the United States*. New York: D. Appleton and Company.

Citizens for the Constitution (A Project of the Century Foundation). 1999. *"Great and Extraordinary Occasions": Developing Guidelines for Constitutional Change*. New York: The Century Foundation Press.

Clark, Bradford R. 2010. "The Eleventh Amendment and the Nature of the Union." *Harvard Law Review* 123 (June): 1817–918.

Cogswell, John Marshall. 2012. *Fix the System: Reform the Constitution*. Buena Vista, Colo.: Campaign Constitution Press.

Colby, Thomas B. 2013. "Originalism and the Ratification of the Fourteenth Amendment." *Northwestern University Law Review* 107 (Summer): 1627–88.

Committee on Federal Constitution, New York State Bar Association. 1982. "Article V and the Proposed Federal Constitutional Convention Procedures Bills." *Cardozo Law Review* 3:529–61.

Conley, Dillon. 1974. "Recommendation for the Establishment of a Permanent Commission of Constitutional Review." *Bureaucrat* 3 (July): 211–24.

Contiades, Xenophon, ed. 2013. *Engineering Constitutional Change: A Comparative Perspective on Europe, Canada and the USA*. London: Routledge.

Cooley, Thomas M. 1878. *A Treatise on the Constitutional Limitations Which Rest upon the Legislative Power of the States of the American Union*. 4th ed. Boston: Little, Brown, and Company.

Cox, Isaac. 1893. *The American Safeguard, or The Constitution of the United States with Its Political History, also Containing a Brief Treatise on Political Economy*. Santa Rosa, Calif.: Sonoma Democrat Publishing Company.

Critchlow, Donald T. 2005. *Phyllis Schlafly and Grassroots Conservatism: 1945 to the Present*. Princeton, N.J.: Princeton University Press.

Currie, David P. "Through the Looking-Glass: The Confederate Constitution in Congress, 1861–1865." *Virginia Law Review* 90 (September): 1257–399.

Dahl, Robert. 2001. *How Democratic Is the American Constitution?* New Haven, Conn.: Yale University Press.

Daly, John Charles (moderator), Paul Bator, Walter Berns, Gerald Gunther, and Antonin Scalia. 1979. *A Constitutional Convention: How Well Would It Work?* Washington, D.C.: American Enterprise Institute for Public Policy Research.

Davenport, John. 2013. "A New American Constitutional Convention." October 1. http://faculty.fordham.edu/davenport/convention.html.

Davis, William C., ed. 2000. *A Fire-Eater Remembers: The Confederate Memoir of Robert Branwell Rhett*. Columbia: University of South Carolina Press.

Dellinger, Walter E. 1987–1988. "1787: The Constitution and 'The Curse of Heaven.'" *William and Mary Law Review* 19:145–61.

———. 1983. "The Legitimacy of Constitutional Change: Rethinking the Amending Process." *Harvard Law Review* 97 (December): 380–432.

———. 1979. "The Recurring Question of the 'Limited' Constitutional Convention." *Yale Law Journal* 88:1623–40.

Denning, Brannon P., and John R. Vile. 2000. "Necromancing the Equal Rights Amendment." *Constitutional Commentary* 17 (Winter): 593–602.

———. 2002. "The Relevance of Constitutional Amendments: A Response to David Strauss." *Tulane Law Review* 77 (November): 247–82.

DeRose, Chris. 2011. *Founding Rivals: Madison vs. Monroe, the Bill of Rights, and the Election That Saved a Nation*. Washington, D.C.: Regnery.

Diamond, Ann S. 1981. "A Convention for Proposing Amendments: The Constitution's Other Method." *Publius: The Journal of Federalism* 11 (Summer): 113–46.

Dillon, Conley. 1974. "Recommendation for the Establishment of a Permanent Commission of Constitutional Review." *Bureaucrat* 3 (July): 211–24.

Dodd, Walter Fairleigh. 1910. *The Revision and Amendment of State Constitutions.* Baltimore: Johns Hopkins University Press.

Donohue, Tom. 2011. *Capitol Bypass: Changing Washington One State at a Time.* N.p.: CreateSpace.

Dranias, Nick. 2014a. "Federalism and Separation of Powers: Introducing 'Article V 2.0.': The Compact for a Balanced Budget." *Engage* 15 (July): 45–53.

———. 2014b. *Introducing "Article V 2.0": The Compact for a Balanced Budget.* Policy Study No. 134. July. Chicago: The Heartland Institute.

Duer, William Alexander. 1856. *A Course of Lectures on the Constitutional Jurisprudence of the United States Delivered Annually in Columbia College, New York.* 2nd ed. Boston: Little, Brown and Company.

Durbin, Thomas M. 1995. *Amending the U.S. Constitution: by Congress or by Constitutional Convention.* CRS Report for Congress. May 10. Washington, D.C.: Congressional Research Service of the Library of Congress.

Edel, Wilbur. 1981. *A Constitutional Convention: Threat or Challenge?* New York: Praeger.

Elliot, Jonathan, ed. 1888. *The Debates in State Conventions on the Adoption of the Federal Constitution.* 5 vols. New York: Burt Franklin.

Ellis, Joseph. 2000. *Founding Brothers: The Revolutionary Generation.* New York: Vintage Books.

Ellis, Sara R., Yusuf Malik, Heather Graves Parker, Benjamin Signer, and Al'Reco Yancy. 2011. "Article V Constitutional Conventions: A Primer." *Tennessee Law Review* 78 (Spring): 663–92.

Elster, Jon. 2000. "Arguing and Bargaining in Two Constituent Assemblies." *Journal of Constitutional Law* 2 (March): 345–421.

———. 1998. "Deliberation and Constitution Making." In *Deliberative Democracy*, ed. Jon Elster, 97–122. New York: Cambridge University Press.

———. 1995. "Forces and Mechanisms in the Constitution-Making Process." *Duke Law Journal* 45:364–96.

———. 2000. "Two Constituent Assemblies." *Journal of Constitutional Law* 2 (March): 345–421.

Enns, Loren J. 2012. *The Sword of Liberty: Returning Power to the American People!* N.p.: Liberty Press, Inc.

Epstein, David F. 1984. *The Political Theory of "The Federalist."* Chicago: University of Chicago Press.

Ervin, Sam J., Jr. 1968. "Proposed Legislation to Implement the Convention Method of Amending the Constitution." *Michigan Law Review* 66 (March): 875–902.

Etcheson, Nicole. 2004. *Bleeding Kansas: Contested Liberty in the Civil War Era.* Lawrence: University Press of Kansas.

Farrand, Max, ed. 1966. *The Records of the Federal Convention of 1787*, 4 vols. New Haven, Conn.: Yale University Press.

Farrar, Timothy. 1867. *Manual of the Constitution of the United States of America.* Boston: Little, Brown, and Company.

Feer, Robert A. 1969. "Shay's Rebellion and the Constitution: A Study in Causation." *New England Quarterly* 42 (September): 388–410.

Feerick, John D. 2014. *The Twenty-Fifth Amendment: Its Complete History and Applications.* 3rd ed. New York: Fordham University Press.

Finkelman, Paul. 1997. *Dred Scott v. Sandford: A Brief History with Documents* (Boston: Bedford Books.

———. 1996. *Slavery and the Founders: Race and Liberty in the Age of Jefferson.* Armonk, N.Y.: M. E. Sharpe.

Fisher, Sidney George. 1872. *The Trial of the Constitution.* Philadelphia: J. B. Lippincott and Co.

Foley, Edward B. 2013. "The Posterity Project: Developing a Method for Long-Term Political Reform." *Oklahoma Law Review* 66 (Fall): 1–20.

The Founders' Constitution. 1987. Ed. Philip P. Kurland and Ralph Lerner. 5 vols. Chicago: University of Chicago Press.

Fritz, Christian G. 2008. *American Sovereigns: The People and America's Constitutional Tradition before the Civil War.* New York: Cambridge University Press.

Fruth, William H. 2010. *10 Amendments for Freedom: How We the People, through the Power of Our State Legislatures, Will Amend the Constitution to Guarantee Our Freedom for All Generations.* Palm City, Fla.: Politicom Corporation.

Fukuyama, Francis. 2014. *Political Order and Political Decay: From the Industrial Revolution to the Globalization of Democracy.* New York: Farrar, Staus and Giroux.

Furey, Francis T. 1889. *An Explanation of the Constitution of the United States of America. Prepared for Use in Catholic Schools, Academies, and Colleges.* New York: Catholic Publication Society.

Gilhooley, Simon J. 2012. "The Framers Themselves: Constitutional Authorship during the Ratification." *American Political Thought* 2 (Spring): 62–88.

Gillette, William. 1965. *The Right to Vote: Politics and the Passing of the Fifteenth Amendment.* Baltimore: Johns Hopkins University Press.

Ginsburg, Tom, Zachary Elkins, and James Melton. 2009. *The Endurance of National Constitutions.* New York: Cambridge University Press.

Glendon, Mary Ann. 1992. "Rights in Twentieth-Century Constitutions." *University of Chicago Law Review* 59 (Winter): 519–38.

Goidel, Kirby. 2014. *America's Failing Experiment: How We the People Have Become the Problem.* Lanham, Md.: Rowman and Littlefield.

Goldwin, Robert A. 1997. *From Parchment to Power: How James Madison Used the Bill of Rights to Save the Constitution.* Washington, D.C.: AEI Press.

Graber, Mark A. 2013. *A New Introduction to American Constitutionalism.* New York: Oxford University Press.

Graham, Fred P. 1963. "The Role of the States in Proposing Constitutional Amendments." *American Bar Association Journal* 49 (December): 1175–83.

Green, Heather. 2012. "The National Popular Vote Compact: Horizontal Federalism and the Proper Role of Congress under the Compact Clause." *Chapman Law Review* 16 (Spring): 211–39.

Grimes, Alan P. 1978. *Democracy and the Amendments to the Constitution.* Lexington, Mass.: Lexington Books.

Grossman, Mark. 2012. *Constitutional Amendments: An Encyclopedia of the People, Procedures, Politics, Primary Documents, Campaigns for the 27 Amendments to the Constitution of the United States.* Amenia, N.Y.: Grey House Publishing.

Guelzom, Allen C. 2005. *Lincoln's Emancipation Proclamation: The End of Slavery in America.* New York: Simon and Schuster.

Guerra, Darren Patrick. 2013. *Perfecting the Constitution: The Case for the Article V Amendment Process.* Lanham, Md.: Lexington Books.

Gunderson, Robert Gray. 1961. *Old Gentleman's Convention: The Washington Peace Conference of 1861.* Madison: University of Wisconsin Press.

Gutmann, Amy, and Dennis Thompson. 2004. *Why Deliberative Democracy?* Princeton, N.J.: Princeton University Press.

Hall, Kermit L, Harold M. Hyman, and Leon V. Sigal, eds. 1981. *The Constitutional Convention as an Amending Device.* Washington, D.C.: The American Historical Association and the American Political Science Association.

Hall, KrisAnne. 2014. *Sovereign Duty.* n.p.: KrisAnne Hall.

Hambleton, C. W. 2014. *The Convention.* The Sons of Liberty Trilogy, vol. 1. N.p.: CreateSpace.

Hamilton, Alexander, James Madison, and John Jay. 1961. *The Federalist Papers.* Clinton Rossiter ed. New York: New American Library. Orig. pub. 1787–88.

Hanlon, Michael C. 2000. "Note: The Need for a General Time Limit on Ratification of Proposed Constitutional Amendments." *Journal of Law and Politics* 16 (Summer): 663–98.

Harmon, John M. 1979. "Constitutional Convention—Limitation of Power to Propose Amendments to the Constitution." 79-75 Memorandum Opinion for the Attorney General. 3 Op. Off. Legal Counsel. October 10. 390–418.

Hartnett, Edward. 1998. "A 'Uniform and Entire' Constitution: Or, What If Madison Had Won?" *Constitutional Commentary* 15 (Summer): 251–97.

Hawley, Joshua D. 2014. "The Transformative Twelfth Amendment." *William and Mary Law Review* 55 (April): 1501–86.

Heideking, Jurgen. 2012. *The Constitution before the Judgment Seat: The Prehistory and Ratification of the American Constitution, 1787–1792.* Ed. John Kaminski and John Leffler. Charlottesville: University of Virginia Press.

Held, Allison L., Sheryl L. Herndon, and Danielle M. Stager. 1997. "The Equal Rights Amendment: Why the ERA Remains Legally Viable and Properly before the Sates." *William and Mary Journal of Women and the Law* 3: 113.

Hendrickson, David C. 2003. *Peace Pact: The Lost World of the American Founding.* Lawrence: University Press of Kansas.

Hill, Scott J., and Adam Wright, eds. 2013. *Amending the Constitution by an Article V Convention.* New York: Nova Science Publishers, Inc.

Hoar, Roger Sherman. 1917. *Constitutional Conventions: Their Nature, Powers, and Limitations.* Boston: Little, Brown, and Company. Reprint. Littleton Colo.: Fred B. Rothman and Co., 1987.

Hoebeke, C. H. 1995. *The Road to Mass Democracy: Original Intent and the Seventeenth Amendment.* New Brunswick, N.J.: Transaction Publications.

Hoffert, Robert W. 1992. *A Politics of Tensions: The Articles of Confederation and American Political Ideals.* Niwot: University Press of Colorado.

Hollis, Duncan B. 2010. "Unpacking the Compact Clause." *Texas Law Review* 88 (March): 741–806.

Hooper, Charles R. 2010. *The Next American Revolution: How to Demand Congressional Reform Now.* Hampton, Tenn.: Watauga Press.

Howard, Philip K. 2014. *The Rule of Nobody: Saving America from Dead Laws and Broken Government.* New York: W. W. Norton and Company.

Hume, Richard L., and Jerry B. Gough. 2008. *Blacks, Carpetbaggers, and Scalawags: The*

Constitutional Conventions of Radical Reconstruction. Baton Rouge: Louisiana State
    University Press.

Huq, Aziz. 2014. "The Function of Article V." University of Chicago Public Law and Legal
    Theory Working Paper no. 470. http://papers.ssrn.com/sol3/papers.cfm?abstract_
    id=2406089. Published in *University of Pennsylvania Law Review* 162, no. 5 (2014): 1165–
    236. Accessed June 27, 2014.

Immarigeon, Jean-Philippe. 2014. "Dissolve Congress: A Cure for Constitutional Crisis."
    Harper's 328 (February): 51–52.

Jameson, J. Franklin. 1898. "Political Uses of the Word Convention." *American Historical
    Review* 3 (April): 477–87.

Jameson, John Alexander. 1887. *A Treatise on Constitutional Conventions: Their History,
    Powers, and Modes of Proceeding.* 4th ed. New intro. John R. Vile. Chicago: Callaghan and
    Company. Reprint. Clark, N.J.: Lawbook Exchange, 2013.

Jarvis, Carl. 2014. *The United States of Dysfunction.* Houston. Tex.: BLSC Media Group.

Jefferson, Thomas. 1964. *Notes on the State of Virginia.* New York: Harper and Row. Orig. pub.
    1785.

———. 1905. *The Works of Thomas Jefferson.* Ed. Paul Leicester Ford. New York: G. P. Putnam's
    Sons.

———. 1862. *The Writings of Thomas Jefferson.* Ed. H. A. Washington. New York: H. W.
    Derby.

Jennings, Thelma. 1980. *The Nashville Convention: Southern Movement for Unity, 1848–1850.*
    Memphis: Memphis State University Press.

Johnson, Samuel. 1967. *A Dictionary of the English Language.* London: SW Strahan; New York:
    AMS Press. Orig. pub. 1755.

Kacprowicz, Charles. 2010. *Reclaiming America through Single Issue Federal Conventions.*
    Spruce Pine, N.C.: Markets Global Publishing.

Kalfus, Mason. 1999. "Why Time Limits on the Ratification of Constitutional Amendments
    Violate Article V." *University of Chicago Law Review* 66 (Spring): 437–67.

Kammen, Michael. 1987. *A Machine That Would Go of Itself: The Constitution in American
    Culture.* New York: Alfred A. Knopf.

Kay, Richard S. 2011. "Constituent Authority." *American Journal of Comparative Law.* 59
    (Summer): 715–61.

———. 1987. "The Illegality of the Constitution." *Constitutional Commentary* 4 (Winter):
    57–80.

Kenyon, Cecelia M. 2003. *Men of Little Faith: Selected Writings of Cecelia Kenyon.* Amherst:
    University of Massachusetts Press.

Keogh, Stephen. 1987. "Formal and Informal Constitutional Lawmaking in the United States
    in the Winter of 1860–1861." *Journal of Legal History* 8 (December): 275–99.

Kerber, Linda K. 1998. *No Constitutional Right to be Ladies: Women and the Obligations of
    Citizenship.* New York: Hill and Wang.

Killenbeck, Mark R., ed. 2002. *The Tenth Amendment and State Sovereignty.* Lanham, Md.:
    Rowman and Littlefield.

Kimball, Dale A. 1966. "The Constitutional Convention, Its Nature and Powers—And the
    Amending Process." *Utah Law Review.* 1966 (September): 390–415.

Kobach, Kris W. 1999. "May 'We the People' Speak? The Forgotten Role of Constituent
    Instructions in Amending the Constitution." *U.C. Davis Law Review* 33 (Fall): 1–87.

———. 1994. "Rethinking Article V: Term Limits and the Seventeenth and Nineteenth Amendments." *Yale Law Journal* 103 (May): 1971–2007.

Kuroda, Tadahisa. 1994. *The Origins of the Twelfth Amendment: The Electoral College in the Early Republic, 1787–1804.* Westport, Conn.: Greenwood Press.

Kyvig, David D. 1996. *Explicit and Authentic Acts: Amending the Constitution, 1776–1995.* Lawrence: University Press of Kansas.

———. 2000. *Unintended Consequences of Constitutional Amendments.* Athens: University of Georgia Press.

———, ed. 1985. *Alcohol and Order: Perspectives on National Prohibition.* Westport, Conn.: Greenwood Press.

Labunski, Richard. 2006. *James Madison and the Struggle for the Bill of Rights.* New York: Oxford University Press.

———. 2000. *The Second Constitutional Convention: How the American People Can Take Back Their Government.* Versailles, Ky.: Marley and Beck Press.

Larson, Edward J. 2014. *The Return of George Washington: 1783–1789.* New York: HarperCollins.

Lash, Kurt T. 2014. *The Fourteenth Amendment and the Privileges and Immunities of American Citizenship.* New York: Cambridge University Press.

———. 1994. "Rejecting Conventional Wisdom: Federalist Ambivalence in the Framing and Implementation of Article V." *American Journal of Legal History* 38 (April): 197–231.

Lauer, B. C. 2014. *I Overthrew the Government and This Is How I Did It.* N.p.: CreateSpace.

Lee, Charles Robert, Jr. 1963. *The Confederate Constitutions.* Chapel Hill: University of North Carolina Press.

Lee, R. Alton. 1961. "The Corwin Amendment in the Secession Crisis." *Ohio Historical Quarterly* 70 (January): 1–26.

Lessig, Lawrence. 2014. "A Real Step to Fix Democracy." *The Atlantic*, May 30, http://www.theatlantic.com/politics/archive/2014/05/a-real-step-to-fix-democracy/371898/. Accessed July 4, 2014.

———. 2012. *Republic, Lost: How Money Corrupts Congress—and a Plan to Stop It.* New York: Twelve.

Levin, Mark R. 2013. *The Liberty Amendments: Restoring the American Republic.* New York: Threshold Editions.

Levinson, Sanford. 2006. *Our UnDemocratic Constitution: Where the Constitution Goes Wrong (And How We the People Can Correct It).* New York: Oxford University Press.

———. 2014. "The Twenty-first Century Rediscovery of Nullification and Secession in American Political Rhetoric: Frivolousness Incarnate or Serious Argument to be Wrestled With?" *Arkansas Law Review* 67 (May): 17–79.

———, ed. 1995. *Responding to Imperfection: The Theory and Practice of Constitutional Amendment.* Princeton, N.J.: Princeton University Press.

Lieber, Francis. 1865. *Amendments of the Constitution, Submitted to the Consideration of the American People.* New York: Loyal Publication Society. Reprinted in Francis Lieber. *Reminiscences, Addresses, and Essays,* 137–39. Philadelphia: J. B. Lippincott, 1882.

Light, Paul C. "Federalist No. 85: Has the National Government Become an 'Awful Spectacle'?" *Public Administration Review* 72, supp. 1 (December 2011): S155–S159.

Lim, Elvin T. 2014. *The Lovers' Quarrel: The Two Foundings and American Political Development.* Cambridge, Mass.: Harvard University Press.

Lincoln, Abraham. 1953. *The Collected Works of Abraham Lincoln*. Ed. Roy P. Basler. New Brunswick, N.J.: Rutgers University Press.

Lising, Douglas J. 2011. *Remember Roscoe Filburn, Amending the Constitution: The Only Sure Way to Limit the Federal Government*. N.p.: Douglas J. Lising.

Lucas, James W. 2010. *Timely Renewed: Amendments to Restore the American Constitution*. N.p.: Constitution Renewal Initiative.

Lutz, Donald. 1988. *The Origins of American Constitutionalism*. Baton Rouge: Louisiana State University Press.

Madison, James. 1973. *The Mind of the Founder: Sources of the Political Thought of James Madison*. Ed. Marvin Meyers. Indianapolis: Bobbs-Merrill.

Maier, Pauline. 2010. *Ratification: The People Debate the Constitution, 1787–1788*. New York: Simon and Schuster.

Main, Thomas J. 2013. *Is the American Constitution Obsolete?* Durham, N.C.: Carolina Academic Press.

Maltz, Earl M. 1990. *Civil Rights, the Constitution, and Congress, 1863–1869*. Lawrence: University Press of Kansas.

———. *The Fourteenth Amendment and the Law of the Constitution*. Durham, N.C.: Carolina Academic Press.

Mann, Thomas E., and Norman J. Ornstein. 2012. *It's Even Worse Than It Looks: How the American Constitutional System Collided with the New Politics of Extremism*. New York: Basic Books.

Manne, Neal S. 1979. "Good Intentions, New Inventions, and Article V Constitutional Conventions." *Texas Law Review* 58 (December): 141–70.

Mansbridge, Jane J. 1986. *Why We Lost the ERA*. Chicago: University of Chicago Press.

Mansbridge, Jane, Cathie Jo Martin, Sarah Binder, Frances Lee, Nolan McCarty, John Odell, Dustin Tingley, and Mark Warren, eds. 2013. *Negotiating Agreement in Politics: Report of the Task Force on Negotiating Agreement in Politics*. Washington, D.C.: American Political Science Association. Available at http://scholar.harvard.edu/files/dtingley/files/negotiating_agreement_in_politics.pdf.

Marks, Frederick W., III. 1971. "Foreign Affairs: A Winning Issue in the Campaign for Ratification of the United States Constitution." *Political Science Quarterly* 86 (September): 444–69.

Mason, Alpheus T. 1964. *The States Rights Debate: Antifederalism and the Constitution*. Englewood Cliffs, N.J.: Prentice-Hall.

Massey, Calvin R. 1995. *Silent Rights: The Ninth Amendment and the Constitution's Unenumerated Rights*. Philadelphia: Temple University Press.

McDonald, Forrest and Ellen Shapiro McDonald, eds. 1968. *Confederation and Constitution, 1781–1789*. New York: Harper and Row.

McLaughlin, Andrew C. 1962. *The Confederation and the Constitution, 1782–1789*. New York: Collier Books. Orig. pub. 1905.

McMillen, Sally. 2009. *Seneca Falls and the Origins of the Women's Rights Movement*. Reprint. New York: Oxford University Press.

Meador, Lewis H. 1898. "The Council of Censors." *Pennsylvania Magazine of History and Biography* 22: 265–300.

Meyer, Howard N. 1973. *The Amendment That Refused to Die*. Radnor, Pa.: Chilton Book Company.

Miller, Keith W. 2013. *True Democracy: Empowering Everyday Americans through Legislative Lottery*. North Charleston, S.C.: CreateSpace Independent Publishing Platform.

Mobley, G. R., and D. E. Mobley. 2014. *We the People: The Strategy to Convene a Convention—For Republic Review*. Hobard, Wash.: Mobius Strip Press.

———. 2013. *We the People: Whose Constitution Is It Anyway?—The Constitutional Fix to a Constitutional Problem*. Hobard, Wash.: Mobius Strip Press.

Monaghan, Henry Paul. 1996. "We the People[s], Original Understanding, and Constitutional Amendment." *Columbia Law Review* 96 (January): 121–77.

Moore, Wayne D. 2013. "Variable Constitutional Authority: Madisonian Founding Perspectives." *American Political Thought* 2 (Fall): 217–58.

Morgan, Iwan. 1998. "Unconventional Politics: The Campaign for a Balanced-Budget Amendment Constitutional Convention in the 1970s." *Journal of American Studies* 32 (December): 421–45.

Morgan, Thomas B. 1963. "Seventeen States Vote to Destroy Democracy as We Know It." *Look* 27 (December 3): 76–88.

Morris, Henry O. 1897. *Waiting for the Signal: A Novel*. Chicago: Schulte.

Morris, Richard B. 1985. "The Mount Vernon Conference: First Step toward Philadelphia." *This Constitution*, no. 6 (Spring): 38–40.

Moyer, Kerry L., and Mark W. Podvia. 2009. *The Citizens' Guide to a Modern Constitutional Convention: Prepared for the Pennsylvania Constitutional Convention Commission*. N.p.: Civic Research Alliance.

Natelson, Robert G. 2010–11. *Amending the Constitution by Convention: A Complete View of the Founders' Plan*, 3 parts. Golden, Colo.: The Independent Institute.

———. 2013. "Founding-Era Conventions and the Meaning of the Constitution's 'Convention for Proposing Amendments.'" *Florida Law Review* 65: 1–76.

———. "James Madison and the Constitution's 'Convention for Proposing Amendments.'" *Akron Law Review* 45: 431–48.

———. 2011, 2013. *Proposing Constitutional Amendments by a Convention of the States: A Handbook for State Lawmakers*. Washington, D.C.: American Legislative Exchange Council.

———. 2014. *State Initiation of Constitutional Amendments: A Guide for Lawyers and Legislative Drafters*. Working Papers. http://dx.doi.org/10.2139/ssrn.2420987.

Neale, Thomas H. 2012a. *The Article V Convention for Proposing Constitutional Amendments: Historical Perspectives for Congress*. Report. October 22. Congressional Research Service.

———. 2012b. *The Article V Convention to Propose Constitutional Amendments: Contemporary Issues for Congress*. Report. July 9. Congressional Research Service.

Nelson, Michael, ed. 2013. *Guide to the Presidency and the Executive Branch*, 2 vols. 5th ed. Los Angeles: Sage.

Nelson, William E. 1988. *The Fourteenth Amendment: From Political Principle to Legal Doctrine*. Cambridge, Mass.: Harvard University Press.

O'Kane, Kevin C. 2014. *The Constitutional Convention of 2022*. N.p.: CreateSpace.

Okrent, David. 2010. *Last Call: The Rise and Fall of Prohibition*. New York: Scribner.

Oliphant, Lincoln C. 1985. "Amending the U.S. Constitution: A New Convention?" *News Letter, University of Virginia, Institute of Government*, October, 7–12.

Orfield, Lester Bernhardt. 1942. *The Amending of the Federal Constitution*. Ann Arbor: University of Michigan Press.

Palmer, Kris E., ed. 2000. *Constitutional Amendments: 1789 to the Present*. Detroit: Gale Group.

Paulsen, Michael Stokes. 1993. "A General Theory of Article V: The Constitutional Lessons of the Twenty-seventh Amendment." *Yale Law Journal* 103 (December): 677–789.

———. 2011. "How to Count to Thirty-four: The Constitutional Case for a Constitutional Convention." *Harvard Journal of Law and Public Policy* 103:677–789.

Payandeh, Mehrdad. 2011. "Constitutional Aesthetics: Appending Amendments to the United States Constitution." *BYU Journal of Public Law* 25:87–130.

Pendergast, Tom, Sara Pendergast, and John Sousanis. 2001. *Constitutional Amendments: From Freedom of Speech to Flag Burning.* 3 vols. Detroit: UXL.

Penello, Penny, ed. 1985. *Electing Delegates to a Constitutional Convention: Proceedings of an Annual Meeting Presidential Showcase Program Held in Washington, D.C., July 1985.* Washington, D.C.: American Bar Association.

Penrose, Mary Margaret. 2011. "Conventional Wisdom: Acknowledging Uncertainty in the Unknown." *Tennessee Law Review* 78 (Spring): 789–805.

Peterson, Merrill D., ed. 1966. *Democracy, Liberty, and Property: The State Constitutional Conventions of the 1820s.* Indianapolis: Bobbs-Merrill.

Pincus, Matthew. 2009. "When Should Interstate Compacts Require Congressional Consent?" *Columbia Journal of Law and Social Problems* 42 (Summer): 511–44.

Platz, William A. 1934. "Article Five of the Federal Constitution." *George Washington Law Review* 3 (November): 17–49.

Ponceau, Peter S. Du. 1831. *A Brief View of the Constitution of the United States Addressed to the Law Academy of Philadelphia.* Philadelphia: E. G. Dorsey. Reprint. New York: Da Capo, 1974.

"The Powers of Constitutional Conventions." 1916. *Harvard Law Review* 29 (March): 528–33.

Pritchett, C. Herman. 1982. "Congress and the Article V Convention." *Western Political Quarterly* 35 (June): 222–27.

"Proposed Legislation on the Convention Method of Amending the United States Constitution." 1972. *Harvard Law Review* 85 (June): 1612–48.

Pulitzer, Sidney. 2012. *Repair Washington: Practical Legislation for a Constitutional Convention.* N.p.: Sidney Pulitzer.

Pullen, William R. 1948. "Applications of State Legislatures to Congress for the Call of a National Constitutional Convention, 1788–1867." Master's thesis, University of North Carolina at Chapel Hill.

Quirk, William J. 2020. *Courts and Congress: America's Unwritten Constitution.* New Brunswick, N.J.: Transaction Press.

Radin, Max. 1930. "The Intermittent Sovereign." *Yale Law Journal* 30:514–31.

Rakove, Jack N. 1986. "The Gamble at Annapolis." *This Constitution*, no. 12:5–10.

———. 1996. *Original Meanings: Politics and Ideas in the Making of the Constitution.* New York: Alfred A. Knopf.

———. 1999. "The Super-Legality of the Constitution, or, a Federalist Critique of Bruce Ackerman's Neo-Federalism." *Yale Law Journal* 108 (June): 1931–58.

Rappaport, Michael B. 2010. "Reforming Article V: The Problems Created by the National Convention Amendment Method and How to Fix Them." *Virginia Law Review* 96 (November): 1509–81.

———. 2012. "Renewing Federalism by Reforming Article V: Defects in the Constitutional Amendment Process and a Reform Proposal." January 18. Policy Analysis for the CATO Institute.

Ratification of the Twenty-first Amendment to the Constitution of the United States. 1934.
　　Department of State Publication No. 573. Washington, D.C.: United States Government
　　Printing Office.

Raven, Rory. 2010. *The Dorr War: Treason, Rebellion and the Fight for Reform in Rhode Island.*
　　Charleston, S.C.: The History Press.

Rees, Gover, III. 1986. "The Amendment Process and Limited Constitutional Conventions."
　　Benchmark 2 (March–April): 66–108.

Rich, Bennett M. 1960. *Major Problems in State Constitutional Revision.* Ed. W. Brooke Graves.
　　Chicago: Public Administration Service.

Richardson, James D. *A Compilation of the Messages and Papers of the Presidents, 1789–1908.*
　　N.p.: Bureau of National Literature and Art.

Roche, John P. "The Founding Fathers: A Reform Caucus in Action." *American Political
　　Science Review* 55 (December): 799–816.

Rodenkirch, John J. 2010. *Constitutional Balance Amendment.* 2nd ed. Carol Stream, Ill.:
　　Explanation Press.

Romney, Dustin. 2014. *Rule of Law: Why and How We Must Amend the Constitution.* N.p.:
　　CreateSpace.

Rosenthal, Alan, Burdett A. Loomis, John R. Hibbing, and Karl T. Kurtz. 2002. *Republic on
　　Trial: the Case for Representative Democracy.* Washington, D.C.: CQ Press.

Rossum, Ralph A. 2001. *Federalism, the Supreme Court, and the Seventeenth Amendment: The
　　Irony of Constitutional Democracy.* Lanham, Md.: Lexington Books.

Rudomanski, Richard. 2014. *Article V.* N.p.: Richard Rudomanski.

Ruff, Karen. N.d. "The Constitution According to English: Article V." Managing an Article
　　V Constitutional Convention: The Con-Con. http://www.slideshare.net/nikihannevig/
　　article-v-public-version.

Rutland, Robert A. 1984. "The Virginia Plan of 1787: James Madison's Outline of a Model
　　Constitution." *This Constitution,* no. 4 (Fall): 23–30.

Sabato, Larry. 2007. *A More Perfect Constitution: 23 Proposals to Revitalize Our Constitution
　　and Make America a Fairer County.* New York: Walker and Company.

Saturno, James V., and Megan Suzanne Lyunch. 1971. CRS Report for Congress: *A Balanced
　　Budget Constitutional Amendment: Background and Congressional Options.* December 20.
　　Washington, D.C.: Congressional Research Service.

Schaller, Thomas F. 1998. "Democracy at Rest: Strategic Ratification of the Twenty-first
　　Amendment." *Publius: The Journal of Federalism* 28 (Spring): 81–97.

Schiller, Wendy J., and Charles Stewart III. 2015. *Electing the Senate: Indirect Democracy before
　　the Seventeenth Amendment.* Princeton, N.J.: Princeton University Press.

Schlafly, Phyllis. 2013a. "Is Article V in Our Future?" *Town Hall Magazine,* August 27, http://
　　townhall.com/columnists/phyllisschlafly/2013/08/27/is-article-v-in-our-future-n1673875/
　　page/full.

———. 2013b. "Mischief-Making about the Constitution." *The Phyllis Schlafly Report,*
　　September. http://www.eagleforum.org/publications/psr/sept13.thml. Accessed June 23,
　　2014.

Schumaker, Robert J. 2014. *Federalist 2doto: Constitutional Convention 2doto.* N.p.: The
　　Schumaker Group.

Schwartzberg, Melissa. 2014. *Counting the Many: The Origins and Limits of Supermajority
　　Rule.* New York: Cambridge University Press.

———. 2009. *Democracy and Legal Change*. New York: Cambridge University Press.

Smith, J. Allen. 1965. *The Spirit of American Government*. Ed. Cushing Strout. Cambridge, Mass.: Belknap Press of Harvard University Press. Orig. pub. 1907.

Smith, James Morton, ed. 1995. *The Republic of Letters: The Correspondence between Thomas Jefferson and James Madison 1776–1826*. New York: W. W. Norton.

Solberg, Winton, ed. 1958. *The Federal Convention and the Formation of the Union*. Indianapolis: Bobbs-Merrill.

Spalding, Matthew, and Trent England. 2011. "Article V: Congress, Conventions, and Constitutional Amendments." First Principles Series. February 10. Washington, D.C.: Heritage Foundation. http://www.heritage.org/research/reports/2011/02/article-v-congress-conventions-and-constitutional-amendments.

Stansbury, Arthur J. 2013. *Elementary Catechism on the Constitution of the United States for the Use of Schools*. Clark, N.J.: The Lawbook Exchange. Orig. pub. Boston: Hilliard, Gray, Little, and Wilkins, 1831.

Stathis, Stephen. 1990. "The Twenty-second Amendment: A Practical Remedy or Partisan Maneuver?" *Constitutional Commentary* 7 (Winter): 61–88.

Stern, Michael. 2011. "Reopening the Constitutional Road to Reform: Toward a Safeguarded Article V Convention." *Tennessee Law Review* 78 (Spring): 765–88.

Storing, Herbert J., ed. 1971. *The Complete Anti-Federalists*. 7 vols. Chicago: University of Chicago Press.

Story, Joseph. 1987. *Commentaries on the Constitution of the United States*. Intro. Ronald D. Rotunda and John E. Nowak. Durham, N.C.: Carolina Academic Press.

Strassner, Howard. 2014. *Bill of Rights for Our Posterity: Journal of the Second Constitutional Convention*. Amazon Digital Services.

Strauss, David A. 2001. "Commentary: The Irrelevance of Constitutional Amendments." *Harvard Law Review* 114 (March): 1457–505.

Street, Alfred B. 1859. *The Council of Revision of the State of New York: Its History, a History of the Courts with Which Its Members Were Connected; Biographical Sketches of Its Members; and Its Vetoes*. Albany: William Gould.

Strout, D. Wayne. 2014. *Restoration: God's Original Plan for America*. Spring Grove, Pa.: WS Press.

Swindler, William. 1963. "The Current Challenge to Federalism: The Confederating Proposals." *Georgetown Law Journal* 52 (Fall): 1–41.

Symposium on the Article V Convention Process. 1968. *Michigan Law Review* 66 (March): 837–1017. Includes articles by Everett McKinley Dirksen; Sam J. Ervin Jr.; Paul G. Kauper; Ralph M. Carson, Robert G. Dixon Jr.; Arthur Earl Bonfield; and Clifton McCleskey.

Taking Back Our Republic. 2010. Thirty-Thousand.org, February 22, http://www.Thirty-Thousand.org.

Tarr, G. Alan, and Robert F. Williams. 2006. *State Constitutions for the Twenty-first Century*. Vol. 2, *The Politics of State Constitutional Reform*. Albany: State University of New York.

Thorpe, Francis N. 1909. *The Federal and State Constitutions, Colonial Charters and Other Organic Laws of the States, Territories, and Colonies Now or Heretofore Forming the United States of America*. Washington, D.C.: Government Printing Office.

Tiedeman, Christopher G. 1890. *The Unwritten Constitution: A Philosophical Inquiry into the Fundaments of American Constitutional Law*. New York: G. P. Putnam's Sons.

Toobin, Jeffrey. 2013. "Our Broken Constitution." *The New Yorker*, December 9, 64–73.

Traynor, Roger J. 1927. "The Amending System of the United States Constitution, An Historical and Legal Analysis." Ph.D. diss., University of California.

Tsai, Robert L. 2014. *America's Forgotten Constitutions: Defiant Visions of Power and Community*. Cambridge, Mass.: Harvard University Press.

Tucker, St. George. 1999. *View of the Constitution of the United States with Selected Writings*. Foreword by Clyde N. Wilson. Indianapolis: Liberty Fund. Orig. pub. 1803.

Tugwell, Rexford. 1974. *The Emerging Constitution*. New York: Harper and Row.

U.S. Department of Justice, Office of Legal Policy, Report to the Attorney General. 1987. *Limited Constitutional Conventions under Article V of the United States Constitution*. September 10. Washington, D.C.: U.S. Government Printing Office.

Van Alstyne, William W. 1978. "Does Article V Restrict the States to Calling Unlimited Conventions Only?—A Letter to a Colleague." *Duke Law Journal*, January, 1295–306.

———. 1979. "The Limited Constitutional Convention—The Recurring Answer." *Duke Law Journal*, September, 985–1001.

Van Sickle, Bruce M., and Lynn M. Boughey. 1990. "Lawful and Peaceful Revolution: Article V and Congress' Present Duty to Call a Convention for Proposing Amendments." *Hamline Law Review* 14 (Fall): 1–115.

Vile, John R. 1991. "American Views of the Constitutional Amending Process: An Intellectual History of Article V." *American Journal of Legal History* 35: 44–69.

———. 1989. "Ann Diamond on an Unlimited Constitutional Convention." *Publius: The Journal of Federalism* 19 (Winter): 177–83.

———. 2011. "The Case against a 'Repeal Amendment.'" *National Law Journal*, January 3, 38–39.

———. 2015. *A Companion to the United States Constitution and Its Amendments*, 6th ed. Santa Barbara, Calif.: Praeger.

———. 1992. *The Constitutional Amending Process in American Political Thought*. New York: Praeger.

———. 1994. *Constitutional Change in the United States: A Comparative Study of the Role of Constitutional Amendments, Judicial Interpretations, and Legislative and Executive Actions*. Westport, Conn.: Praeger.

———. 2005. *The Constitutional Convention of 1787: A Comprehensive Encyclopedia of America's Founding*. 2 vols. Santa Barbara, Calif.: ABC-CLIO.

———. 1993. *Contemporary Questions Surrounding the Constitutional Amending Process*. Westport, Conn.: Praeger.

———. 2006. "The Critical Role of Committees at the U.S. Constitutional Convention." *American Journal of Legal History* 48 (April): 147–76.

———. 2015. *Encyclopedia of Constitutional Amendments, Proposed Amendments, and Amending Issues, 1789–2015*. 4th ed. Santa Barbara, Calif.: ABC-CLIO.

———. 2014. *Essential Supreme Court Decisions: Summaries of Leading Cases in U.S. Constitutional Law*. 16th ed. Lanham, Md.: Rowman and Littlefield.

———. 1998. "Francis Lieber and the Process of Constitutional Amendment. *Review of Politics* 60 (Summer): 525–43.

———. 1986. "Judicial Review of the Amending Process: The Dellinger-Tribe Debate." *Journal of Law and Politics* 3:21–50.

———. 2013. *The Men Who Made the Constitution: Lives of the Delegates to the Constitutional Convention*. Lanham, Md.: Scarecrow Press.

258   Selected Bibliography

———. 1990. "Permitting States to Rescind Ratifications of Pending Amendments to the U.S. Constitution." *Publius: The Journal of Federalism* 20 (Spring): 109–22.

———. 1991. "Proposals to Amend the Bill of Rights: Are Fundamental Rights in Jeopardy?" *Judicature* 75 (August–September): 62–67.

———. 2014. *Re-Framers: 170 Eccentric, Visionary, and Patriotic Proposals to Rewrite the U.S. Constitution.* Santa Barbara, Calif.: ABC-CLIO.

———. 1991. *Rewriting the United States Constitution: An Examination of Proposals From Reconstruction to the Present.* New York: Praeger.

———. 1980. "The Supreme Court and the Amending Process." *Journal of the Georgia Political Science Association* 8 (Fall): 33–66.

———. 1993. "Three Kinds of Constitutional Founding and Change: The Convention Model and Its Alternatives." *Political Research Quarterly* 46 (December): 881–95.

———. 2014. *The United States Constitution: Questions and Answers*, 2nd ed. Santa Barbara, Calif.: ABC-CLIO.

———. 2015. *"The Wisest Council in the World": Restoring the Character Sketches by William Pierce of Georgia of the Delegates to the Federal Convention of 1787.* Athens: University of Georgia Press.

———. 2012. *The Writing and Ratification of the U.S. Constitution: Practical Virtue in Action.* Lanham, Md.: Rowman and Littlefield.

———, ed. 2011. *Proposed Amendments to the U.S. Constitution, 1787–2001.* 4 vols. Clark, N.J.: The Lawbook Exchange.

———. 1993. *The Theory and Practice of Constitutional Change in America: A Collection of Original Source Materials.* New York: Peter Lang.

Vile, John R., and David L. Hudson Jr., eds. 2013. *Encyclopedia of the Fourth Amendment*, 2 vols. Los Angeles: Sage Reference.

Vile, John R., David L. Hudson Jr., and David Schultz, eds. 2009. *Encyclopedia of the First Amendment*, 2 vols. Washington, D.C.: CQ Press.

Vile, John R., William Pederson, and Frank J. Williams, eds. 2008. *James Madison: Philosopher, Founder and Statesman.* Athens: Ohio University Press.

Virginia Commission on Constitutional Government. 1967. *The Reconstruction Amendments Debates.* Richmond: Virginia Commission on Constitutional Government.

Vorenberg, Michael. 2001. *Final Freedom: The Civil War, the Abolition of Slavery, and the Thirteenth Amendment.* New York: Cambridge University Press.

Vose, Clement E. 1972. *Constitutional Change: Amendment Politics and Supreme Court Litigation since 1900.* Lexington, Mass.: Lexington Books.

———. 1979. "When District of Columbia Representation Collides with the Constitutional Amendment Institution." *Publius: The Journal of Federalism* 9 (Winter) 115–25.

Walker, Bill. 2011. "The Article V Convention: Discussing the Reality Versus the Fantasy." *Thomas M. Cooley Law Review* 28:21–36.

Waugh, John C. 2003. *On the Brink of Civil War: The Compromise of 1850 and How It Changed the Course of American History.* Lanham, Md.: Rowman and Littlefield.

Webb, Derek A. 2012. "The Original Meaning of Civility: Democratic Deliberation at the Philadelphia Constitutional Convention." *South Carolina Law Review* 64 (Autumn): 183–219.

Weber, Paul J. and Barbara A. Perry. 1989. *Unfounded Fears: Myths and Realities of a Constitutional Convention.* New York: Praeger.

Webster, Noah. 2008. *Sketches of American Policy*. Intro. John R. Vile. Clark, N.J.: The Lawbook Exchange.

White, Laura A. 1965. *Robert Barnwell Rhett: Father of Secession*. Gloucester, Mass.: Peter Smith. Orig. pub. 1931.

Wilkey, Malcolm R. 1995. *Is It Time for a Second Constitutional Convention?* Commentary by Walter Berns, Terry Eastland, Phyllis Schlafly, Edwin Meese III, Michael E. DeBos, Dwight R. Lee, and Michael Stokes Paulsen. Ed. Roger Clegg. Washington, D.C.: National Legal Center for the Public Interest.

Williams, Robert F. 1996. "Are State Constitutional Conventions Things of the Past? The Increasing Role of the Constitutional Commission in State Constitutional Change." *Hofstra Law and Policy Symposium* 1:1–26.

Wilson, Jack A. 2010. *Republic Lost*. Lawrenceville, Ill.: Jack A. Wilson.

Wilson, Woodrow. 1961. *Constitutional Government in the United States*. New York: Columbia University Press. Orig. pub. 1908.

Wolfe, Christopher. 1979. "Woodrow Wilson: Interpreting the Constitution." *The Review of Politics* 41 (January): 121–42.

Wood, Gordon. 1969. *The Creation of the American Republic, 1776–1787*. New York: W. W. Norton.

Wood, Stephen B. 1968. *Constitutional Politics in the Progressive Era: Child Labor and the Law*. Chicago: University of Chicago Press.

Wooster, Ralph A. 1962. *The Secession Conventions of the South*. Princeton, N.J.: Princeton University Press.

Young, Daniel T. 2007. "Disarming the Constitutional Time Bomb: Making Sense of Article V and the Possibility of a Second Constitutional Convention." BA thesis, University of Virginia.

Ziegler, Mary. 2009. "Ways to Change: A Reevaluation of Article V Campaigns and Legislative Constitutionalism." *Brigham Young University Law Review*, 969–1010.

Cases

Baker v. Carr, 369 U.S. 186 (1962).

Barron v. Baltimore, 32 U.S. 243 (1833).

Brown v. Board of Education, 347 U.S. 483 (1954).

Chisholm v. Georgia 2 U.S. (2 Dal.) 419 (1793).

Civil Rights Cases, 109 U.S. 3 (1883).

Colegrove v. Green, 328 U.S. 549 (1946).

Coleman v. Miller, 307 U.S. 433 (1939).

Dillon v. Gloss, 256 U.S. 368 (1921).

District of Columbia v. Heller, 554 U.S. 570 (2008).

Dodge v. Woolsey, 59 U.S. 331 (1885).

Frontiero v. Richardson, 411 U.S. 677 (1973).

Gideon v. Wainwright, 372 U.S. 335 (1963).

Hawke v. Smith I, 253 U.S. 221 (1920).

Hawke v. Smith II, 253 U.S. 231 (1920).

Hollingsworth v. Virginia, 3 U.S. (3 Dal.) 379 (1798).

Idaho v. Freeman, 529 F. Supp. 1107 (1981).

Kelo v. City of New London, 545 U.S. 469 (2005).

Kimble v. Swackhamer, 439 U.S. 385 (1978).

Leser v. Garnett, 258 U.S. 130 (1922).

Luther v. Borden, 7 How (48 U.S.) 1 (1948).

Mapp v. Ohio, 367 U.S. 643 (1961).

Marbury v. Madison, 5 U.S. 137 (1803).

Marsh v. Chambers, 463 U.S. 783 (1983).

McCulloch v. Maryland, 4 Wheaton (17 U.S.) 316 (1891).

McDonald v. Chicago, 566 U.S. 3025 (2010).

National Prohibition Cases, 253 U.S. 350 (1920).

Oregon v. Mitchell, 400 U.S. 112 (1972).

Plessy v. Ferguson, 163 U.S. 537 (1896).

Powell v. McCormack, 395 U.S. 486 (1969).

Reed v. Reed, 404 U.S. 71 (1971).

Reynolds v. Sims, 377 U.S. 533 (1964).

Scott v. Sandford, 60 U.S. (19 How.) 393 (1857).

Slaughterhouse Cases, 16 Wallace (83 U.S.) 36 (1873).

Smith v. Union Bank of Georgetown, 30 U.S. (5 Pet.) 518 (1831).

Town of Greece v. Galloway, No. 12-696 (2014).

U.S. Steel v. Multistate Tax Commission, 434 U.S. 452 (1978).

U.S. Term Limits v. Thornton, 514 U.S. 779 (1995).

Virginia v. Tennessee, 148 U.S. 503 (1893).

Weeks v. United States, 232 U.S. 383 (1914).

Wesberry v. Sanders, 376 U.S. 1 (1964).

Whitehill v. Elkins, 389 U.S. 54 (1966).

INDEX

www.ingramcontent.com/pod-product-compliance
Lightning Source LLC
Chambersburg PA
CBHW010114270326
41929CB00023B/3349